FROM THE GROUND UP
THE FIRST FIFTY YEARS OF McCAIN FOODS

DANIEL STOFFMAN

IN COLLABORATION WITH
TONY VAN LEERSUM

Produced on the occasion of its 50th anniversary by

McCAIN FOODS LIMITED
BCE Place
181 Bay Street, Suite 3600
Toronto, Ontario, Canada
M5J 2T3
www.mccain.com
416-955-1700

For copies of this book, please contact:
McCain Foods Limited,
Director, Communications,
at growingtogether@mccain.com
or at the address above

This book was printed on paper containing post-consumer waste, which saved:
- 42 trees
- 29 million BTU's of energy
- 4,626 pounds of greenhouse gases
- 15,163 gallons of water
- 2,509 pounds of solid waste

Calculation based on research by Environmental Defense and members of the Paper Task Force.

Copyright © McCain Foods Limited 2007

All rights reserved. No part of this book, including images, illustrations, photographs, logos, text, etc. may be reproduced, modified, copied or transmitted in any form or used for commercial purposes without the prior written permission of McCain Foods Limited, or, in the case of reprographic copying, a license from Access Copyright, the Canadian Copyright Licensing Agency, One Yonge Street, Suite 1900, Toronto, Ontario, M6B 3A9.

LIBRARY AND ARCHIVES CANADA CATALOGUING IN PUBLICATION

Stoffman, Daniel
From the ground up : the first fifty years of McCain Foods / Daniel Stoffman in collaboration with Tony van Leersum.

Includes index.
ISBN: 978-0-9783720-0-2

1. McCain Foods Limited – History.   2. McCain, Wallace, 1930– .
3. McCain, H. Harrison, 1927–2004.   I. Van Leersum, Tony, 1935– .   II. McCain Foods Limited   III. Title.

HD9217.C34M338 2007   338.7'664028530971   C2007-903193-5

Project management and design: Counterpunch / Linda Gustafson
Editor: Judy Phillips
Printed in Canada by Friesens Printers

PHOTO CREDITS: Many of the photographs are from the extensive picture archives, both historical and contemporary, that McCain agronomists and other employees have contributed to, including the photographs of Erika Fitzgerald, Erik Haasken, Luis Lago Castro, David Morgan, Ghislain Pelletier, David Pullan, John Walsh, Tony van Leersum, and many others. The collection of historical photographs is maintained by Dawn Shaw at Florenceville, New Brunswick.

Other photographs are by: Keith Blackmore (107), Bart W. Bradbury (164), The Woodstock *Bugle* (126), Carl Court (61 left), Doug Forster (x), Mark Howard (174), Mike Kipling (38), Michael Mahovlich / Masterfile (138 right), Trish McCain (ii), Diana Murphy (140), Mike Ridewood (133 various), Henk Ruitenbeek (129, 133 various), Clive Schaupmeyer (124), Eerik Schipper (68), Sid Tabak (i, vii–ix, 93, 138 left, 139 top, 144, 159, 161, 162, 163, 238, 239), and Graeme Williams (192).

Efforts have been made to locate the copyright owner of the photographs used in this publication. We would be happy to include any omissions in future editions.

CONTENTS

Foreword   by Wallace McCain / x

Preface   by Janice Wismer / xii

Chapter One   **THE BEGINNING** / 1

Chapter Two   **CROSSING THE ATLANTIC** / 39

Chapter Three   **ACROSS THE CHANNEL** / 69

Chapter Four   **DOWN UNDER** / 103

Chapter Five   **THE HOME FRONT** / 125

Chapter Six   **SOUTH OF THE BORDER** / 165

Chapter Seven   **NEW WORLDS TO CONQUER** / 187

Chapter Eight   **A WORLD OF CHANGE** / 225

Afterword   by Dale Morrison / 240

Acknowledgements / 242

Index / 244

NOBODY, LEAST OF ALL THE McCAIN BROTHERS, IMAGINED THAT THE LITTLE FROZEN FOODS PLANT THEY OPENED IN 1957 WOULD, BEFORE THE CENTURY WAS OVER, MAKE FLORENCEVILLE THE FRENCH FRY CAPITAL OF THE WORLD.

TOP: Harrison McCain and
BOTTOM: Wallace McCain, c.1980s.
FACING PAGE: The Florenceville plant by night, 2006.

WALLACE MCCAIN

FOREWORD

Wallace McCain, 2003.

I am writing this on my own behalf and on the behalf of my brother Harrison. We were a team. I wish he were here to add his own, most distinctive, voice, but I think I know what he would feel and say.

We were two young guys, eager to have a business we could call our own; eager to succeed. We never really started out with grandiose ambitions. We used to think just maybe we could build a business that might make a million dollars. And, we never really did it for the money. We just thought business was fun – it was a game and a challenge. We liked building things, and we loved the people we worked with. That's why we did what we did.

Our success wasn't because we were great financial engineers – we weren't. It wasn't because we had the very best plants – often we didn't. And our success wasn't because we built a sophisticated strategic plan – in fact, we never prepared one in all our years! We had some good timing, and we had some good luck. But mostly, we were able to build a team of truly great people. People who cared a lot. People who didn't care so much about the material things of power, title, and money; they just wanted to get things done (quickly), just like Harrison and me, and they wanted to make a difference. People who were honest, hard working, persevering, direct, and dedicated to success; people who shared our dreams – that's what made McCain Foods Limited a smashing success.

This book, on the occasion of our fiftieth anniversary, will tell the story of hundreds of those very people. It tells stories of our victories, and some of our failures (we had many, but we learned from them). It tells war stories and love stories (we all loved the business). This book is an important collection of stories to describe the past: fifty years of success led by two people but driven by thousands. I am proud of what we accomplished together. I am proud of the unique relationship Harrison and I had, with the support of our older brothers, even after what transpired and when he passed away. I am proud of all the people described in these stories, and they should be equally proud, because it is their story also.

One of the things that made Harrison and me pretty good leaders was that we always looked forward, never back. After these stories get told and the memories are embedded, it is just as important for us to keep facing forward into the future. No matter how good Harrison and I, and our people, were in our day, it should never be the same. Great companies renew themselves. The McCain family has renewed itself – from a family business into a business family. And just as important, McCain Foods is renewing itself under exceptional professional management, with the world's best professional management techniques of large global enterprises. That means change, and of course change can be difficult, but it is necessary to perpetuate the legacy that Harrison and I, and the people described in these stories, have built. Inside difficult change is opportunity, and we have the opportunity now to take a great twentieth century organization and make it a great twenty-first century organization.

I believe in that. I know Harrison would believe in that. And I think the hundreds of people who were our partners would also believe in that. In fact, it's just as exciting today as the day in February 1957 when we turned on our first fryer to make a McCain frozen french fry.

On behalf of Harrison and me – thank you all for fifty amazing years.

G. Wallace F. McCain
Toronto, Canada
March 2007

JANICE WISMER

PREFACE

Janice Wismer at the McCain offices at BCE Place in Toronto, Canada, 2005.

There is a certain simplicity to life at McCain that many large, public companies today are trying to achieve. Underlying that simplicity is a purposeful resolve to win. That winning attitude is deeply ingrained in the culture of McCain, a culture that values treating all people at all levels – customers, employees, and suppliers – with respect. That a small-town Canadian business could become, fifty years after its founding, a global mega-brand and one of the world's most respected companies is a testament to the loyalty and efforts of its employees.

It doesn't matter where you travel with McCain in the world, whether it be Ballarat, Australia; Scarborough, England; Johannesburg, South Africa; or the place that started it all, Florenceville, New Brunswick, the stories of the founding fathers and the vision that they inspired to build the finest global food business in the world, are endless. Woven through all these stories are common threads: The joy of watching young people develop and rise through the leadership ranks. The constant craving to learn on the fly. The acceptance of mistakes in the pursuit of excellence. Embracing the local culture and respecting small-town values wherever McCain developed operations. The great pride in being a family business in a global village.

This book is an attempt to tell the whole tale of Canada's most successful entrepreneurs – Wallace and Harrison McCain – but it's really a book about great leadership. There is so much for us all – current and future employees – to learn from within these pages. Even the story of how this book came to be holds a lesson: that it is the stories we share that help us to grow and keep our culture constant and rich.

It was at the first board meeting of the McCain Learning Centre – governed by talented McCain leaders from around the world – that the seed was planted to write this book. The McCain Learning Centre itself was the product of a vision set out with the launch of a new strategic plan in 2004. Its mission is clear: to provide the tools for all employees to continuously learn and grow, achieving excellence in every job every day, making McCain the preferred choice in all our markets. The board, which represents the interests of employees around the world, strongly believes that sharing the experiences, entrepreneurship, and sheer fortitude of the remarkable people who built McCain into the global force it is today would inspire in our employees the caring, committed attitude that has carried McCain forward and that will take us to the next level of performance.

We have all been chosen – and have chosen ourselves – to be a part of this family. We have been given a great gift – a global success story, a place where we can learn, grow, and be valued for our contributions. It's up to us now to be the standard-bearers for the future. I have every confidence that we will continue to make the family proud.

Janice Wismer
Vice-President, Human Resources
McCain Foods Limited
Toronto, Canada
May 2007

CHAPTER ONE

THE BEGINNING

In 1955, Harrison and Wallace McCain were looking for a business to start. Both had been working for one of Canada's most successful entrepreneurs, K.C. Irving. But neither intended to spend a lifetime as an employee. They had learned a lot and now they were ready to run a company of their own.

They had plenty of street smarts, loads of ambition, and all the energy and confidence they would need to be successful entrepreneurs. They also had some money they had inherited from their father, A.D. McCain, who had built a business as an exporter of potatoes to the Caribbean and Latin America and was a successful stock market investor. What Harrison, then twenty-eight years old, and Wallace, twenty-five, didn't have was a good idea.

It was almost three years since they had started talking about launching a business and still they hadn't hit upon that elusive something they really wanted to do. They had thought about, and rejected, dozens of schemes and suggestions, from buying a seat on the Montreal Stock Exchange to setting up a Coca-Cola distributorship to operating a laundry business.

Harrison had spent five years as a sales manager for Irving Oil. "I had an excellent time there," he said in an interview in 1997. "But I had an overriding drive to be in business for myself. I thought something would turn up some day. And one day I decided nothing was going to turn up." So he resigned from Irving Oil to devote himself full time to the search for a business opportunity.

While Harrison was exploring possibilities, Wallace who had just married, continued working for the Irving hardware chain, Thorne's Hardware. One day in January 1956, Harrison called Wallace to tell him their elder brother, Bob, had suggested they consider the frozen food business.

FACING PAGE: Potato harvesting in the early days of McCain Foods. Mechanical lifters pulled the potatoes out of the soil and pickers piled them into barrels. Local schools closed for weeks during the annual fall harvest.

A.D. McCain and McCain Produce

It was natural, Harrison McCain said, that he and his brothers would earn their livings in the potato business. "Our father was a potato dealer and a farmer. Our grandfather was a farmer. Our great-grandfather was a farmer and a land-clearer. He saw a piece of woods, cleared a farm, and started growing potatoes."

Clearing land was back-breaking labour – chopping down pine trees and burning the stumps. Farming too was hard work, but hard work alone wasn't enough. Success in farming also required good business skills.

Harrison and Wallace McCain always said they knew nothing about the frozen food business when they started McCain Foods in 1957. But they had grown up immersed in a world of agriculture and business. As for hard work, that was a way of life in the McCain family.

Wallace and Harrison were the two youngest of Andrew and Laura McCain's six children. In 1909, Andrew, known by his initials A.D., started a potato export company, McCain Produce, in partnership with his father to export seed potatoes. When the Americans placed high tariffs on potatoes, A.D. McCain travelled to the Caribbean and South America to find new markets. He also proved to be a shrewd investor, amassing a small fortune in the stock market, as well as extensive landholdings in Carleton County.

When A.D. McCain died in 1953, his widow Laura ("Mrs. A.D."), who had been a school teacher before her marriage and then a homemaker, took over the family business. "Dad never talked business at home," Wallace McCain recalls. "After he died, my mother ran McCain Produce. Andrew and Bob, my brothers, worked for Mother. She had no business experience, and yet she made more money than Dad did in the stock market." Andrew, the eldest of the McCain brothers, became president of McCain Produce, developing new markets for the company in the Mediterranean countries of Europe and North Africa.

Agricultural industries are marked by boom and bust cycles as food prices rise and fall. Consequently, McCain Produce would make money one year and lose the next – one reason Laura McCain did not want all her sons to continue in the produce business and why A.D. McCain insisted they attend university. It also led to Bob McCain's interest in the more stable processing side of the food business, prompting him to suggest to his brothers that they start a frozen foods factory.

As of 2007, Stephen McCain, a son of Harrison and Wallace's brother Andrew, and Vernon Thomas were co-managing directors of McCain Produce. They have had to contend with a major challenge: the nations of South America, Europe, and North Africa have banned the importation of North American potatoes. The official reason is to prevent the spread of plant diseases. In response, Stephen McCain and Thomas have successfully repositioned McCain Produce's business by developing new markets for table potatoes and plant protection materials.

Stephen McCain is also chairman of McCain Fertilizer, which operates factories in New Brunswick, Prince Edward Island, and Maine.

TOP LEFT: McCain Produce potatoes are loaded onto a ship in Saint John, New Brunswick.
ABOVE: A McCain Produce building in Florenceville. Seed potatoes stored here are shipped to international markets.

LEFT: The McCain plant, on the left bank of the Saint John River, dwarfs the village of Florenceville, 1981. The village is clustered around a bridge downriver; Harrison and Wallace's houses are on the right bank of the river.
RIGHT: Florenceville's famous partially covered bridge, spanning the Saint John River.

New Brunswick potatoes were being shipped to Maine, where they were processed as french fries, frozen, and packaged. Canadian peas were also being frozen in the United States. Why not freeze Canadian potatoes and peas in Canada?

The brothers, who had been close since childhood, were intrigued by the idea. Neither knew anything about freezing food, a technology then in its infancy. On the other hand, they were no strangers to the food business. The McCain family had been involved in agriculture, in one way or another, since it had first arrived in Canada from Ireland in 1825. Harrison and Wallace had grown up in Florenceville, a farming community. As boys, each had his own cow to milk before going to school.

Before working for Thorne's, Wallace had sold insecticides and fertilizers for Green Cross, a job that required him to travel around the Maritime provinces calling on farmers. "I learned more about agriculture doing that than I had at home," he says. "I sold fungicides for potatoes, so I learned a little about potatoes."

The more the brothers found out about frozen food, the more interested they became. They liked the notion of being innovators in a new branch of food processing. It seemed like the right idea at the right time. Within a month, they had decided to build a factory to freeze potatoes and other vegetables. And they decided to do it where the raw materials were located, in their hometown of Florenceville.

That was the beginning of McCain Foods Ltd. On February 23, 1957, the plant opened on what had been a cow pasture on the shore of the Saint John River. Every hour, the new factory, with thirty workers, produced almost seven hundred kilograms of frozen produce. Total sales that first year were $153,000.

By 2007, as McCain Foods prepared to celebrate its fiftieth anniversary, annual sales were around $6 billion, with 77 percent of those sales outside Canada. The company

Harvesting potatoes near Florenceville, 2005.

was producing close to half a million kilograms of potato products per hour, as well as a host of other frozen food items. It had twenty-one thousand employees working in fifty-seven factories in fifteen countries on six continents. Yet its home base is still the rural village of Florenceville, where a road sign at the town limits declares: "Florenceville – French Fry Capital of the World."

The sign is not a boast but a simple statement of fact. Almost all eaters of french fries at some point will eat a McCain french fry, whether or not they are aware of it. McCain french fries are everywhere – in McDonald's and KFCs and thousands of other restaurants and supermarket freezer compartments in more than a hundred countries. One of every three french fries sold worldwide is a McCain french fry, which translates into one hundred million servings of McCain french fries each and every day.

Canada doesn't have many brands recognizable to consumers around the world. Canada Dry and Canadian Club originated in Canada but the companies that produce them are no longer based there. BlackBerry, the wireless email device; Bata footwear; Four Seasons hotels; and Harlequin, the romance book publisher, are Canadian-based global brands. So is McCain, still owned by the McCain family and so popular internationally that, in 2003, A.C. Neilson, the marketing information company, named it a "global mega brand."

Yet, back in 1956, Harrison and Wallace were not even dreaming of creating a multinational business empire. "We just wanted to get something going, make some money," recalls Wallace. "I know it never crossed my mind that we would be an international global business."

A good product is an essential ingredient of business success. So is hard work. And so is good timing. Harrison and Wallace McCain had picked the perfect time to start a frozen food business. They were entering a new industry just when the technology that made the industry possible was being developed. At the same time, the Canadian population was growing rapidly, thanks to the loudest baby boom of the industrialized world and a high rate of immigration. More people meant more mouths to feed and more business for food processors.

More important still, a momentous social change was getting underway, one that would fuel the growth of the industry through the 1960s and beyond: the entry of ever-increasing numbers of women into the labour force. With both partners working, families had less time and energy to prepare meals. Anything that made the task easier – frozen french fries, for example – was welcome. The proliferation of fast food restaurants was also in part the result of the entry of married women into the labour force. Families with two wage earners had less time to cook at home and more disposable income to spend in restaurants. Eating out, once reserved for special occasions, became routine.

Before World War II, only a minority of Canadians owned cars. During the 1950s, car ownership increased rapidly. To cater to hungry drivers, the restaurant industry built drive-in and other quick-service restaurants. French fries, which can be eaten without utensils, were the perfect food for the automobile era.

In 1948, brothers Dick and Mac McDonald revamped their restaurant in San Bernardino, California, to feature counter-style quick service, offering fifteen-cent hamburgers and ten-cent servings of french fries. Ray Kroc bought the right to franchise McDonald's from the brothers and, in 1955, opened his first McDonald's outlet in Des Plaines, Illinois. The first Kentucky Fried Chicken opened in 1952. But it wasn't until the 1960s that these and other chains began to spread rapidly across

North America, then to Europe and the rest of the world. McCain grew along with them as one of their most important suppliers.

It is fitting that one of the world's major frozen food companies is based in Canada because it was the Inuit of Canada's Far North who invented frozen food. Their favourite method of freezing a fish was to toss it on the ice as soon as it was caught. The Inuit knew hundreds of years ago that a fish frozen quickly in the dead of winter tasted better when thawed than did a fish frozen more slowly in the spring or fall, when temperatures were milder.

The Florenceville plant up and running in 1957.

When food is frozen slowly, ice crystals form that damage the food's cellular structure, thereby also damaging its colour, texture, and flavour. Quick-frozen food, on the other hand, is virtually indistinguishable from fresh once it has been thawed. Clarence Birdseye, of Brooklyn, New York, studied biology and then worked as a fur trader in northern Labrador, where he figured all this out by observing the Inuit. Back in the United States, Birdseye invented a "quick freeze machine" and, in 1925, founded Birdseye Seafoods.

The business was not successful because the public, based on previous experience, disliked frozen food. As well, few grocery stores had freezers, and home refrigerators lacked freezer compartments. Four years later, Birdseye sold his company to General Foods, which kept the brand name but split the word in two – "Birds Eye." Gradually, the frozen food business picked up and, during the 1950s, it enjoyed explosive growth as American families, now equipped with modern fridges and home freezers, discovered the joys of TV dinners and frozen orange juice.

At the age of fifteen, Jack Simplot leased an Idaho potato farm and became one of the biggest shippers of potatoes in the western United States. The J.R. Simplot Dehydrating Company perfected a new method of dehydrating potatoes and, during World War II, became an important food supplier to the U.S. military. After the war, Simplot decided that frozen foods were the wave of the future. And what better product to offer than the french fry, which was becoming increasingly popular and yet was so time-consuming to prepare?

The problem was that raw potatoes that had been cut up and frozen turned to mush when thawed. Ray Dunlap, a scientist working for Simplot, solved the problem. He found that pre-cooking the potato stabilizes it so it can be frozen and thawed later without breaking down the cellular structure. It took several years of work, but Dunlap and Ray Kuenemann, another Simplot food scientist, came up with a frozen fry as good as a fresh one. In 1953, Simplot started selling them – just as, on the other side of the continent, Harrison and Wallace McCain were looking for a business to start.

While Harrison and Wallace were working for Irving, their brothers, Andrew and Bob, were operating McCain Produce, the family produce firm. It raised cattle and shipped seed potatoes around the world. Like all growers, the firm wanted more stability in the market for its products.

It was the search for stability, says Bob's son Andrew, that piqued his father's interest in the frozen vegetable business. Andrew is chairman of McCain Foods Group Inc., the official name of "Holdco," the family holding company that owns the shares of McCain Foods Limited. "My father originated the idea of a frozen food company," he says. His father was thinking not just of himself but of the other farmers in Carleton County who were at the mercy of fluctuating potato prices. If a factory could be built in the area to process potatoes and other vegetables, the result would be increased demand for the raw materials and, Bob hoped, more predictable prices.

Bob and Harrison visited a french fry plant owned by John Baxter in Corinna, Maine. As Wallace McCain recalls it, Baxter's advice was "Don't do it." The raw material for processed french fries was better in the west, they were told. Idaho, not New Brunswick, was the place to be.

TOP: Bob McCain shows a visitor Thomas Equipment's AirVac harvester, which separates stones from potatoes.
BOTTOM: Andrew McCain, 1980.

But the McCain brothers didn't have enough money to go into business in Idaho even if they had wanted to. Anyway, they were set on Florenceville. It was home, it had plenty of potatoes, and the New Brunswick government was prepared to help them obtain financing to build a factory that would provide an important new market for New Brunswick farmers and boost the province's economy.

Harrison and Wallace each put in $30,000, and their elder brothers, Andrew and Bob, contributed $20,000 a piece. Harrison and Wallace each owned one-third of the

Harrison reviews construction plans with Bob and Andrew. The steam peeler behind them could handle 135 kilograms of potatoes at a time.

company shares. Andrew and Bob, who were receiving salaries from McCain Produce, which they managed, each got one-sixth. McCain Foods Ltd. and Carleton Cold Storage Ltd., the company set up to own the cold storage facility, issued a total of $420,000 worth of bonds, which were guaranteed by the province of New Brunswick.

"That was a big deal for us," recalls Wallace, because the government guarantee allowed the new company to borrow money at an interest rate it could afford. "Who was going to buy McCain Foods bonds without a guarantee? Nobody. And it didn't cost the government anything except the risk it took." The brothers also persuaded the Carleton County Council to temporarily forgo property taxes on McCain Foods.

Under a program to encourage construction of cold storage facilities to help farmers, the federal government provided Carleton Cold Storage with an $87,000 grant. To qualify for this grant, Carleton Cold Storage had to be a public company. McCain Foods owned shares in the company and eventually bought all of them. (It absorbed Carleton Cold Storage in 1979.)

Harrison and Wallace paid a visit to the Bank of Nova Scotia in Saint John, where they met with the bank's supervisor for New Brunswick and Prince Edward Island. They wanted a $150,000 line of credit that would be used as working capital, with the new company's inventory and receivables as security. As they were making their pitch, the supervisor interrupted them. It so happened that the president of the bank, Horace Inman, was touring the province and was about to visit the branch. The McCain brothers would have to wait until the president's visit was over. Then they would be able to continue making their case for the bank's support.

"Inman was a very outgoing guy," recalls Wallace. "He sees us sitting there in the anteroom, waiting, so he asks who we are, and we told him."

Inman knew the McCain family from his time as supervisor of the bank in New Brunswick. He said, "You want to start a frozen food business? That's interesting. Did you get the money?"

"We don't know yet."

"Don't go anywhere."

Inman went into the supervisor's office. He came out fifteen minutes later and

The McCain family, left to right: Harrison, Wallace, Bob, Laura, Rosemary, Andrew, Jed Sutherland (Marie's husband), Marie, Billie, Margie, Marjorie.

confronted the brothers. "Your grandfather did business with this bank, too," he said. "He owed this bank a lot of money, and when he owed it he was actually broke. But your father paid all the money back. We never lost a nickel from any McCain. You've got your money."

Raising money for a factory was one thing; actually building it was another. Wallace and Harrison were salesmen. They knew nothing about building a manufacturing facility. But good leaders recognize their limitations, and the brothers, as they built the company, repeatedly recruited the best talent they could find in manufacturing, engineering, agronomy, and finance, among other fields. They began that pattern in Florenceville by seeking help from Olof Pierson.

Pierson had designed the Baxter plant in Corinna, Maine, and the McCains wanted him to design theirs. Wallace recalls Pierson, a graduate of the Massachusetts Institute of Technology, as brilliant but disorganized: "He smoked a lot. He would come in and talk about what we were going to do, and he would draw something on the back of his cigarette package. He never wrote anything down. He had it all in his head."

Sometimes Pierson would forget things – such as the motors that were needed to run the conveyor belts on the production line. It didn't occur to him to get them until Wallace asked him about it, shortly before the factory was scheduled to open. On the other hand, he was inventive and liked to design new machinery. This was important

THE BEGINNING 9

LEFT: Harrison and Wallace at the site of the Florenceville factory, 1956.
RIGHT: Opening ceremony, February 23, 1957. Wallace McCain (far left) watches on as New Brunswick premier Hugh John Flemming (far right) and Milton Gregg, federal minister of labour, cut the ribbon.

because the frozen food industry was still young, and its machinery and methodology were far from fully developed.

While the factory was being built, Wallace and Harrison moved their young families from Saint John, a big city by New Brunswick standards, to the village of Florenceville, home to just a few hundred people. Wallace's wife, Margaret (or Margie, as she is known), recalls the house she and her family moved into as small, cold, mouse-infested, and having a leaky roof. It was only later, once the company was successful, that the couple obtained a mortgage from the bank to build a better house, on a site overlooking the Saint John River. Wallace and Margaret hired an architect to design a $40,000 house, but Wallace couldn't raise more than $30,000 from the bank. He solved the problem by having the contractor "cut off" a third of the rooms, at the back of the house.

Harrison and Marion (Billie) McCain built a house next door to Wallace and Margie. Both houses were enlarged in later years, though the original fronts remain in place.

The official opening of the McCain Foods factory was a major event, not just for Carleton County but for all of New Brunswick. Premier Hugh John Flemming cut the ribbon for the factory and Milton Gregg, the federal minister of labour, came from Ottawa to do the same for the cold storage unit. They were among the seven hundred people who crowded into the Florenceville high school for the opening ceremonies and speeches.

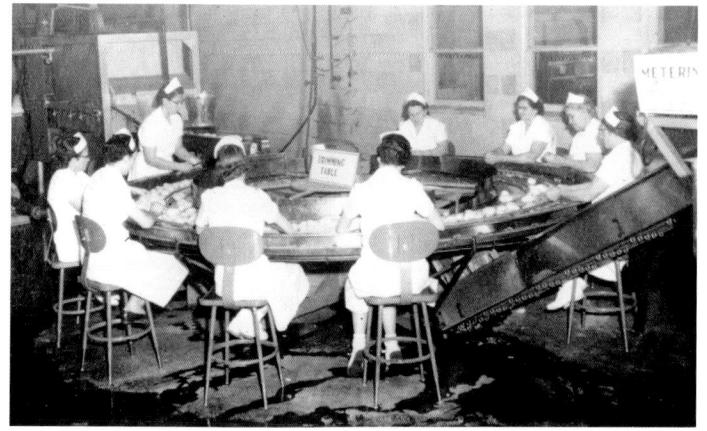 

LEFT: The trim table, 1957. This was "positive trimming," in which each potato was individually trimmed.
RIGHT: Opening-day tour: Wallace explains the packing area to Minister Gregg (centre), while Harrison chats with Premier Flemming.

Few of them understood how big a challenge the McCain brothers had set for themselves. Florenceville and its surroundings were farm country – not home to the skilled trades people needed to keep a large manufacturing operation going. Wallace McCain recalls going to garages looking for mechanics who would be able to maintain the equipment in the new factory. "No one knew anything about the technical part of the business," he says. "There were no machines like that around Florenceville."

Fortunately, Frank Hickling, who had assisted Olof Pierson in designing the plant and had been maintenance manager of the Birds Eye plant in Maine, stayed on as mechanic and plant manager. He had never finished high school, but he was smart and he knew how to run a frozen food factory. Nobody else did. "If we hadn't had him, I don't know what we would have done," says Wallace. "Nobody else had any experience."

There was rarely a dull moment. The fryers sometimes overheated, causing the accumulated potato crumbs or oil filter paper to burst into flames. Wallace says he used to make sure he had his clothes within easy reach when he went to bed in case he was called out to one of these fires in the middle of the night. (Now all McCain plants use heat exchangers with high-pressure steam systems to heat the fryers. They also have flame extinguishing systems in the hood above the fryers, thereby eliminating the risk of fires.)

One of Pierson's innovations was a machine that used steam to peel the skin off the potatoes. It was shaped like an oil drum and had a door on the side through which the potatoes were loaded. The only problem was that sometimes the pressure of the steam would blow the door off.

TOP: Unloading barrels of potatoes onto the production line, 1957.
BOTTOM: Packing frozen french fries into cartons by hand.
FACING PAGE: In 1959, McCain was producing frozen potato patties, broccoli, and peas. The middle photo shows employees Frank Hickling and Gene Bulmer receiving an order of fresh broccoli; the truck bears the old McCain Produce logo.

Flying doors were just part of the local colour at the McCain Foods factory. Another feature were the hunters and fishermen tramping through the factory with their trophies to be stored in the public lockers the McCains had included in the cold storage area in order to qualify for the federal grant. But these were the least of the problems. The brothers quickly realized that John Baxter, who had cautioned against basing a potato-processing business in New Brunswick, was right. "Our first products were greasy, black fries," Wallace says. "If there was such a thing as Grade F, that was what we were producing. We had never heard of sugar content in potatoes, or ACD [darkening caused by a chemical reaction in some potatoes after they have been cooked]."

The problem was simple: the local potatoes weren't good raw material for french fries. "We should have gone west … even to Manitoba or Alberta," Wallace says. "We didn't. We thought New Brunswick had the best potatoes in the world, but it probably had the worst for processing. The potato growers were growing good seed potatoes, but the poorest you could imagine for processing into frozen french fries."

To make good french fries, you need a long potato consisting of at least 20 percent solids – a potato such as the Russet Burbank, a variety prominent in the U.S. Pacific Northwest, which produces a long, crisp french fry. New Brunswick, with its short growing season, didn't grow the Russet Burbank, a long-season variety. Instead, farmers in the Saint John River Valley and neighbouring Aroostook County in Maine grew round potatoes such as the Kennebec and Katahdin. Easterners found these varieties tastier than the Russet Burbank as table potatoes. But they are far from ideal for french fry processing because of their round shape and lower solid content, which result in a short, moist, or limp french fry. And the stony soil of New Brunswick is also less than perfect for potato growing, since the stones can damage the potatoes during harvesting.

Not only were the potatoes less than ideal, but the farmers didn't know how to handle them properly. Potatoes produced for the fresh table and seed market – the only market the growers knew – are stored at low temperatures to keep them firm and prevent sprouting. But at low temperatures the potato transforms its starches into sugar, which caramelizes when the potato is fried. This produces a dark brown french fry. And consumers do not want dark brown french fries; they want light golden ones. So the growers needed to be educated on how to grow, store, and handle potatoes destined for processing.

In the beginning, McCain Foods had no choice but to do the best it could with what farmers delivered to its plant. In the early 1960s, over farmers' protests, it introduced the Russet Burbank to New Brunswick. But because of the shorter growing season, the potatoes were smaller than the ones grown in Idaho.

Happily for McCain, Donald Young, a plant biologist and specialist in potato variety breeding at the Agriculture Canada Research Centre in Fredericton, was trying to develop a processing potato better suited for the short eastern Canadian growing season. In 1983, he succeeded. The new potato, called the Shepody, was a boon for McCain and has since become one of the three most grown varieties in North America. Because of McCain's efforts, the Shepody is now grown around the world.

"Don made an enormous contribution to McCain Foods," says Wallace, "first through the Shepody variety, and later in a number of projects, from teaching and guiding our global team of agronomists for many years, to greatly improving yields in Manitoba and research in areas where we planned to build."

Since its first french fries weren't top quality, it was just as well that McCain, in its early period, was well diversified into other vegetables. For a while, frozen peas were a big part of the business, along with french fries. McCain also packed strawberries, broccoli, cauliflower, beans, and Brussels sprouts. Later, however, the company decided to focus on french fries and stopped processing vegetables other than potatoes.

In the long run, having to struggle to obtain the kind of potatoes it needed benefited McCain by forcing it to acquire expertise in agronomy. Tony van Leersum, who joined McCain in 1978 to head European operations and later became corporate vice-president for agriculture, believes this expertise enabled the company to operate successfully wherever it went. Because its major competitors, Simplot and Lamb Weston, enjoyed an ideal growing environment in the U.S. Northwest, they lacked experience in adapting to less favourable locations. As a result, the U.S. french

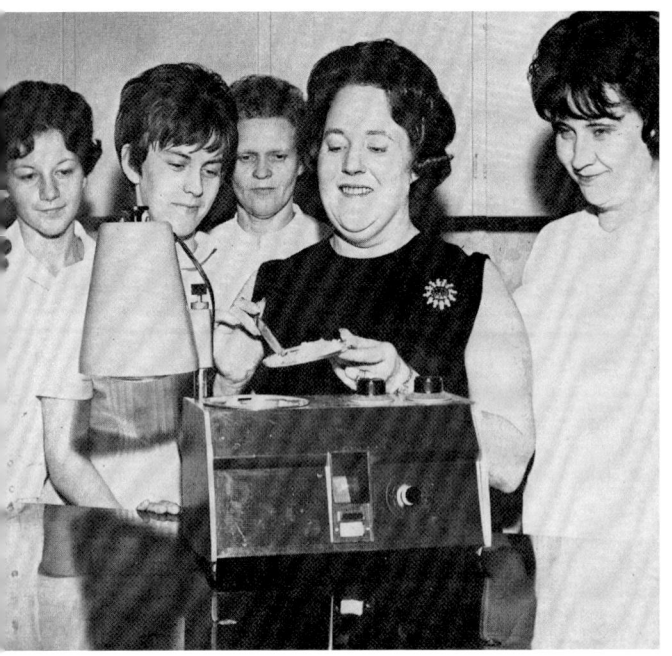

TOP: Jean Lawler and team in the test lab. Lawler was a stickler for quality: if she didn't approve of a batch, it wasn't shipped.
BOTTOM: Betty Betts in the quality-control lab, 1959.

fry giants have had less success in expanding outside North America.

The knowledge that McCain Foods began to acquire in Florenceville in 1957 is being applied today in locations as far-flung as China and India. "Today we will not invest in production facilities in a market until we know exactly where to grow the potatoes and where the best potatoes are," says Terry Bird, vice-president of corporate development and emerging markets. "In China, that took us seven years. We would go to one area, we'd grow, we'd test. Then we would try someplace else."

The location of the best place to grow determines the location of the factory. "It takes a kilogram of potatoes to make half a kilogram of french fries. If your factory is hundreds of kilometres away from where the good potato fields are, that adds a lot of cost to the operation," Bird explains. "We want the fields within a hundred kilometres of the factory."

Although the Florenceville plant had many inadequacies during its early years, McCain Foods has never depended on technology and machinery for its success. Its success was, and still is, based on people. In his Christmas message in the company paper, *The Star,* in 1972, Harrison McCain said: "We well know that people, not buildings and equipment, are the chief asset of our group, and we know that our continuing growth is strictly conditional on the loyalty and efforts of our employees." By saying this, he wasn't just being nice – he was speaking as the realist that he was.

Especially in the early days, it took phenomenal efforts to make a success of McCain Foods. "Most people don't realize just how hard Harrison and Wallace worked to get this business off the ground," says Allison McCain, chairman of McCain Foods. "They put their heart and soul into it."

Recollections of veteran employees published in the twenty-fifth-anniversary edition of *The Star* capture the flavour of those early times. Here's Betty Betts describing the beginning years at the Florenceville plant:

The first summer that I worked on peas, Harrison ran the line and Wallace worked in the field. It would be ten, eleven at night and Wallace would come dragging in, and would he ever be tired. They worked, they really worked! They know where their first dollar came from because they worked for it. They would tell us everything that was happening, everything that they were going to do and how we were part of it. And we really believed that we were part of the McCain family, believe you me!

Betty Betts is a good example of the kind of person who helped build McCain Foods. So is Lester Cox, or "Bud." Dubbed the "granddaddy of all supervisors" by *The Star*, Cox trained more than fifty production management trainees and supervisors. He joined McCain as a labourer in the cold storage building two years after the company began production in Florenceville. At the time, the freezing of the product, the packaging, and the shipping were part of the cold storage department. Work that today is done by machines, such as packing the frozen food in plastic bags, in those days was done by humans. Seven-day weeks of fourteen-hour days were common. Management, including Harrison and Wallace, helped out wherever help was needed.

Cox recalled labouring alongside the bosses in the cold storage. "Wallace McCain must have fired me a hundred times," he told *The Star* in 1992. "You had to think and act like them in order to survive. They like people to do things their way. If you do, you will make out okay."

Among the future supervisors Cox trained were members of the younger generation of McCains, including Allison, Scott, Michael, and Peter, as well as several other university graduates who would later become directors of McCain companies. "I trained them pretty hard; they knew what work was, anyway," Cox said. He trained these younger McCains in what he called "the McCain way," which means getting the job done quickly and efficiently. He told them, "Maybe later I will have to work for you, but now you work for me, and you do as I say."

In the *Star* article on Cox, Scott McCain explained the McCain way like this: "Our production people have been trained over the years to say, 'Don't tell me it can't be done, just do it.' … If it means you have to run seven days a week, do it. If the line

Bertha Lunn kisses Harry Kinney at his 1983 retirement party, as (left to right) production manager Scott McCain, production foreman Sherdon Cox, and production supervisor Bud Cox watch on. Plant manager Murray Lovely is on the right.

THE BEGINNING 15

Laura (Mrs. A.D.) McCain

Mrs. A.D. was Florenceville's leading philanthropist, involved in a wide range of community activities, from starting a Boy Scout troop to founding the Florenceville public library. She collected used clothing at her house so that anyone in need could drop by and choose an item. She ran her own social housing program, renting out about a dozen houses in the town at low rents.

"If someone in Florenceville needed help, she was the one they went to," says McCain Foods chairman Allison McCain. "Maybe someone needed help with a mortgage; the bank wasn't interested in people who had no resources, so they went to her. If people got let go at the factory, they would go to her and say, 'I really need that job.'

"Once when I was the production manager I fired a guy – it was the right thing to do. The next day, when I walked into the personnel manager's office, he was on the phone. 'The production manager just walked in and he was the one who fired him, so you can talk to him,' he said into the phone before handing it to me. Turned out it was my grandmother on the other end.

"The guy I had fired had gone to her. We didn't end up taking him back, but I do know of a couple of cases where people did end up coming back to work for us because of her intervention."

Laura McCain was also well known for her driving. "We used to be terrified," recounts her grandson Andrew McCain. "She insisted on giving us a ride home from school if she happened to be there. It was absolutely terrifying to be in the car with her going over the bridge. She could barely see over the wheel, and she would be driving almost a hundred kilometres an hour. But she always got us home safely."

The bridge in question is old and narrow. Mrs. McCain's car was big. "She waited until there wasn't any traffic and then scooted across down the middle of the bridge," recalls retired McCain food scientist Paul Dean. If a local resident happened to be driving on the bridge in the oncoming direction, that driver knew to back up and let Mrs. McCain pass.

She kept a close watch on her own children, not only when they were growing up but also as adults. Joe Palmer, former owner of Day & Ross and a friend of the McCain brothers, sometimes received phone calls from Mrs. McCain asking that he intervene to change some behaviour of which she disapproved. As Palmer recounts in his biography, Mrs. McCain would call, state the problem, and then hang up before Palmer had a chance to reply and without saying goodbye. A typical call would go like this: "Joe, this is Laura McCain. I wish Wallace wouldn't swear so much. He'll listen to you." Then she would hang up.

Palmer estimated he received two dozen such calls about Mrs. McCain's four sons. "In twenty-four or twenty-five phone conversations, I never once got a word in before she hung up. She was a great woman, and I had a world of respect for her."

TOP LEFT: Laura McCain and family: (left to right) Wallace, Eleanor, Harrison, Laura, Mr. A.D., Marie, Bob, Andrew.
RIGHT: Mrs. A.D., the family matriarch, was as famous for her driving as she was for her philanthropy.

could run ten thousand pounds per hour, the McCain way would be to have it run at twelve thousand pounds. Ten isn't acceptable. It was an attitude of never saying no. Never giving up. As a company, we have survived for thirty-five years using that philosophy."

Bud Cox made another contribution to McCain Foods: he had nine children and all of them worked for the company at one time or another. On one night shift, his son Tony was working under his supervision. During the shift, Bud fired and rehired him twice. As of 2007, six Cox offspring were McCain employees.

Cox and others who worked at McCain in the early days had to be generalists. If a machine needed fixing, you figured out how to fix it, even if you didn't know how to fix machines. Cox said: "We trained ourselves, got a little manual, called the serviceman, who probably didn't know more than we did. If we were lucky we bought a piece of equipment that would work and give the results we wanted. If we bought a piece, put it in the line, didn't get results, then we had to figure out what we had to do to that piece to make it work."

Sometimes innovative methods were employed. In one legendary incident, an engineer and a production supervisor were trying to figure out what was wrong with the freezing tunnel. To investigate, they donned snowmobile suits and rode through the tunnel on the belt. On another occasion, when an underground pipe plugged and attempts to unplug it were unsuccessful, someone decided to shoot a gun into the pipe to clear it. It didn't work.

The McCains knew they needed good people if their business was to succeed, and so they went looking for them. They tried to lure an engineer named Carl Morris from the Birds Eye plant just across the border in Maine. Morris declined. "I didn't think they were going to amount to much," he explains. How, he thought, could such a small company compete with the likes of General Foods?

McCain was packing some products under the Birds Eye label, and Morris had met the two brothers during his visits to Florenceville to ensure its production was

TOP: Carl Morris (right) with Dave Morgan, winner of a 1969 safety contest for his suggestion to install Dutch doors in the mezzanine of the Florenceville building.
BOTTOM: Marilyn Strong, 1971. Strong joined McCain in 1961 as Harrison's secretary.

TOP LEFT: Bob Ferguson, New Brunswick snack foods sales supervisor, next to a McCain potato-chip truck.
TOP RIGHT: Pop-a-Doodle production, 1970.
BOTTOM: McCain chips came in a variety of flavours.

up to Birds Eye standards. "I got to know Harrison and Wallace quite well," he said, "and we became good friends."

Although he turned down the job offer, Morris still got involved with the company. "I became the first engineer to consult for McCain – without pay. If they were working on a project, such as putting in a new blancher, they would say, 'How big do you think that ought to be?' We would be having dinner and I would draw it on a napkin."

Gradually, Morris changed his opinion: maybe Harrison and Wallace would amount to something after all. He liked their ambition to develop the company and their ability to make decisions quickly. General Foods never made a wrong decision, he says, but the company leaders took so long to make it that any advantage was often lost.

So, on April Fool's Day 1962, Morris started working at McCain Foods as plant manager. He relished the chance, absent at Birds Eye, to work in an environment where decisions were made quickly and where it was permissible to make mistakes. "If you were wrong, you got a heck of an education and you probably didn't make that mistake again. If you were right, you were so far ahead of everybody else that it was a major coup for the company."

Early errors by McCain Foods included a foray into the popcorn business. The product was called Pop-a-Doodle and had a sweet topping on it. One Christmas, the McCain marketers had the bright idea of offering two-foot-long bags of Pop-a-Doodle coloured red and green. Almost none sold.

In the 1970s, the company operated a snack food division with a factory in Saint-André, close to Grand Falls, producing potato chips. But the freight costs to major Canadian markets were too high to gain a significant market share, so the business was sold. McCain then decided to focus exclusively on frozen foods, which it produced at its original plant in Florenceville and at a bigger one in Grand Falls, opened in 1971.

McCain switchboard operators Helen Hallett and Mabel Carter.

Like other McCain veterans, Morris describes the early days as fun. Part of that fun came from participating in an ambitious project: to build McCain Foods into the biggest french fry producer in the world. "If Wallace and Harrison had started to make eyeglasses or footballs, they'd have had the same vision – to be the biggest in the world," says Morris. "They would have had the same goal and they would have accomplished it. Because they were very ambitious. And just a helluva lot of fun to be around."

Yet Morris also recounts a brutal work schedule: "I am not kidding when I say we worked seven days a week, eighteen hours a day." But the work was enjoyable because everyone pulled together. "Lots of times there would be two truckloads that had to go to Toronto or somewhere and there weren't enough bodies to load the trucks. So we'd all go over, Harrison and Wallace included, and load trucks."

Some managers would view hard labour as beneath them. But Wallace and Harrison weren't professional managers. They were entrepreneurs with everything riding on the success of their fledgling company. For them, loading trucks was a way to make good on promises to their customers, to earn the respect of their employees, and perhaps most important of all, to learn the business.

In later years, they took what they had learned in Florenceville around the world, to France and South Africa and Argentina and many other countries, where they

Les McIntosh, personnel manager; Tim Bliss, chief engineer; and Don Wishart, purchasing manager, 1969.

built factories to process potatoes and other raw materials into frozen food products the consumers of the world wanted to buy. "How did they know how to do something in Australia?" asks Carl Morris. "Because in Florenceville they had done every job that was to be done: harvesting potatoes, cutting them, sorting them, cooking them, packaging them, putting them in the cold storage, loading them on the trucks."

While Wallace and Harrison were learning the basics of the manufacturing process, they were also learning how to run an organization and how to recruit the talent without whom they knew they would never realize their ambitions. Morris went on to become vice-president of manufacturing for McCain Foods Canada, then senior vice-president, and then launched McCain's business in Japan and South Korea as president of McCain Japan.

Another key early recruit was Tim Bliss, who also joined in 1962 and became corporate vice-president of engineering. Bliss was a friend of Wallace McCain's from their college days at the University of New Brunswick. Both spent summers as officer cadets in the University Naval Training Division and during the summer of 1951 were stationed together at Esquimalt, on Vancouver Island. Their ship took a one-month training cruise to Hawaii, where they spent seven days. Once they had completed their time in Esquimalt, they returned to New Brunswick via the Panama Canal on a cruiser, the HMCS *Ontario,* accompanying a destroyer returning from the Korean War.

Bliss likes to point out that he didn't use his friendship with Wallace McCain to get a job at McCain Foods. He was working for Engineering Consultants Inc., a firm owned by Irving, when he heard that McCain was looking for an engineer. "Irving and McCain had a gentleman's agreement not to rob management personnel from one other," Bliss recalls. "So McCain couldn't contact me, but I could contact them."

Bliss called not Wallace but Harrison McCain, who, after consulting with Wallace as he always did, promptly hired Bliss. Morris and Bliss provided the expertise Wallace and Harrison themselves lacked. "They made a dramatic hit with the company," Wallace says, "because one understood production and one understood engineering, which Harrison and I knew nothing about."

One advantage of living and working in a village is that you don't waste time com-

muting to and from work. Bliss soon discovered the advantage of living five minutes from the plant: he could get there quickly when he was awakened in the middle of the night.

"One night that we were running peas, I came into work three times. And one Christmas Day, I got a phone call at eight in the morning from the watchman. He said, 'You'd better come up here and have a look. A wall of that new cold store we're building out back just fell down.' So I went to the plant in the howling wind and blowing snow. We went out and had a look. There wasn't anything we could do except survey the damage and start Boxing Day to fix it."

Bliss enjoyed working in a place where a constant sense of urgency prevailed: "It was a case of production trying to keep up with sales. We just couldn't make enough product." The factory was shut down in the summer because it ran out of potatoes – there wasn't yet technology to store them year round. But that didn't mean work stopped. The production downtime was used to build additions to the factory and upgrade equipment in order to increase the plant's output and keep up with soaring demand. And in the couple of months before the new season's potatoes arrived, the factory processed other vegetables.

That McCain's french fries had become so popular so quickly was a testament to the selling skills of Harrison and Wallace. "We produced some damn poor products, but

LEFT: At the 1976 International Food Show, London, England.
RIGHT: Harrison promotes McCain products at a 1970 food show.

ABOVE: Wallace and Dick McWhirter in Australia, 1968.
FACING PAGE: A sampling of the product line of the early 1970s.

Harrison was a superb salesman. We both did a lot of sales work, and we sold the product," says Wallace. Fortunately, they had little competition. Zeropac, a Quebec company, was the only other processor of standalone frozen french fries in Canada at the time. Fraser Vale, of Chilliwack, British Columbia, produced frozen fries but only to include as part of a package of fish and chips.

The early years were ones of constant travel across Canada for Wallace and Harrison. Each spent around 150 nights a year away from home. Usually, at least one of them was on the road. After Morris and Bliss arrived, the brothers knew the factory would be in good hands, so both of them often travelled at the same time. Harrison and Wallace sometimes had to walk down the production line to borrow travel money from the workers. There were no credit cards, automatic teller machines, or extended banking hours then, and the employees knew how important the sales trips were to the company's success. "Harrison would get two dollars from one person and five dollars from another," says former employee Florence White. "He would always pay back the money. The faith everyone put in him was amazing."

In the 1960s, North American demand for french fries was growing by around 20 percent a year. This demand was fuelled by the explosive growth of quick-service restaurants. One early McCain customer was A&W, which opened its first Canadian restaurant in Winnipeg in 1956. But the biggest buyer was Kentucky Fried Chicken. At the time, most Kentucky Fried Chicken outlets were using fresh potatoes for their french fries, as many continued to do until the late 1970s. However, Wallace and Harrison persuaded some outlets to switch to frozen. Wallace recalls: "When we went to a town, the first thing we asked was, 'Is there a Kentucky Fried Chicken here?' They were big users." At the time, the individual franchisees made their own decisions as to which french fries to use; such decisions are now made by the corporate office.

These early sales trips were gruelling. Harrison and Wallace quickly figured out that winning over chefs was the quickest way to success in the food service market. So they spent their days on the road demonstrating frozen french fries to chefs in restaurant kitchens. After a day of demonstrating, their clothes smelled of frying oil. To get rid of the odour, they hung their suits out the windows of their modest hotel rooms to air out overnight.

This was the beginning of the end-user system of selling to the food service industry that became one of the most important drivers of McCain's success in Canada and around the world. Like many great ideas, the end-user system is common sense. The traditional way for a manufacturer to get its product to a customer is to convince a distributor of its worth and leave it to the distributor to sell it. But the distributor has lots of products to sell. So why not go directly to customers with just one product – yours – and demonstrate its superiority?

Dick McWhirter, a salesman who came to McCain in 1960 from Kellogg, perfected the end-user system. The purpose of the system, which is still used by McCain salespersons all over the world, is to persuade chefs who have always prepared their french fries from fresh potatoes that frozen fries are a better choice. This was especially difficult when frozen french fries were still a novelty. Chefs had always prepared fries from fresh potatoes and doubted that a frozen product would be accepted by their customers. Moreover, fresh potatoes were cheap – around one and a half cents a kilogram at the time, while McCain was asking nine cents a kilogram. Why pay more for processed, frozen ones?

The best way to make the case for frozen fries is to do a side-by-side comparison. The salesperson has the chef peel, cut, and cook fresh potatoes. The raw potatoes are weighed before being prepared and the oil level in the frying pan is measured. Meanwhile, the McCain rep prepares the frozen fries. Then he or she compares the preparation time, the weight of the finished product, and its appearance, taste, and texture. Finally, the sales rep calculates the per-serving cost, including labour, of each method.

In this test, the advantages of McCain frozen french fries become clear. The chef sees that the apparent lower cost of fresh potatoes is illusory: once fresh potatoes have been peeled, cut, and cooked, ten kilograms of potatoes yields less than two kilograms of fries. Frozen fries absorb less oil than fresh fries and take less time to prepare, thereby reducing labour costs. Moreover, their quality is more consistent throughout the year. In the spring, for example, raw potatoes that have been in storage for months tend to be high in sugar, resulting in soggy fries that are unappetizingly dark. And of course there is another advantage: with frozen fries, there are no peels and starchy water that need to be disposed of.

McCain chicken picnic, 1973: (left to right) Harrison, Tim Bliss, Carl Morris, Dick McWhirter (his face partially blocked), and Archie McLean (vice-president of marketing).

Sometimes, an unconvinced customer offers to take a case to try out the product. "If he does that, you know you are not going to keep the customer," says Wallace. "So you say, 'You've got to use this for a month before you can know for sure.' If you can hold the customer for a month – we have found from experience – he has let the guy who ran the peeler go, so that restaurant won't be going back to raw potatoes."

McWhirter was the second salesman hired by McCain. The first, Ralph Orr, also came from Kellogg. Orr worked the Maritime provinces while McWhirter was based in Hamilton, Ontario. A third salesman, Peter Laurie, worked out of Ottawa. One day when Laurie was visiting the Florenceville headquarters, Harrison challenged him to a sales contest in nearby Woodstock. The challenge was to see who could sell the most product on the main street, with each taking one side of the street. Harrison won but, says Laurie, that was because Harrison knew Woodstock better than he did and picked the side with the most potential customers.

McWhirter was appointed sales supervisor for Ontario, then national sales manager. In 1969, he became vice-president of sales. Like Carl Morris, McWhirter left a huge American company to come work for a small Canadian one. In a *Star* interview in 1983, McWhirter said he had two reasons for joining what was then an almost unknown company. First, he could see that grocery stores were starting to install frozen food sections and he thought frozen foods had big potential for future growth. Second, he was impressed by the McCain brothers.

As a Kellogg salesman, McWhirter had never had to demonstrate how to prepare Corn Flakes, so selling frozen french fries was a new challenge for him. "When I talked to a chef, I was selling to the buyer who bought the product, cooked the product, tasted the product, and served the product. No hot air – I had to know my facts and sell with enthusiasm."

One of his major responsibilities, at a time when McCain was just beginning to assemble a sales force, was to find people who would excel at selling products whose worth was, to many, still unproven. Just because someone had worked at a major food processor such as Campbell, Kraft, or Kellogg was no guarantee that person could sell McCain frozen french fries. Quite a few did join up, McWhirter said. "Just like

Harrison

During the latter years of the 1970s, fundraisers in Toronto were busy calling Canada's captains of industry to solicit money for the construction of a new home for the Toronto Symphony Orchestra. In exchange for the largest donation, they were offering naming rights for the spectacular new hall designed by prominent Canadian architect Arthur Erickson. Among those called was Harrison McCain. Would he be prepared to contribute $5 million in exchange for the right to name the new hall?

"Yes," he said, "I would. Name it the Florenceville Dance Hall and you've got your money."

The offer was declined and instead the new building was named Roy Thomson Hall, in honour of the late media magnate, in exchange for a $4.5 million donation from the Thomson family. Paul Tellier, a long-time member of the McCain Foods board, is sure that Harrison would have written a cheque if Toronto's cultural elite had been willing to accept the colourful name he proposed.

Harrison McCain was almost as famous for his sense of humour as for his brilliance as an entrepreneur and businessman. The stories of his escapades would fill a book.

In the mid-1960s, Stanley Wagner visited Harrison in Florenceville. Wagner owned Caterpac, a British food distributor that McCain Foods wanted to acquire. He was known as a jokester, so Harrison thought he would play a joke before Wagner had a chance to. As Harrison described the episode years later in an interview, he and Wagner talked in his office at McCain Foods until late afternoon. Harrison then invited him home for dinner. On the way, they drove through Florenceville's low-income neighbourhood. Harrison pulled into the driveway of an unkempt, decrepit house and said, "Well, here we are."

Wagner was speechless.

An old woman was hanging out underwear on the clothesline, the garments flapping in the wind. Harrison said, "There's Billie hanging out my drawers."

"Stanley's mouth dropped open," Harrison recalled. "He didn't know what to say."

Harrison contentedly watched Wagner "writhe and suffer" for a minute. Then he backed his car out of the

Harrison, Connie Bliss, and Shirley Morris sing Christmas carols at the Florenceville McCain Christmas party, 1970.

driveway and drove home, where Harrison's wife, Billie, awaited them.

Harrison was good at seizing opportunities to have some fun. James Downey, former president of the University of New Brunswick and a close friend, told the story of Harrison's visit to a posh restaurant in London, England. He was standing near the door waiting for a friend, and, as usual, was nattily dressed. An older man accompanied by a young woman arrived and, mistaking Harrison for the head waiter, asked to be shown to a quiet table. "This way, sir, madam," said Harrison, leading them to a table and taking the order for "champagne." Harrison then informed the head waiter of what he had done and conveyed an order for the most expensive bottle of bubbly.

For Downey, this story told a lot about Harrison McCain – quickness of mind, acting ability, and sartorial elegance combined with a lack of pretension. "Most of us, and certainly most CEOs, would have felt sufficiently offended to be mistaken for a waiter that we would have put the snotty gent to rights immediately."

Wallace

Margaret McCain likes to say that her husband, Wallace, is bilingual – he speaks Maritime English and cursing. No one felt the brunt of his salty language more than ice hockey referees when they made what Wallace considered unfair calls against the Potato Kings, a Florenceville team sponsored by McCain Foods during the 1970s.

"Wallace was an enthusiastic hockey fan," recalls Ian Cameron, who played left wing and centre. "His language at the games was just awful. To hear him yelling and screaming at referees would just turn your hair."

So keen a fan was Wallace that he selected employees for McCain Foods on the basis of their hockey skills. Most turned out to be excellent employees and in some cases strong managers. Cameron, for example, has worked in senior management positions for McCain Foods for three decades.

The Potato Kings played in the Republican League, an amateur circuit in New Brunswick. Many of the players worked for McCain. Tim Bliss, vice-president of engineering, was the team's coach. In 1972, Bliss heard that Cameron and Bill Adams, both recently hired by Day & Ross, McCain's trucking company, were good hockey players. Adams, who became a McCain vice-president, had rated a tryout with the Toronto Maple Leafs.

"Pretty soon they were in Florenceville working as production management trainees and playing hockey," recalls Bliss, who says about eight McCain employees were hired to strengthen the Potato Kings.

When Bliss got too busy to be the head coach, McCain hired John French, who had played professional hockey in the World Hockey Association, to replace him as head coach and work in the accounting department.

For Wallace, sometimes the welfare of the team took precedence over that of the factory. On one occasion, Bert Inman, a good player, was called away from the fryer when nobody else was present to operate it because Wallace wanted him to travel to Campbelltown to play for the team.

"Wallace was a big supporter of our team and the game of hockey," says French. "If he had customers or employees in from out of town and there was a game on, that's where they ended up, whether they wanted to be there or not."

Wallace played on the Florenceville high school hockey team and then on the junior varsity team during his one year at the University of New Brunswick. "I was never much of a player, but I had a lot of fun at it," he says.

After a few years, the Potato Kings folded. "It started out for a laugh because I liked hockey and there wasn't much to do in Florenceville," says Wallace. But after a few years, he decided that the $50,000 a year it was costing McCain to sponsor the Potato Kings was too much, especially since the championship seemed out of the team's reach. "I don't like to lose," Wallace says.

His son Scott, now a Maple Leaf Foods executive, carries on the family hockey tradition as majority owner of the Saint John Sea Dogs of the Quebec Major Junior Hockey League. Scott also played for the Potato Kings. "He was a great player," says Wallace.

TOP LEFT: The Potato Kings in action, 1979.
TOP RIGHT: The 1974–75 Potato Kings, with Bill Adams in hockey uniform at bottom left. Coach Tim Bliss is on the far right, middle row, with manager Don Wishart beside him.

I had decided to take a chance on McCain Foods, I guess my enthusiasm convinced them to take a chance with me, and with McCain. For many of them, it proved to be a very satisfactory career." As the years went by, however, the company preferred to hire inexperienced people rather than recruit veterans from other companies. "Training them ourselves, we have better results," McWhirter said. "More loyalty and fewer bad habits."

McWhirter enjoyed a challenge, and one of the biggest during the early years was trying to persuade western Canadians to buy french fries processed in the east. "We had a lot of fun in the 1960s selling in western Canada," he told *The Star*. "I mean, who wanted to buy a truckload of frozen potatoes from New Brunswick? The first question from the distributor was, 'Where the hell is Florenceville?' Also, many distributors said, 'You're crazy, McWhirter, we've got enough potatoes here in Manitoba and Alberta to satisfy us all.'" In addition to helping introduce McCain to western Canada, McWhirter pioneered sales in Singapore, Australia, and the Caribbean.

Another important early recruit was Carl Ash, who joined McCain in 1965 as comptroller. When Ash applied for the job, Harrison asked Ken Cossaboom, who was then accountant for McCain, to speak with Ash and get back to Harrison with his opinion. Cossaboom said, "The signature on his CV is 'C. Ash.' So I think he is the right man to handle the company's finances."

McCain Foods has been a financial success from the beginning. Its first operating statement, for the period ended May 31, 1957, showed a profit of $1,822, and the company has made money ever since – an almost unheard of achievement. It was growing rapidly, but rapid growth is no guarantee of increased profits. Costs must be kept under control. Harrison and Wallace McCain knew that if they were to manage McCain's growth effectively, they would need better financial information than they were getting.

At the time, Ash was manager of finance at the Dominion Bridge Company in Montreal. But he had grown up in Nova Scotia and New Brunswick and wanted to return to the Maritimes. Every year, he and his wife drove to Amherst, Nova Scotia,

Harrison and Wallace on a Thomas Equipment tree shearer, 1969.

Wallace and Harrison at the Florenceville plant, 1970.

for their summer holidays. "There wasn't any Trans-Canada Highway then," Ash told *The Star* in 1987. "The main road went right alongside the McCain plant. Each year I drove by, the company was larger. I always had in my mind that at some point in my career I would like to join a company that had started out small and was expanding."

In 1965, an employment agency was advertising for a comptroller. The ad didn't name the company but did say it was located in northwestern New Brunswick near good hunting and fishing. Recalls Ash: "I said, 'It can only be McCain Foods.'" After he applied for the job, Wallace and Harrison McCain invited him for an interview and hired him.

The fly-fishing suited Ash, but the budgeting process at McCain Foods needed work. One manual accounting machine served the entire company. "They had virtually no systems at all," Ash told *The Star*. "You have to plan where you are going and you have to know what your costs are – it was a real challenge because there wasn't anything to start with."

Ash designed the management control report (MCR), which Bruce Terry, who became director of finance in 1990 and later CFO of McCain Foods Limited, describes as "the bible of the company." Ash had been trained in standard cost accounting at Dominion Bridge and he introduced that approach at McCain. "Standard costing drives you toward understanding where you are overachieving and where you are underachieving," explains Terry. "Underachievement is where you are losing. So this approach allows you to identify and focus on the big issues."

Bill Mabee, who was vice-president of finance and later succeeded Ash, played an important role in the successful implementation of MCR, working with managers of the different functions within the company to help them get used to the new system. "They all needed to learn to speak the language of the other disciplines," he recalls. Mabee spent a lot of time with Carl Morris translating McCain's manufacturing processes into a system of administrative control.

Wallace and Harrison soon became strong believers in the MCR and used it to help them guide the company's fortunes for more than four decades. "At every monthly management meeting we combed through the variances in the MCR," says

Terry. And the MCR created a low-cost mentality at McCain which, in Terry's view, drove the company's worldwide success. "In manufacturing, he who has the lowest costs wins. You have to market, you have to do everything else right, but if you can't do it at the lowest cost, somebody else can ultimately copy you and take away your business."

Yet another early hire who became a McCain mainstay was Paul Dean, who arrived in 1959 to take charge of quality control. A native of upstate New York, Dean studied food science at the University of Georgia and turned down eight job offers to come to Florenceville and work for McCain. Recruiting highly qualified individuals to come to out-of-the-way Florenceville has always been a challenge but, in Dean's case, the location was an attraction. He came for the climate, preferring the cool Canadian weather to what he would have experienced had he chosen to work for Coca-Cola in Atlanta or one of the other U.S. companies that wanted him.

Like Carl Morris, Dean thought at first that the ambitious McCains might be overreaching. "Harrison would say he was going to be the largest french fry producer in the world. I used to roll my eyes. I didn't think it was possible because the Americans were so big. But he had great single-mindedness of purpose. He put the blinders on, and he was headed right that way."

Dean echoes many employees who say that one of the satisfactions of working for the company was the variety of the work. "It was management by crisis. You never knew what you were going to be doing on a given day."

There was an urgent purpose to it all – the desire to keep getting bigger and better. But this came with a price: hard work that could wear a person down. "We couldn't get enough help," Dean recalls. "We were always short of production people and supervisors. So we worked six or seven days a week. Harrison and Wallace worked that way, and they expected everyone else to. I just got worn down." Dean left McCain for the federal government food research station at Kentville, Nova Scotia, where he worked for six years before returning to McCain.

Like Terry, Dean believes that attention to detail, especially on the cost side, has a

Wallace and Harrison discussing robotics in 1972. By 2007, most of McCain's packing departments were roboticized.

LEFT: Wallace and Harrison listen as Carl Ash addresses McCain employees at the 1977 Christmas party.
RIGHT: Carl Ash at his desk, 1987.

lot to do with the company's success. At one point, Dean spent several months looking into whether McCain should make its own cheese for its pizzas rather than continue to rely on an outside supplier. Once he had everything figured out, including the design for a production line, he took the proposal to Wallace, who immediately spotted a flaw. It takes a hundred kilograms of milk to make twenty kilograms of cheese. The rest is whey, a milky water that has little value (though in dried form, it is used in some food products). "Wallace saw right away that it would be too expensive for us to try it," says Dean. (Although McCain Foods did not end up making cheese at its New Brunswick plants, it later bought several cheese plants in Ontario.)

Archie McLean came aboard in 1972 as vice-president of marketing, eventually rising to the position of president and CEO of McCain Foods Canada Ltd. Soon after joining McCain, he found that 55 percent of consumers were preparing their french fries in the oven rather than deep-frying them, resulting in a french fry lacking in crispness.

"We should have a product that can be heated in the oven but tastes like it was prepared in the deep fat fryer," he said.

Carl Morris set to work in the test kitchen to turn McLean's vision into reality. He succeeded in developing a process that gave oven-prepared fries a deep-fried crispness and flavour. Part of the process was patented and, in 1975, McCain launched

Superfries, which quickly became a resounding success, increasing retail sales of McCain fries by 30 percent. They are also a bestseller in Great Britain and Australia as "Oven Chips" and in Europe as "1.2.3 Frites" or "Just Au Four."

Part of the exhilaration of building McCain Foods was that it was a learning experience for everyone, including all its senior executives. Nobody in the company had an MBA. Instead, the executive ranks were filled with young, energetic managers who weren't afraid to try new things and who knew how to learn from their mistakes.

The first overseas employee hired was Charles "Mac" McCarthy, who joined in 1965 to launch a British branch of McCain Foods. He had a good job with an English frozen food processor, Eskimo Foods. So why leave to join a risky foreign start-up? "It was the people," he says. "The people with Harrison and Wallace – Andrew and Bob, Timmy Bliss, Carl Ash, Carl Morris, Don Wishart, Bob Wishart, Paul Dean,

and lots more – all good fellows, all working hard, all enthusiastic, just a great crowd, and none of us was a sophisticated business operator. We learned as we went on. We had our experience, and that taught us what to do the next time."

Good people are vital to building a great company, and so is money. Just as McCain had the perfect timing for starting a frozen french fry company, so it was fortunate in its choice of banker. The Bank of Nova Scotia has strong roots in the Maritime provinces and is the most international of the Canadian banks. While some Canadian banks dislike lending money against foreign receivables, Scotiabank, which had branches in Jamaica before it had one in Toronto, tends to be more understanding of the needs of companies doing business internationally. Historically, says former chairman Cedric Ritchie, the bank grew by financing the trade in sugar, rum, and molasses from the south for codfish and lumber from the north.

Ritchie grew up in Upper Kent, near Florenceville, and started his banking career in nearby Bath. He knew the McCains before he started his ascent up the executive ladder, which culminated in his appointment as chairman and CEO in 1974, a position he held until he retired in 1995.

TOP: Archie "Only the Bold Will Prosper" McLean, 1982.
MIDDLE: The launch of Superfries gave McCain its most successful product to date.
BOTTOM: Mac McCarthy, 1977.

The Florenceville plant in winter, early 1970s.

"Without Cedric we could not have built this business," says Wallace. "Mostly deals were done by phone, no big documents needed. There was trust. It helped that he came from the same province, he knew where we came from, he understood us and what we were doing. He knew we were honest and responsible people."

When Harrison travelled, he carried a letter signed by Ritchie saying that the Bank of Nova Scotia would honour a cheque for any amount signed by Harrison McCain. Bruce Terry tells of the time Harrison flew to Australia to buy a business for $15 million with a cheque. The Australian company's bank said it couldn't accept a cheque for such a large amount. Harrison produced Ritchie's letter, the banker called Canada, and the cheque was honoured. Wallace's son, Michael, who during the 1990s ran McCain's U.S. business, used to say that Harrison and Wallace had a simple financial strategy: 1-800-CALL-RITCHIE.

Cedric Ritchie says Wallace and Harrison inspired confidence from the first. "They were likeable, ambitious, very energetic. They knew where they wanted to go, and they knew how to get there. There wasn't much grass growing under their feet."

As a native of the Saint John River Valley, Ritchie is particularly impressed with the economic benefits the success of McCain has brought to the area. "Potatoes are a seasonal industry. The crop all comes off in six weeks in September and October. Before McCain started, most of the crop was shipped to Montreal and Toronto. The glut would reduce the price. McCain brought stability to the marketing and to the price. More importantly, it brought the value-added processing to the area, and that created steady employment. Before, it was all seasonal employment."

The farmers obtained price stability by signing pre-season contracts to sell all or some of their crop to McCain at a set price. The growers still had crop risk, but McCain Foods took on the market risk. As it turned out, during most of the 1960s and 1970s, the contract price was higher than the market price at the time of delivery.

From the beginning, transporting was a major problem for McCain. Florenceville is far from the company's major Canadian markets and as production levels soared

Gail Seeley hands documents to the driver of a Day & Ross double trailer "B-train," c.1970.

during the early years, getting the goods to the customers on time became increasingly difficult.

Elbert Day and Walter Ross founded Day & Ross in 1950. They had one truck for hauling potatoes from New Brunswick to Quebec. Joe Palmer, a colourful New Brunswick grower turned entrepreneur, later bought a share of the company. Once the Florenceville factory was opened, it didn't take long for McCain Foods to become Day & Ross's biggest customer. In 1965, it bought majority ownership of the company; Palmer retained a small interest and stayed on as president.

As McCain grew, so did Day & Ross, and by the end of the 1960s it owned four hundred trucks. The company had good returns for many years but then got into financial difficulty. New management was later able to overcome those problems and reshape Day & Ross into one of Canada's most successful trucking lines and a significant contributor to the overall success of McCain Foods.

As the 1960s began, McCain Foods' sales were growing ever larger each year. Florenceville was becoming more prosperous. The shops were bustling and people were driving newer cars. One payday, just to demonstrate the importance of McCain to the local economy, the company paid everyone in two-dollar bills, which soon overflowed the tills of the local storekeepers.

Harrison and Wallace weren't paying themselves lavish salaries or dividends.

They were bringing home only $100 a week when employees such as Frank Hickling were earning $150. Everything the company earned was being ploughed back into it. "Some people are in business to clip dividends or make a certain amount of profit," Harrison told *Canadian Business* magazine. "We're in business to grow."

By the end of the 1960s, growth was well underway. In his 1968 Christmas message to employees, Harrison remarked that McCain had already become the largest frozen vegetable company in Canada and one of the largest frozen french fry producers in the world.

Much bigger companies saw what the McCains were accomplishing and wanted in. Heinz, Imasco, General Foods, and others offered to buy McCain Foods. The brothers could have sold and retired from fourteen-hour workdays to lives of leisure. "We never considered it," says Wallace. "It never crossed our minds." For them, building a great business was more fun than sailing or playing golf.

"You're in love with the game," Harrison explained to *Executive* magazine. "The game is action, what's going on. There's something new all the time – buying companies, building factories, hiring guys, motivating people, seeing advertising programs, taking positions on commodities, borrowing money, settling lawsuits."

George McClure, an economist who had held senior government positions, joined McCain in 1970. He was attracted by the energy and optimism that the company's leaders brought to work with them every day. They were going to do big things and nothing was going to stand in their way. "It was a sense," says McClure, "of 'the world is our oyster.'"

TOP: The September 1967 edition of *Executive* magazine featured the McCains.
BOTTOM: George McClure, 1970.

Maritimers are international traders. Their own home markets are too small to sustain large businesses, so they need to look elsewhere, not only west to the rest of Canada but south to the United States and east across the Atlantic. It did not escape the notice of the McCains that the freight rate from New Brunswick to England was lower than the rate to Vancouver. Nor did they fail to observe that nobody was making any serious attempt to sell frozen french fries to the British, a nation of chip eaters. A vast market was there for the taking.

"Our dad was an exporter of seed potatoes and he taught us the world is small," Harrison McCain told the *Toronto Star* in 1975. "We were lucky to have our vision of

Florenceville employees celebrate McCain's twenty-fifth anniversary.

the whole world as a market. Our business succeeded because we didn't want to sit here on our arse in New Brunswick."

Being part of the McCain team in its first decades was exhilarating, in part because the McCains were so quick to pounce on new opportunities. "It was ready, fire, aim," says McClure. "We were out to dominate the processed-potato business in the world. It was a crazy goal but we just had an intuitive feeling that we could do it. It was a remarkable feeling, and you can't duplicate that in many jobs … The best thing and the thing that appealed to me most was a great sense of adventure."

As the 1960s progressed and the company continued to grow, the McCains were having far too much fun to even think about selling the company. The adventure was just beginning.

Special thanks also to ...

McCain has survived and thrived with the dedication and generous hard work of so many people over the years, people whose contributions and stories would fill many books. Some have been named and quoted in this one, or appear in the pictures.

Because there is not enough room to honour and acknowledge everyone, thirty long-term McCain employees and retirees were asked to name candidates for a list of employees who became legendary and who helped build the company in some significant way. Many more could be added to this list if space allowed.

The real aim of this list, however, is to convey to readers that the success of McCain Foods Limited is based on many more people, at all levels of the company, than those who are given voice or face here.

CANADA

Ken Antworth
Dwight Arbeau
Camile Beaulieu
Alberta Bell
Nelson Bernier
George Bourgoin
Bob Brown
Ken Brown
Dan Chartier
Bob Chernecki
Tom Davidson
Wayne Devine
Steve Dowbiggin
Marie Giberson
Doug Howatt
Bob Hurst
Burt Inman
Harold Kilfoil
Gilles Laforge
Kevin Lelievre
Angus "Gus" Lyall
Claude Lord
Alden Lunn
Peter Mabee
Wanda McCarthy
Wilfred McCarthy
Dave McInroy
Ron Minty
Alton Morrell
Ken Nichols
Elaine Norton
Dave O'Brien
Bev O'Keefe
David Parfitt
Ray Peterson
Jean Pinette
Madeline Post
Reg Reid
Arthur Rioux
Winston Ruff
Ken Seeley
Leonard Slipp
Peter Smith
Stan Spavold
Les Thomas
Allen Tompkins
Lloyd Tompkins
Jeff Vesey
John Walker
Bud White
Gilbert White
Gilbert Whittaker

UNITED KINGDOM

Gussie Archer
Robin Batten
Peter Beswick
John Collins
Geoff Dent
Pat Drummond
Peter Eddleston
Dave Ferrar
Pam Hume
Colin Jenkinson
Julie Leivers
Allan Milton
Don Morris
John Sissens
Barry Tetley
Bob Thompson
Ernie Thompson

AUSTRALIA / NEW ZEALAND

Warner Blake
Damien Varnis
Ian Wilmot
Bob Wilson
Trevor Wilson

CONTINENTAL EUROPE

Rinus Ars
Rob Buurma
Bram de Kok
Anton Roos
Ad Traas

OTHER

Pierre Chamas
Steve Prater

CHAPTER TWO

CROSSING THE ATLANTIC

Harrison McCain stood on a hill in the seaside town of Scarborough, on England's Yorkshire coast, and stared in amazement. Then he turned to Wallace McCain and Mac McCarthy and said, "You must both have been drunk when you bought this piece of land."

The land in question was to be the site of a McCain Foods factory. On completion, in 1969, it would become the company's first manufacturing facility outside Canada. But it was hardly an ideal spot to build a frozen foods factory. The sloping terrain would increase construction costs and result in awkward internal arrangements, such as the cold storage area being almost two metres above the rest of the plant. However, it was the best site available at the time.

Scarborough, England, bears no resemblance to the sprawling suburb, part of the Greater Toronto megalopolis, that is its Canadian namesake. Rather, it is a beach resort on the North Sea with a permanent population of about fifty thousand, rising to two hundred thousand in the summer.

It wasn't the company's first choice – that had been McCarthy's hometown of Grimsby, close to Lincolnshire's potato country, where McCain Foods already had an office. But no suitable site was available there and so the company settled on Scarborough. Scarborough did have several advantages, including an abundant supply of both water and labour. Wastewater from the plant could be piped directly into the North Sea. Also, Scarborough was in a depressed area where the British government was prepared, in an effort to attract industry and create jobs, to subsidize construction of factories. And its municipal council was eager to attract McCain because a food processing plant would be an ideal complement to the short summer tourist industry that employed many female workers in hotels and restaurants for three months but left them without jobs the rest of the year.

FACING PAGE: North Yorkshire, with the purple heather fields of the moor in the distance.

McCain's first overseas plant was in Scarborough, England. Scarborough Castle, on the North Yorkshire coast, can be seen at cliff's edge.

In retrospect, the decision taken in 1967 to build a factory in Britain and become a major producer of frozen food in that country was a masterstroke, a perfectly timed move that would begin the transformation of a small Canadian company into a global powerhouse. Of course, Wallace and Harrison McCain couldn't know that at the time. What they did know was that if McCain Foods was going to continue to grow, it had to expand outside Canada. Building a plant in Britain was a gamble, but it seemed like one they had to make.

The alternative of expanding into the United States might, at first glance, seem the more logical choice. After all, it was right next door, its people spoke the same language, and it was the biggest french fry market in the world. The problem was that it was also the most competitive french fry market in the world. In the early 1950s, Simplot had led the way in developing the technology to make frozen french fries. Then, in 1960, Gilbert "Gib" Lamb, president of Lamb Weston, an important producer of frozen peas, turned his attention to frozen potatoes. By the latter years of the 1960s, the two companies were well entrenched as the dominant frozen french fry processors in the United States. McCain Foods didn't have the financial muscle to take them on.

Great Britain was a different story. Here was a nation of fifty million people, just a day's trip from Florenceville. Its people also spoke the same language as Canadians

– more or less. It didn't matter that they called french fries "chips." What mattered was that chips were one of their favourite foods and per capita consumption of them was among the highest in the world. Best of all, the American french fry giants weren't there in a big way. "Our major competitors grew up in the United States and stayed in the United States," explains McCain Foods chairman Allison McCain, who worked for the company in Britain for sixteen years before returning to Canada. "Because their own domestic market is so large, they didn't have as much need as we did to expand internationally."

This didn't mean that McCain had no competition in Great Britain. Other companies were producing frozen chips there, but the market wasn't nearly as developed as in the United States: McCain Foods could build a new market for its products rather than having to wrest existing market share from others.

Harrison and Mac McCarthy, 1970.

Exporting to Great Britain from Canada was not a good long-term option after the pound sterling sharply devalued, as it meant Canadian-made products were not competitive in price with locally produced products. In addition, because of the primitive shipping methods of that era, McCain's products often arrived badly damaged. If McCain wanted to sell chips in Britain, it had to make chips in Britain.

McCain Foods was not a newcomer to the British market when it made the decision to build a factory. It had been present since 1960, when Harrison McCain went over to try to unload surplus peas. At the time, McCarthy was production director for Eskimo Foods, a processor of frozen fish, chicken, and vegetables. It just so happened that Britain had a pea shortage just when McCain had a pea surplus. The young company urgently needed to sell the peas because it did not have the money to finance another year's production with the previous year's still unsold.

"I wrote to the Canadian High Commission to give me addresses of people who freeze peas in Canada," says Mac, who insists on going by his nickname (indeed, being addressed as such testifies to the unusual degree of informality at McCain at the time, especially in England). "One of them was McCain Foods. The very next day I had a phone call from a fellow saying, 'I'm Harrison McCain. Can I come and sell you some peas?'"

Wallace and Harrison in 1967, at the opening of Thomas Equipment.

Surprised by the speed of the response, Mac replied, "I wrote only yesterday."

Harrison said, "I haven't got the letter. I've been in London for a week."

"I believe in fate," said Mac. "Come down now.

"I bought two hundred tons of peas from him, which he was delighted to sell me. I later discovered they had an excess from the year before, so it was very good for them."

The two businessmen had dinner together and then Mac returned Harrison to his hotel. It was not one of the grand London hotels that he would later frequent as the company became more prosperous but a small inn with a few rooms over a pub. By the time they got there, it was locked for the night.

"I took him to my house and he slept in one of the kids' bedrooms," says Mac. "We stayed up until the early hours of the morning learning about each other, putting the world to right, and I can clearly remember saying as he retired to go to bed, 'I have never met anyone who can speak so long and so fast as you.'

"He said, 'You should meet my brother, Wallace. He's a ball of fire.'

"I thought, 'Gosh, the two of them together must be a real ball of fire.'"

By selling Canadian-grown peas in Britain and forging a relationship with a British wholesaler, Harrison McCain was groping his way toward the beachhead strategy that would serve the company so well in the decades ahead: from that point on, McCain always entered a new market by exporting product to it from its factories elsewhere, thereby establishing a beachhead. Only when the McCain brand was well established would it begin production in the new territory.

At first, however, McCain did not sell its own brand in Britain. Instead it shipped french fries and other items produced at Florenceville to be sold under the brands of Eskimo and other British packers. Every four months or so, Harrison McCain showed up in England to make deals.

"Every time he came over, we met," says Mac. "Sometimes he stayed with us. We always did something together. He was always enthusiastic about everything he did, and I loved it. We became very, very close friends."

Harrison decided he wanted Mac to work for McCain Foods – in Canada. He refused. "The beer was too cold and there was no cricket and there wasn't really the football that I was used to here. It wasn't my life. I didn't want to do that."

Mac had a better idea: he would stay in Britain, McCain would launch its own operation there, and he would run it.

Harrison wasn't sure that was a good idea. McCain was selling its products to food packers in the United Kingdom who might not appreciate a supplier going into competition with them. But McCain was going to lose that business anyway, replied Mac, because eventually the major companies would decide to process their own products.

In 1965, Mac came to North America on a business trip. "I went to see Harrison and Wallace every weekend, and on the third weekend they agreed to start a company in England."

And so, at the age of thirty-seven and with a wife and five children to support, Mac left a good job with a strong company to launch the first foreign subsidiary of a small Canadian food processor that nobody in Britain and even few Canadians had ever heard of. Clearly, he had great confidence in the potential of the business.

McCain's first U.K. headquarters was Mac's Grimsby home, where his wife, Sheila, handled phone calls, dealt with bills of lading for imported food from Canada, and did the typing. He spent his days on the road trying to convince wary British restaurateurs of the merits of frozen chips. Those were his pioneering times, he recalls – years of long workdays and seven-day work weeks.

He relied on the same system of demonstrating the product in restaurant kitchens that had worked so well in Canada, having been perfected by Dick McWhirter. It was, Mac points out, the same system used for many years by door-to-door vacuum cleaner salespeople: "You know, somebody comes in and vacuums the carpets. 'Oh, that's a wonderful vacuum cleaner, I'll buy it.' Well, with our french fries, we would go in and try to persuade the caterer to allow us to fry our french fries and compare the quality and cost with the product they were using – usually chips made from fresh potatoes." Most restaurants in those days did not have freezers, and McCain would sometimes supply one as a way of getting its frozen chips accepted.

In 1965, McCain bought the London-based company Caterpac, a group of twelve frozen food distributors. The following year, the name was changed to McCain International Ltd. and later to McCain Foods (GB) Ltd., when the Florenceville-based sales organization McCain International was established. McCain Foods GB is responsible for Great Britain – England, Scotland, Wales – as well as for Northern Ireland and the Republic of Ireland.

At first, Mac concentrated his efforts entirely on the food service industry, as that was the fastest way to acquire volume. Once demand had been created by selling to the end users, McCain chose wholesalers to distribute the product.

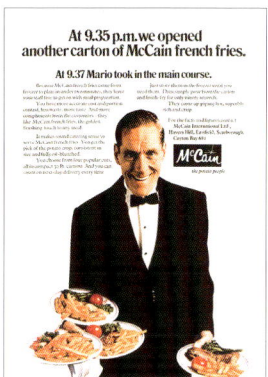

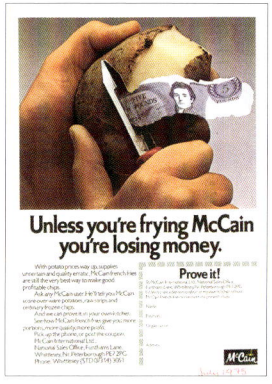

Ads targeting the food service industry, comparing the advantages of McCain frozen french fries with those of fresh potatoes. Ads top and middle, 1966–67; bottom, 1975.

LEFT: Construction of the Scarborough plant begins: Mac McCarthy at the sod-busting.
RIGHT: The Scarborough plant under construction, as seen from the bottom of Havers Hill.

In October 1965, Mac recruited Hal Kinder to join McCain's new British venture as accountant. Kinder, with remarkable foresight, could see that the fledgling Canadian company had a good chance at success. It was "in the right place at the right time," he recalled in a 1984 interview in the McCain's *Star*. "The frozen french fry market in Britain really hadn't been exploited. The market was absolutely new … We had the product and we had a unique way of selling the product."

Good leadership is indispensable to both building a company and inspiring confidence in employees. In Mac, McCain Foods had chosen just the leader it needed to build the company in the United Kingdom. It was his presence that prompted Kinder to leave a good job as chief accountant in a retail group of companies: "I can remember meeting Mac for the first time. It was really his personality and enthusiasm that told me the company was going to succeed … Mac described the operation of McCain Foods in Canada to me and said that the intentions were to develop a market from scratch for McCain Canadian products, which would lead eventually to an investment in a manufacturing unit. This might take two years, three years, ten years – there was no real time frame planned. It depended on the success of the effort."

At that time, Kinder was one of only four McCain employees based outside Canada. The others were Mac, a secretary, and Harry Harrison, who handled orders and logistics.

Just as the beachhead strategy was first developed for McCain's U.K. and, later, Australian markets, so was the policy of exporting the company's accumulated knowledge and expertise by sending experienced personnel from an established location to help get things started at a new one. Shortly after Kinder came aboard, McCain sent four people from Canada to train a British sales force in the end-user system.

McCain joins in Scarborough's annual carnival in the summer of 1968. Its float, consisting of a tractor and a Thomas Equipment harvester, announced the company's impending arrival.

It worked. "Everybody involved in the company in those early days was so enthusiastic about the growing achievements," said Kinder. "Each week and each month we saw improvements on the previous period."

The company's intense focus on producing one product, french fries, for one market segment, the food service industry, enabled it to boost volumes quickly. Before long, McCain had the problem every manufacturer wants – it couldn't keep up with demand. "We had to import all the product from Canada, and this was becoming a problem in organizing the number of shipments that we needed to maintain supplies, as the volumes were growing so quickly," Kinder said.

And so, just two years after launching McCain Foods in Britain, the company made the decision to build a factory. The plant in Scarborough would become, for a time, the largest french fry plant in the world outside North America. Although the $2.6 million McCain invested does not seem so large in light of the far greater

LEFT: Mrs. A.D. McCain and her four sons – (left to right) Wallace, Andrew, Bob, and Harrison – at the Scarborough opening.

RIGHT: Mac assists Mrs. A.D. at the official unlocking of the plant.

sums the company has invested in other countries since, it was nevertheless a big risk – McCain wasn't yet financially strong enough to sustain a major failure. If the factory failed, so would the company.

In early 1968, work started on the Scarborough hillside, and in March 1969 the factory was ready. All four McCain brothers attended the opening ceremonies, along with their mother, Laura. It was a major event in the town and local dignitaries were present to see Mrs. McCain unlock the plant door and proclaim, "May God bless this factory and all who work in it."

For the first few months, it seemed she hadn't been heard. The Scarborough plant experienced major problems, caused by equipment that didn't work properly and by employees who didn't know how to use the machinery that did work. "It was a nightmare," says Wallace McCain. Adds Mac: "It was the only bad time for me after joining McCain."

Almost every morning, the motors powering the apparatus in the potato-receiving area were burnt out and needed to be rewound. The design of the steam boilers didn't allow for sufficient expansion, and so the ends sometimes blew off, halting production. The peeler, which used caustic soda to soften the potato skins, frequently broke down.

And then there was the problem of waste disposal: french fry processing involves getting rid of large quantities of potato peels.

The Scarborough operation pipes its effluent up the hill and then down into a bay about three kilometres from the factory. But in the early days, the pump often malfunctioned, flooding the plant with effluent. The pipe also broke several times, causing even worse flooding. Even when the pump did work, it didn't succeed in getting the waste out into the North Sea, where it could break down. Although peel and

LEFT: Margie and Wallace McCain at the Scarborough opening reception, along with:
MIDDLE: Sheila and Mac McCarthy, and
RIGHT: Billie and Harrison McCain.

excess bits of potato were, in theory, supposed to be screened out before the effluent was piped out to the ocean, in practice this didn't always happen.

"We had loads of complaints about potato peels on the beach," says Ken Wilmot, who was production supervisor at the time and later became quality-control manager and then technical manager. "There was a rock formation on the sea side of the pipe discharge which held in everything and didn't allow it to get out to sea. We had to blast that rock away eventually so that the effluent could get taken out to sea."

(McCain has long since upgraded its waste treatment techniques. All suspended solids are now removed before the effluent is pumped into the North Sea through a two-kilometre-long pipe. In 1997, measures were taken to ensure that European Economic Community bathing-water standards for Scarborough beaches are sustained.)

The rough start-up was painful, but it was probably inevitable. McCain built the Scarborough plant the same way it had built the Florenceville factory and the same way it was building the company as a whole: through a process of trial and error. The new factory was much larger than the one at Florenceville, and some of the machinery in it was the first of its kind. But Scarborough was an invaluable learning experience for McCain. The company put the lessons learned there to use immediately in building another new plant, in Grand Falls, New Brunswick.

Harrison McCain had the problems in Scarborough on his mind at nine o'clock one sunny Florenceville morning in the spring of 1970 when he walked over to the production area to talk to Milford Kinney, one of his most experienced managers. As Kinney recalls it, they sat down on a junk pile behind the plant.

Harrison said, "We've got trouble in England, and I want you to go and straighten it

Leaving for England: (left to right) Murray and Beatrice Lovely, Dennis and Esme Jesson, Milford and Margaret Kinney, and Clarence and Elaine Antworth.

out. I want you to go for a year. Take three people with you – a supervisor for each shift and some guy you can train for a plant manager, and when you get that done, you can come home. Come and see me in Wallace's office at one o'clock and tell me who you are going to take."

This is but one example of the trait Kinney and many other McCain employees cite as a reason for the company's rapid growth under the leadership of the McCain brothers: quick decision making. The McCains did not procrastinate when it came to making decisions. Kinney didn't feel he was being ordered to go to England – just strongly encouraged. "If you thought you could do a job, you didn't say no to them," says Kinney, who was eighty-four in 2007. "I am sure if I had a good reason, I wouldn't have had to go."

Murray Lovely and Clarence Antworth accompanied Kinney to England that fall, along with Dennis Jesson, an Englishman who had been hired in Britain and had been training in Florenceville, most recently as cold store manager. (At the time, "cold store" included freezing, packaging, and shipping the product.) Kinney became production manager while Lovely and Antworth worked as shift supervisors. At the same time, Mac McCarthy's brother James, who had been plant manager at Scarborough, became manager of the U.K. division of Thomas Equipment, McCain's farm equipment company. Kinney, Lovely, and Antworth stayed for one french fry season, from August to May 1971, when the factory ran out of potatoes to process. Back in Florenceville, Lovely became legendary for his skill as plant manager at the flagship McCain factory, where he trained many other plant managers from many countries.

Dennis Jesson stayed on as factory manager and eventually became production director of the British company. Jesson was an Oxford graduate who had played three varsity sports and was an Oxford Triple Blue. (A "blue" is awarded to athletes at Oxford and Cambridge who compete at the highest level of university sport.) It was often said that Jesson's management style resembled his style on the rugby field, where he let no obstacles stand in his way. Although rugby can be a brutal game, it also requires coordination of the roles of the fifteen players on the team. And, unlike Canadian or American football, there are no timeouts.

Steve Bullock, a Yorkshire native who worked at Scarborough as training manager,

  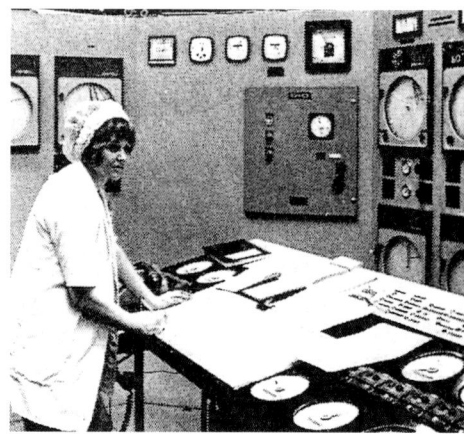

Operations at the Scarborough plant, 1971: (left to right) taking a sample for grading; Dennis Jesson and engineer John Irons; an unidentified technician in the control room.

credits Jesson with bringing order to the Scarborough operation. Bullock cites, as an example of Jesson's practical approach to problem solving, his method of ensuring that the women selected to work on the trim table would not get overly excited when a field mouse showed up among the potatoes. "Buy some mice and put them in a box," Jesson ordered. "When you open the box, some of the women will scream. Those are the ones we do not want on the trim belt. Send them to the packaging department."

Jesson had a simple strategy for overcoming problems and making a resounding success of the Scarborough plant: bull-headed determination, careful organization, and non-stop work. If he hadn't succeeded, McCain would not have been able to meet the growing demand and might have lost its chance to claim a major share of the British market. Jesson went on to become managing director of another french fry company in England acquired by McCain, Potato Allied Services, in Grantham. After his retirement, he helped launch a new McCain factory in Argentina.

Jim Evans, who joined McCain in 1967 in the engineering department at Florenceville, experienced a bit of culture shock when he started work in England not long after the Scarborough plant opened. Florenceville may be rural and isolated, but most of the workers at the original McCain factory had telephones and cars. Not so for their Scarborough counterparts in 1970.

Evans, who was production manager for the day shift, sometimes arrived at work to find a note left by the night manager noting a mishap that had occurred. "I couldn't just call him up to get more information, like I could in Canada," says Evans. "Not just labourers, even most of my supervisors were not 'on the phone,' as they said. So I had to send somebody out to 'knock him up' before I went home so that I could talk to him

Scouting a field of a purple-flowered potato variety for disease.

and find out what happened when, say, the end blew off the pipe. And since hardly anyone had a car, the person who went to get him would usually go on a bicycle."

Lack of storage capacity at the plant was a major problem. The storage problems were compounded by the wide variety and erratic quality of the raw potatoes coming into the plant. McCain has two grades of french fry – the top or "McCain grade," and a lower grade, usually containing a higher proportion of shorter fries, that is packed under the Caterpac label in Britain, Favorita in continental Europe, and Valley Farms in Canada and elsewhere. If the plant is depending on truck deliveries and the suppliers can't be counted on to deliver the desired grade, production is disrupted. And that's what happened at Scarborough.

When the potatoes arrived at the plant, they were tested for size and colour. The McCain-grade potatoes went in one bin and the lower grade ones in another. But the bins were relatively small – holding only enough potatoes for about two hours worth of processing. If the plant was processing chips to be sold under the McCain brand and too many trucks came in with the lower grade potatoes, there was no place to put them. As well, the plant lacked space to store enough plastic bags and boxes to pack the finished product.

Most of the potatoes came from Yorkshire and the adjoining county of Lincolnshire, a journey of up to three hours. Trucks that didn't arrive at the scheduled time could cause production to stop if there weren't enough raw potatoes on hand.

The raw materials were also a problem. English farmers, like the Canadian farmers in the Saint John River Valley, were used to producing table potatoes for the retail market: they weren't set up to switch overnight to potatoes suitable for processing. Cultural differences complicated matters. New Brunswick growers were often small operators scraping out a living, eager to supply to an important new customer. The English farms tended to be large estates, some of them centuries old, run by professional managers.

"These farmers were descended from families that had been in farming for hundreds of years," recalls Evans. "The farmers would drive up in a Land Rover or a

LEFT: Harvesting potatoes in England.
RIGHT: Sampling potatoes early in the growing cycle. The number of tubers on each plant is an indicator of crop size.

Mercedes. They were used to growing certain varieties that suited their customers or their type of earth or their part of the country, and some smartass guy from the colonies comes over and tells them to grow Russet Burbank. They said, in effect, to take a hike." Although Russet Burbank was the preferred potato for french fries in North America because of its length, it was not grown in Britain at the time.

French fry manufacturing then was labour intensive. Electronic defect removal systems had not yet been invented, and McCain depended on short-term female labour to operate the trim table. The company invited prospective employees for coffee at a local nightclub on Saturday mornings. Advertisements showing women in bikinis read "Come work with us for eight weeks and earn money for a vacation in the sun." The workers were each offered a free hairdo and, because they had to stand for long periods, the services of a chiropodist.

All the effort and aggravation of getting the Scarborough plant running smoothly had a huge payoff for McCain. As the 1970s began, the company had the largest french fry factory outside North America just when demand for that product was about to take off, both in Britain and continental Europe. The same social and economic trends that favoured the french fry business in North America were appearing across the Atlantic. Women were entering the workforce in growing numbers, increasing the demand for frozen food that could be quickly prepared after the work day.

To appeal to that same demand for convenience, the major fast food chains were expanding out of their North American base. Kentucky Fried Chicken (which changed its name to KFC in 1991), Burger King, and McDonald's all set up shop in Britain, and all three became McCain customers. Mac is especially proud that the British branch made the first McCain sale anywhere to McDonald's. The deal gave

LEFT: MacFries coming off the line, late 1970s.
RIGHT: Trimming in the early days was labour-intensive.
BELOW: The Russet Burbank.

the company a boost because other potential buyers saw the success McDonald's was having using fries supplied by McCain.

Mac deserves credit for the McDonald's breakthrough, according to Wallace McCain. It helped that a U.K. dock strike was forcing McDonald's to fly its fries in from Idaho at high cost, making a local source of supply all the more attractive. At the same time, he had to overcome a handicap in dealing with McDonald's, namely that Harrison and Wallace had seriously annoyed the chain's top executives by refusing to let its representatives visit McCain's Grand Falls factory. "We told them we knew how to make fries and did not need them to check or teach us," Wallace says. "Supplying them in the United Kingdom broke the ice, also with the decision makers in Canada, the United States, and elsewhere."

The fundamental characteristic of a chain is that customers are served the identical product no matter whether the outlet they enter is in Mexico City or Manchester. This is what gives a chain its advantage over individual restaurants: a new outlet of a ubiquitous chain like McDonald's has loyal customers the day it opens its doors because those customers have enjoyed its food in other locations. In contrast, a new non-chain restaurant must build its business from scratch.

Because of its desire for uniformity, McDonald's wanted Russet Burbank fries, just like the ones it served in the United States. "Eventually," says Mac, "we gave them their Idaho potatoes right here in Yorkshire, but it took time."

It wasn't just a matter of picking up the phone and telling suppliers to start supplying Russet Burbank. If McCain wanted a new variety of potatoes produced in Britain, it was up to McCain to develop seed potato production. Because of European plant health regulations, North American potatoes could not be imported into Britain.

LEFT: The pizza line in Scarborough, c.1979.
RIGHT: Mac adjudicating a McCain pizza eating contest, 1980.

McCain was granted permission to import, under strict quarantine, just eight Russet Burbank seed tubers. Over a period of five years, these were multiplied until there was enough seed to grow potatoes for processing.

To make quality seed available to the contract growers, McCain bought a Scottish seed potato company and established McCain Potatoes GB, in Montrose, Scotland. The new subsidiary was successful and, because of McCain's efforts, British growers were able to produce Russet Burbanks for McDonald's and for the rest of the rapidly growing McCain Foods (GB) business.

Sales were so strong that the Scarborough plant was expanded in 1972, with the addition of a second production line at a cost of $3.2 million, a dehydration line, and more storage space. And when Scarborough could no longer satisfy the demand, the company opened a second British plant, at a cost of $16 million, in Whittlesey, a town of fifteen thousand in Cambridgeshire. This plant at the time was the largest frozen food factory in the world, with an annual capacity of two hundred thousand metric tons of potatoes. Cedric Ritchie, then chairman of the Bank of Nova Scotia, officiated at the opening.

Establishing itself as a major force in the British food industry made McCain an international company, and that had important repercussions. For one thing, it made the company more attractive to Canadians as a place to work, since a job at McCain Foods held the possibility of foreign travel.

Allison McCain had no intention of working in the family business when he visited England in 1975. He had lunch in London with his uncle Harrison McCain and Mac McCarthy; they suggested he tour the Scarborough plant and the new one in Whittlesey, which had just started production.

LEFT: Mac and Sheila McCarthy with Wallace at the opening of the Whittlesey plant, 1976.
RIGHT: Harrison speaking at the Whittlesey opening ceremony.

He was impressed. "The guys there were all excited about what they were doing. I decided that's the kind of environment I liked. I went home and I went to see Harrison and said, 'I want a job.'" The international aspect was a big attraction for Allison: "I had the travel bug."

For prospective British employees, McCain appealed for another reason: its informality and lack of bureaucracy. Nick Vermont became managing director of McCain GB in 1998 and in 2005 was named regional CEO for Britain, Ireland, South Africa, and eastern Europe. He first joined the company in 1983 as the product manager for chips after working for the catering division of British Rail. The British national railroad was organized along military lines, he says, and "everything was done by numbers and processes and procedures.

"British Rail was very slow and bureaucratic. I remember coming to my first interview at McCain. I was being interviewed by a senior product manager and he reported to the marketing director, who reported to the managing director, who reported to Harrison McCain. So it was a much flatter chain of command, and I knew things would happen fast."

Steve Bullock, retired personnel manager, and John Blackburn, retired training manager, both joined McCain in the early 1970s, and both were impressed by the informality of the workplace. This reflected the personalities of the McCain brothers but also that of Mac McCarthy. Although English, he had none of the stuffiness Canadians sometimes associate with English people. He would stop and talk to everyone, regardless of their position in the company, and make sure everyone knew what was going on and what management was thinking about. For example, if heavy rains were affecting a harvest, employees would be warned of the problems they could expect.

In 1982, McCain bought the french fry plant of Potato Allied Services (PAS) in Grantham from Salvesen Group, a refrigerated transport company. Working for a company that is taken over by a competitor is always unnerving, and Graham Finn, who had been with PAS since 1969, didn't know what to expect. He was amazed by the attitude of his new bosses when he first met Harrison McCain and Mac: "Here were the owner of the company and the boss in England talking to you about the business. They were absolutely awesome – they could talk about the FFA [free fatty acid] level in the fryer, asked you about the retention time and temperature in the blancher, what your blanching losses were, your giveaways in the packaging department, the fan capacity and stack height in the potato storage, which Delta-T you would normally use for ventilating. They knew everything there was to know about our business.

"I remember coming out of the first meeting with them wet as a dish cloth. They tested you, what you knew, what you thought. Salvesen's would not know a potato from a turnip; these guys knew more than you did. It was a complete revelation. The transition went very smoothly."

Finn liked the new environment so much that, as of 2007, he was still working for McCain GB, as associate director of agriculture. As he recalls, what impressed him and his colleagues most of all was that suddenly they were being treated as people. "With PAS we were a number; with McCain we became persons, with names."

The U.K. employees had a boss who was comfortable with North American informality. "There's nobody in my company in Britain who called me anything but 'Mac,' whether they swept the floor of the factory or they were the marketing director," Mac McCarthy says. "I was 'Mac' to every single person. And Harrison was 'Harrison' and

TOP LEFT: Opening of the Whittlesey plant: (left to right) Harrison, Eleanor, Billie, Jed Sutherland (Marie's husband), Marie, Wallace, Margie, and Patrick Johnson (Eleanor's husband).
TOP RIGHT: A tour group at the plant opening stops to watch the action at the trim table.
BOTTOM: Graham Finn, associate director of agriculture, 2007.

Nick Vermont, 2006.

Wallace was 'Wallace' throughout the whole company. If you overstepped the mark you knew who was the boss, but there were no airs and graces."

In the McCain philosophy, trying and failing is better than not trying at all. And mistakes are all right as long as they aren't repeated. Harrison McCain introduced Nick Vermont to that philosophy during a meeting in 1984, a year after Vermont joined the company as product manager for chips.

"I had run a consumer promotion that had come in something like five times over budget in terms of redemption and therefore cost. And I had spent about two weeks of sleepless nights wondering how I was going to tell Harrison this. And I gingerly got up and did my presentation and in the end I said, 'Well, I do have to confess that I got it horribly wrong and it's cost five times what it was budgeted for.'"

Harrison replied, "Nick, Nick, I don't mind if you were five times over budget, don't mind that at all, if it meant you sold five times as much, and I don't mind anybody making a mistake once. But just never make the same mistake again."

An English potato field.

Allison McCain held a series of jobs in Britain after being trained in Florenceville and working for three years as manufacturing director in Australia. His first British assignment was as plant manager at Scarborough. He then became director of manufacturing for McCain GB, deputy managing director, managing director, and finally CEO. He points out that while the U.K. company had autonomy, "there was a Canadian flavour to it or, more precisely, a Harrison and Wallace style of management to it. We've been able to take the best elements of what we do in Canada and apply them elsewhere without going in with a formula that says, 'This is the way you are going to do it.'

"A lot of American companies have more control from head office. Instead, we have a managing director reporting to head office and the other people reporting to him. I used that as a positive in England when I hired someone. I would say, 'You don't have to worry about working for somebody in Canada, you work for me. I have to worry about working for somebody in Canada.'"

CROSSING THE ATLANTIC

McCain gives out free samples to launch its retail products in England, c.1976.

The ability to make decisions quickly gave McCain a big advantage over its competitors. In the mid-1980s, the Scarborough and Whittlesey plants had a severe problem with potato blight, a devastating disease in which a fungus causes internal rot. In the past, it has destroyed entire potato crops and led to mass starvation, as with the Irish potato famine of the 1840s, when one million people died.

The factories could control the advance of the disease by using fans in the potato storage areas, but they didn't have enough of them. "I remember going with Allison to see Mac to tell him we needed to increase the fan capacity promptly, and it would cost us £275,000," says Finn. "Mac understood immediately, and said, 'Let me call Harrison to give him a chance to have his input.' He called and, ten minutes later, said, 'Okay guys, go ahead.'"

The building of the British and Australian businesses set a pattern that would be followed wherever in the world McCain decided to go. The first step is to establish a market by importing McCain products to sell to the food service industry. Then, if the market potential is sufficient and good potatoes can be grown at a competitive cost, McCain either builds or buys a factory to produce locally. The final step is to enter the retail market.

McCain entered the British retail market in 1976. Since then, its retail french fry business has been hugely successful. Happily for McCain, the British supermarkets were moving to central warehousing systems rather than requiring processors to ship products directly to individual stores. This made it easier for a new competitor to enter the market because it would not have to acquire a fleet of trucks to deliver to hundreds of locations all over the United Kingdom.

Mac gives credit to Roger Lillyman, his first marketing director, for establishing a successful retail business in the United Kingdom. The big breakthrough occurred in 1978 when McCain GB launched Oven Chips, the British version of the product known in Canada as Superfries. Although market research for fries that could be baked in the oven wasn't favourable, McCain had seen the success of the product in Canada and had confidence consumers would accept it once they understood they could have deep-fried taste without the inconvenience, smell, and danger of deep-frying at home.

McCain succeeded in retail through consistent advertising, aggressive selling, and product quality. By focusing on one product, Oven Chips, McCain stole the frozen chip market away from its competitors, including Birds Eye, Findus, and Ross. Steady innovation helped increase both the chip market and McCain's share of it. The company relaunched Oven Chips on a regular basis with new cuts and fresh marketing. And, in 1985, it introduced Micro Chips, which could be prepared in the microwave.

During the late 1980s and early 1990s, although McCain's retail business continued to grow, private labels were growing faster and overall market growth was declining. McCain revolutionized the market again in 1997 by introducing McCain Home Fries, a thick-cut chip that used coating technology to deliver a crispy outside and a moist, fluffy texture inside, just like a British homemade chip.

Home Fries were an overnight success. Despite an initial dip in Oven Chip sales at the time of the launch, the total sales of Home Fries and Oven Chips by 2007 was almost two and half times McCain's chip sales before the launch of Home Fries. Today McCain has more than a 50 percent share of the British frozen chip market, a share five times bigger than the next brand. Private labels are McCain's main competition.

"McCain in Great Britain today is primarily a potato business," says Nick Vermont, "but this hasn't been for lack of trying other product categories." Indeed, buoyed by the success of Oven Chips, McCain GB tried to establish itself as a broad frozen food business during the 1980s. It launched a range of products, including pizza, ready meals, breakfast meals, frozen orange juice, desserts, fish products, and snack foods. Some of these categories were already successful in Canada. But the same competitors that McCain had quickly beat in the french fry market were well established and committed to these categories – and better prepared for another attack from McCain. While McCain was a brand leader in the retail market for frozen pizza for many years, its other categories were not as successful and have since been dropped.

In 1983, McCain GB acquired Britfish, a frozen fish supplier in the Yorkshire city of Hull. However, the competition from Birds Eye was too strong and McCain decided to get out of the retail frozen fish market.

The evolution of Oven Chips: (top to bottom) 1985, the first health positioning – 40 percent less fat than deep frying; 1991, the focus is on 5 percent fat and the use of sunflower oil; 1998 sees a broader health message; 2006, the It's All Good campaign – just potatoes and sunflower oil.

CROSSING THE ATLANTIC

Home Fries: (top to bottom) 1997, original launch packaging; 2003, "Taste the chip from heaven!"; 2006, a new look for the It's All Good campaign.

Today the Hull factory produces appetizers and finger foods for Britain and continental Europe.

McCain never sold any vegetable other than potatoes in the U.K. retail market, though they were an important part of McCain's food service assortment in the early years of production in Scarborough. Eventually, McCain GB withdrew from vegetables to focus on its rapidly growing potato business.

McCain was also unsuccessful in its attempt to implant its farm equipment company, Thomas Equipment, in Britain. The Canadian harvesters weren't well adapted for English fields and soil conditions, and Bobcat, a U.S. company, proved a tough competitor against Thomas's skid steer loaders.

In the first years of the new century, the issue of health and its relationship to what we eat became increasingly important both in North America and Europe, especially Britain. Fast food, in particular fried foods, were attacked as unhealthy and as major contributors to obesity, cancer, diabetes, and other ailments. Oven Chips had originally been promoted for their convenience. In 1985, well before the health issue rose to prominence, McCain GB repositioned its product as the healthy way to eat french fries.

Because french fries are a more significant part of the U.K. dining-at-home menu than the North American, McCain, with its Oven Chips, has had a positive impact on the British diet. In the past, most homes had a deep fryer, which produced much greasier chips while also risking burns and fires. McCain Oven Chips not only are healthier than those deep-fried chips, they are safer. Oven Chips now account for 90 percent of all frozen chips sold in British stores. McCain estimates that since the launch of Oven Chips, some twenty million pans of fat, containing half a billion calories, have been removed from the British diet.

Although McCain had been selling a healthy french fry for nearly twenty years, that wasn't enough to overcome the barrage of negative publicity that came to a head in the spring of 2005. Chef Jamie Oliver's "Jamie's School Dinners" campaign was aimed at improving the food served in schools, including reducing the amount of fried foods. At the same time, scares involving food additives resulted in more than four hundred items being removed from store shelves. McCain products weren't implicated, but these incidents weakened consumers' confidence in convenience foods. Politicians, doctors, nutritionists, and the food industry were all drawn into a national debate about health, obesity, and food quality. Critics of globalization jumped into

the fray, targeting international food brands for special abuse. McDonald's became the poster child for bad nutrition.

According to John Young, who became managing director of McCain GB in 2005, frozen french fries have been "unfairly demonized, not based on any facts but on misguided perceptions." Consumer research revealed that many people thought all chips were high in fat, and many didn't even know that Oven Chips were made from fresh potatoes. For the first time in twenty-five years, the British retail market for frozen chips stopped growing.

In September 2006, McCain relaunched the brand with a campaign based on the slogan "It's all good." The campaign included new packaging, new products, and new advertising on TV, radio, and in movie theatres, as well as promotion through posters, the press, the internet, and points-of-sale. The goal was to overcome consumer confusion and shatter the myth that all french fries are unhealthy.

"The simple premise," says Young, "is that McCain is a good company making good food from simple, wholesome ingredients simply prepared – it's all good."

"McCain's job," says Sue Jefferson, McCain GB's marketing director, "is to meet the need of consumers. We have a history of responding to consumers' needs. That's why we began using sunflower oil in 1988, when consumers asked for healthier choices. And when consumers became concerned about genetically modified foods, McCain communicated that its retail chips were made from Maris Piper, a traditional British variety. The big issue now is to give consumers the facts to help them make informed choices."

McCain GB is a major force in the British food industry. It has won several awards from McDonald's. The trade publication for British grocers named it the best branded frozen food supplier three years in a row. In 2003, McCain's Home Fries won

TOP LEFT: McCain demonstrates potato growing to school children in the London borough of Hackney as part of the It's All Good campaign.
TOP RIGHT: Commercial still from the It's All Good TV campaign, 2006.

ABOVE: Print ads for the So Good for You campaign, which preceded the It's All Good campaign.

ABOVE: The career of a chip: an It's All Good campaign print ad.

the Queen's Award for Enterprise: Innovation. And, in 2005, McCain was named a British superbrand by the Superbrands Organization, which promotes achievements in branding.

Peter Burman joined McCain in 1970 and has spent his entire career with the company, mostly in manufacturing jobs of increasing responsibility. He was responsible for production in Burgos, Spain, then became plant manager in Hoofddorp, the Netherlands; then manager of the pizza plant in Scarborough; manufacturing director for McCain Foods USA; manufacturing director of McCain Alimentaire in Harnes, France; and then production director for McCain GB. In 2006, he was appointed the British company's manufacturing and innovations director.

Burman exemplifies McCain's manufacturing culture. Having started the process of management training and people development in Britain, he has seen many changes, not least in processing technology. Larger scale production lines, automation, computerization, and electronic defect removal have dramatically increased production per man-hour. Meanwhile, hot-air drying before frying and coating have significantly improved product quality.

Perhaps the biggest change Burman has witnessed is in the french fry market itself, from rapid growth to slow growth. "You just assumed it was going to keep growing at 15 percent a year," he says. "Because it was growing, the biggest problem was just supplying sales and keeping up. But in later years, the problem is getting more sales to keep the factories going."

Ian Cameron, too, has had an international career with McCain. In 1972, Joe Palmer hired him straight out of university to work for Day & Ross, McCain's trucking company. Within a year, he had joined McCain Foods at Florenceville and later worked as plant manager in Australia before becoming manufacturing director for McCain Foods USA in Maine. In 1983, while Cameron was working in the United States, Harrison McCain asked him if he was interested in the position of factory manager at the Whittlesey plant.

Cameron said, "Not really. I've been away from home for five years."

Harrison said, "You'll enjoy it. Just go for a couple of years, we'll get somebody else trained and you can come back."

So Cameron agreed to go to England for two years. That was in 1983. In 2007, he was still there. "Business was growing like mad; I had an important job. After a while,

Retired McCain GB employees with management, 2007. Front row: (left to right) Robin Negus, Peter Burman, Val Walker, Hal Kinder (retired), Pam Procter, Mac McCarthy (retired),* Mick Baddley (retired),* Ken Campbell (retired), Ken Wilmot (retired).*
Back row: Dave Chelley, Richard Harris (retired), John Young, Bob Briggs (retired),* Mick Robinson (retired), Steve Bullock (retired), Eion Johnston, Dave Elliott (retired),* Malcolm Howes (retired), Fred Johnson (retired), John Blackburn (retired), Derek Hood (retired), Doug Hague (retired),* Alan Pickup (retired),* Nick Vermont, Alan Drury (retired),* Ian Cameron.
Asterisks indicate retirees with thirty-five years or more of service. The other retirees all have between twenty-five and thirty-five years of service.

this became home." He has never lost his Maritime accent, but he has two grown sons who speak like the Englishmen they are.

Having worked in Australia and the United States under Wallace's supervision, and in the United Kingdom under Harrison's, Cameron is well placed to compare the two McCain brothers who built the company. "Wallace is more of an operations person. Dealing with Wallace, you had to justify every penny you spent, whereas Harrison was a little bit less critical. When we had a meeting, he would have more to say about marketing and sales. They were great as a team. I sat in many meetings with either or both of them and also with Mac McCarthy, who was like the third brother. They had enthusiasm and foresight. Sometimes you didn't have to have 99 percent of the facts. They would just say, 'That's the right thing to do, let's do it.'"

Allison McCain, 2004.

By 2007, things were different. The company was much bigger, and it was being run by professional managers who were responsible to the owners, rather than by the owners (and founders) themselves. As a result, a decision on a capital expenditure that might have been approved after just one phone call now may require board approval and inevitably takes longer.

Nevertheless, Britain, along with Australia, is one of the McCain outposts where the original McCain company culture remains strong. In both cases, there was a strong relationship with one of the founding brothers over many years. Both are also English-speaking Commonwealth countries with close ties to Canada.

"We say there is one culture [across McCain] but that is not exactly right," says Vermont. "It depends on the extent of the influence Wallace and Harrison have had on those businesses, how long those businesses have been part of McCain, how much they have been added to by acquisitions, and the continuity of management."

Britain was the first McCain operation outside Canada, and both founders, in particular Harrison, spent a lot of time there. Their influence persists. Vermont worked with Harrison for nearly twenty years, and several others who were or are still active in the company also worked with him for a long time. Several either came from or worked in Florenceville at some point in their careers.

The success of McCain in Britain paved the way for the success that followed in continental Europe. McCain used its U.K. products to build a beachhead on the continent before it began production there.

The head of the U.K. operation played a vital role in establishing the European operations as vice-chairman of the European companies. "Mac looked and sounded British but spoke and acted European" says Tony van Leersum, who became managing director for Europe in 1978. "In those years, when the company allowed us only one transatlantic phone call per week, Mac was Mr. McCain–in–Europe for us, and the best coach you could wish for."

McCain could not have made a better choice to lead its first foreign venture. He was referred to as the "third McCain" because he had the same combination of energy, decisiveness, and bluntness that made Harrison and Wallace such a formidable force in building their company. "Mac had a temper, but he was so motivating, everybody would do anything for him," says Ken Wilmot.

Howard Mann, who preceded Dale Morrison as president and CEO of McCain Foods Limited, paid tribute to this "third McCain" when Mac retired in 1998, praising him for his ability to get to the core of complex issues. "One of his great strengths is his willingness to give a clear, concise opinion – he is a very difficult man to misunderstand."

Not only was Mac passionately devoted to his work, he was also a philanthropist with a keen interest in both theatre and sports. He was president of local cricket clubs and the driving force behind the building of a live theatre venue in Scarborough. He involved the company in community causes, reflected today in the name of Scarborough's soccer arena: McCain Stadium.

"I was fortunate to go to the United Kingdom as manufacturing director working for Mac McCarthy," says Allison McCain. "I am certain the mix of McCain and McCarthy made us one of the early leaders in the United Kingdom of progressive management practice. McCain GB was always considered to be the 'jewel in the crown' of the group – it was profitable, growing, and very solid. I suspect that was extremely important in the early days of our expansion internationally. It gave us the confidence and the resources to push farther into Europe.

"I enjoyed my years at GB. It's a wonderful country. The people made the work fun: they were experienced, extremely loyal, and proud of their success – and justifiably so."

McCarthy served in key roles in several British food organizations. In 1993, Queen Elizabeth invested him as Commander of the British Empire in recognition of his contribution to the British food industry. He was made Honorary Freeman of the Borough of Scarborough in 1996.

As McCain Foods grew and expanded around the globe, clashes arose between the corporate head office in Canada, which wanted modern, unified systems to link the branches, and the heads of the local operations, who guarded their autonomy. None was more jealous of his autonomy than Mac. Take, for example, the initiative

TOP: Mac McCarthy, 1988.
BOTTOM: Mac McCarthy was awarded the Commander of the British Empire, New Year's Eve 1993 honours list.

Canadian, eh?

During a royal visit to New Brunswick, then premier Frank McKenna mentioned to Prince Charles that the province is the home base of an important multinational company, McCain Foods.

Not so, replied the Prince. He was well acquainted with McCain, he said, and knew it was a British company.

The Prince's error was a common one. In fact, few people know that the world's largest producer of french fries originated in the Maritime province of New Brunswick and still maintains factories there and offices in the village of Florenceville.

Mac McCarthy recalls a meeting attended by a British agriculture minister who cited "the great example of that British company McCain Foods, which started from small beginnings in Scarborough."

Informed McCain was Canadian, he shot back, "It's not. I know the people there, and it's definitely an English company."

Tony van Leersum remembers flying from Florenceville to Chicago in 1985 with Harrison and Wallace McCain to try to persuade McDonald's CEO Fred Turner to buy McCain french fries. "You must be tired after that long flight," Turner said. The McCain executives were baffled by the comment until they realized that Turner assumed they had flown in from Britain where, he thought, McCain had its head office.

Unlike IKEA, which makes a point in its advertising to identify itself as Swedish, McCain has chosen not to emphasize its origins. This, says Nick Vermont, CEO of McCain Foods GB, "is a reflection of the considerable autonomy each of the local companies has had in the areas of marketing and advertising and the way in which the brand is presented to the consumer. We found that consumers in Britain do not think of McCain as being Canadian – British or perhaps Scottish, but certainly not Canadian."

Harrison McCain cared about whether people bought his product, not whether they knew the company's nationality: "We're a British company in Britain and a Canadian company in Canada."

in the early part of the 1980s to centralize the company's financial administration. The various McCain companies around the world were asked to send their financial figures by satellite to Florenceville, where a monthly profit-and-loss statement was to be created. Mac refused.

"No financial figures leave our office before I have had a look at them and agree with the conclusions," he said. "Not even to Harrison. I will not agree to anything that means that Harrison will have figures before I have seen and agreed to them." The program was not implemented. (By 2007, however, 97 percent of McCain's transactions worldwide were being processed at the Florenceville Data Processing Centre, but each operating managing director or president sees the results before they are published in Canada.)

Yet, Mac did understand the need to change with the times. In 1996, Anil Rastogi, corporate vice-president and chief information officer, wanted the U.K. operation to buy £300,000 worth of personal computers. He was told, "Mac will never agree to do this." So Rastogi went to see him in England. He entered the office prepared for a difficult hour of explaining. Mac started by asking him why McCain should spend so much money on new computers. Rastogi, in five minutes, summed up his reasons.

Mac said, "We cannot stop progress, can we?" and authorized the expenditure on the spot.

Success in business never happens without risk, the risk being the possibility of failure. Mac McCarthy took a risk when he left a secure job to launch a small, unknown Canadian company in Britain. The McCains also took a risk in Britain and continued to take risks as they planted the McCain flag around the world. "For many years, maybe ten, as with any small business growing rapidly, you bet the bundle every year, year after year," Harrison McCain told *Executive* magazine in 1984. "If you're wrong once, you're out. We kept pushing the business as hard as we could, borrowing all we could, building and borrowing and building. We were risking it all on deal after deal."

By successfully establishing itself in Britain, McCain Foods acquired a strong position in a market twice the size of its home market. And just across the English Channel, there were more deals to make and other markets to conquer.

ABOVE: Mac and Wallace.
FACING PAGE: Harrison and Mac at the Scarborough plant. Mac has just received his twenty-five-year pin.

CHAPTER THREE

ACROSS THE CHANNEL

It was a sunny day in August 1971 and George McClure was about to leave for the Netherlands to launch the continental European division of McCain Foods. McClure; his wife, Donna; and their four children were sitting in a car in the driveway of Harrison McCain's house in Florenceville. In a couple of minutes they would be on the highway en route to the Fredericton airport, the first leg of a trip that would end in Amsterdam.

As their driver turned the ignition, Harrison McCain leaned into the car and looked McClure in the eyes. "I guess I should tell you what your mandate is," he said. "Your mandate is to dominate the frozen french fry business in Europe."

The recollection brings a smile to McClure's face. "That was so typical of Harrison," he says. "It was the only instruction I ever got."

Some mandate. A small food-processing company based in a New Brunswick village was supposed to dominate a vast, multilingual continent with a population of more than four hundred million. It didn't faze Harrison McCain that the continent he proposed to dominate with McCain french fries was where the french fry had been invented, about 170 years earlier.

Nobody knows the genius's name, but it's generally accepted by culinary historians that it was a Belgian, sometime around the start of the nineteenth century, who first dropped a potato strip into boiling fat, thereby creating the first frite. "We call them French fries, but they really are Belgian fries," says Jean Bernou, who is French.

Bernou heads McCain's European operations, presiding over a division that, in 2005, had almost $900 million in sales and spans thirty-five countries and twenty-four languages. McCain operates eight factories on the continent, including one at

FACING PAGE: A potato field and traditional windmill in the Netherlands.

Annemarie Oosterhoff Harbo, country manager, Denmark.

Matougues, in France's Champagne district. It is the most modern McCain factory anywhere, producing thirty metric tons of fries an hour.

In the fall of 1971, however, McCain had no European factories and no European customers. It didn't even have an office. Its European operations consisted of one employee, thirty-five-year-old George McClure, working out of his house in the Netherlands. The employee had an impressive title – managing director of McCain Europa – but he had never sold a french fry, or anything else for that matter, in his life.

McClure did, however, have a wealth of experience in academia and the civil service. After serving in the Royal Canadian Navy, he had obtained a PhD in economics from the University of California. He worked as an economic planner for the state of Hawaii; was a management consultant; taught at the Royal Military College in Kingston, Ontario; served as an economic advisor to the Nova Scotia government; and then was appointed Atlantic program director for the federal department of regional economic expansion. In that capacity, he chaired a federal–provincial committee on Atlantic transportation. At a meeting in Fredericton in 1969, Harrison McCain made a presentation on behalf of Day & Ross. As usual, Harrison made a strong impression. "He was," recalls McClure, "energetic, dynamic, and self-confident."

McClure must have made a good impression too because Harrison invited him to dinner. Afterward, Harrison told McClure, "Keep in touch. Keep in touch," repeating himself, as was his habit.

McClure had already decided he wanted to switch to the private sector. "I knew that if I stayed in government too long, it would be hard to leave," he says. "I was looking around and I got a call from Harrison, who asked me to consider McCain Foods." He went to Florenceville to talk to Harrison and Wallace. Moving from Ottawa to a village in New Brunswick wasn't a problem for McClure because he was used to small towns, having grown up in Georgetown, Ontario. The drawback was the size of the company – by big business standards, McCain Foods, with only $40 million in annual sales, was still small potatoes.

"But I just had a gut feeling," McClure says. "These guys were going places. They were optimistic, ambitious, hard driving. You just had a sense when you met them that you had met somebody special." The other attraction was the prospect of living abroad later, which appealed to both McClure and his wife.

He started work in July 1970 as Harrison's assistant and spent the next few months learning all aspects of the business, from agriculture to sales, and did some acquisitions for Day & Ross. In January 1971, Harrison sent him on a scouting mission to Europe. Harrison said, "Put your hands in your pockets and just walk around Europe and learn all you can about potato growing and potato processing."

Most of Europe's potatoes are produced in the northern part of the continent. So McClure went to the Netherlands, Belgium, France, Germany, Denmark, and Sweden and talked to everyone he could find who knew something about potatoes and potato processing. He learned that the Netherlands was the heart of the European potato industry. It had the best soil and the best climate for potatoes, and it produced them more efficiently than other European countries. The Netherlands is small, but most of its land is arable, and it was growing twice as many potatoes as all of Canada and as much as Germany or France.

George McClure and his family, 1971.

When he returned to Canada, McClure prepared a report on his findings. To his delight, Wallace and Harrison read it immediately. "That is very flattering to an employee," McClure says. "I have worked for other organizations and written detailed reports and nobody would read them for weeks and weeks. Harrison and Wallace always had a sense of urgency. They were very responsive."

In the 1980s, Harrison and Wallace decided they would each oversee different foreign markets, with Harrison assuming responsibility for Europe. But in the early days, they were still running the whole company together. So it was a joint decision of both brothers, following McClure's report, to make the Netherlands McCain's base of operations in Europe even though Germany and France were the largest markets.

McClure and Harrison McCain both thought being an outsider was an advantage for McCain Foods. Despite the existence of the European Economic Community, few companies in the 1970s operated across Europe. "We didn't have any baggage," says McClure. "We decided we would be Europe-wide and would look at Europe as a single market. A lot of companies weren't thinking that way."

McClure didn't know anybody in the Netherlands, so he went to the Canadian embassy in The Hague to see if it could offer any help. The commercial officer there was going on home leave for two months, and he offered McClure the use of his office. The officer's assistant helped with communications and arranging appointments.

Medaillon D'Or: McCain Europa BV received a gold medal from a European food organization for its frozen mini pizzas, 1981. Pictured are Harrison; Iet van den Boom, the first female manager at McCain; and Tony van Leersum.

McCain had a two-pronged strategy. First it would do what it had done in England, Australia, and the United States: establish a beachhead by shipping in McCain products from elsewhere and trying to sell them. One shipload arrived from Canada, and subsequent ones came from the Scarborough plant in England. Second – and this was a departure from what had been done in England – instead of building a processing plant, McCain would try to buy one or more existing plants. This would be quicker than building a new plant and would come with a customer base.

McClure had left a prestigious job, one that was worthy of a PhD in economics, in which he dispensed economic advice to cabinet ministers. Now here he was on the streets of Amsterdam, knocking on the doors of restaurants, trying to persuade skeptical Dutch cooks of the virtues of frozen french fries from Canada.

It wasn't easy, especially when the combination of freight charges and import duties made the McCain product more expensive than locally produced french fries. "It was very discouraging," says McClure, "because the prices were high and people would say, 'Why do we need french fries from Canada? We've got the biggest french fry processors in Europe right here in the Netherlands.'"

He had to convince the chefs that the frozen fries were of better quality and more convenient than the chilled fries – which were cooked and delivered the same day and had a shelf life of only a few days – that many of them were using. With persistence, McClure succeeded in getting some orders and arranged for a distributor with a cold storage warehouse in the port city of Rotterdam to handle the McCain products.

The next step was to hire two salesmen, Dick van Dalen in the Netherlands and Pierre Jar in Belgium, and an assistant, Iet van den Boom, who could communicate with customers in Dutch, English, French, or German. Now McClure could focus on his main job: building a McCain presence on the continent by buying existing factories.

He started negotiating with two french fry processors. One, Huzo, was located in Lewedorp, in Zeeland province, while the other, Favorita, was in the town of Werkendam, in the province of North Brabant. "The Werkendam factory wasn't very good," says McClure, "but we were desperate to get a base." Tim Bliss, vice-president of engineering, came over from Florenceville to look at the factory and

LEFT: The Werkendam plant, 1972. The office is in the trailer to the right of the factory.

RIGHT: A truck carrying a load of potatoes arrives at the Werkendam factory.

decided that, with a few upgrades, it would be workable. Harrison McCain and Mac McCarthy also had a look and agreed the Werkendam plant would do as McCain's initial European base.

The factory had Dutch management and Turkish workers. Anton de Boef, who was skilled both in factory management and sales, had worked for the previous owners and stayed on as director of sales.

Wayne Hanscom, who arrived in the Netherlands a year later to be the accountant for the European operation, has vivid memories of the Werkendam plant. "It was in an industrial zone, with other buildings and plants all around it," he recounts. "Our office was in a trailer next to the plant. George was in there, and me and a secretary. If I walked from my end of the trailer, the whole thing tipped, and if George walked to my end, it would tip. So the three of us had to be careful how we positioned ourselves."

With Werkendam in place as a McCain factory, McClure turned his attention to Lewedorp, and the deal with Huzo was sealed two months later. John Huige, son of one of the brothers who had owned the Lewedorp plant, stayed as manager. Both deals cost McCain less than it would have cost to build new plants. With the two acquisitions, McCain overnight became a player in the french fry business in four countries. Each plant had different customers in the Netherlands. Favorita also did business in Germany, while Huzo shipped french fries to Belgium and France.

With imports continuing from Scarborough, the company now had three plants manufacturing product to sell in Europe. However, the English potatoes could not be mixed with the Dutch Bintje potatoes because the English potatoes had white flesh while the Dutch ones had yellow. So the English shipments were earmarked

German sales team in 1981 at a meeting in the resort town of Winterberg. Front row: (left to right) Yke Veraart, Hartmut Boesch, Richard Flor, Gisela Muenker, Johanna Christine Goenner, Reinhard Schacht, A. Harrison of Benton and Bowles, Tony van Leersum. Back row: (left to right) Dieter Weinreich, Edgar Thiel, Stefan Mieth, Roland Zwick, Leo Deiting, Josef Schmidt, Friedbert Schelling.

for France, and the Dutch production was shipped to other European countries where consumers preferred yellow-fleshed potatoes.

For every successful acquisition, there are usually several that don't succeed. The German plant owned and operated by Ernst and Hildegard Schnetkamp is one such example. Ernst had been captured by Canadian soldiers in 1945, and he liked to say, "Now you're trying to capture me again." That was because McCain Foods badly wanted his plant. George McClure and later Tony van Leersum made repeated visits, trying their best to make a deal, and Harrison McCain visited the Schnetkamps several times, but they refused to sell.

In 1972, McClure hired a multilingual American, Percival Stybr, as sales manager for all of Europe, leaving John Huige to concentrate on agriculture and manufacturing. Styber's job was to build a sales team in the major markets of Germany and France and to supervise the expansion of McCain into other countries, including Italy, Austria, and Denmark. By now, McCain was one of the few companies that had sales in more than half a dozen European countries.

It was around this time that Hanscom, a New Brunswick native, showed up at McClure's house. He had been working as accountant for McCain's Australian operation, which, like Europe, was in its start-up stage. Hanscom was in his twenties and more interested in exploring the world than building a career. He had joined McCain in Australia, where he had been working for an accounting firm. Before that, he had been in Florenceville working on McCain's books while employed by a Canadian accounting firm. Wallace McCain, on his way home from Japan, interviewed Hanscom on a park bench in Melbourne and offered him the job.

Hanscom accepted on the understanding that it was temporary. When he announced he was leaving, informing Wallace that he and his wife, Margaret, were going to travel overland to Europe via India, Afghanistan, Iran, and Turkey, Wallace told him that if he could get to the Netherlands in four months, he could go to work there for McClure. Hanscom agreed.

LEFT: George McClure (left) and Harrison McCain (right) with the Schnetkamp family in Muenster, Germany, c.1985.
RIGHT: Lewedorp, 1983. A worker sorts potatoes as Paul van der Wel (third from left) and John Huige (far right) look on. The Canadian ambassador to the Netherlands is standing next to Huige.

Hanscom was a slim man, and the rigours of the journey left him even slimmer; by the time he got to the Netherlands, he weighed fifty-five kilograms, the same weight as the two suitcases he was carrying. He arrived just before Christmas as McClure and family were about to depart for a holiday in Spain. Recalls McClure: "I gave him the keys to the mini and the house and said, 'Settle in and put some weight on.'"

Hanscom remembers his time in the Netherlands as a great learning experience. "George was the best mentor you could ever imagine. He would confide in you, bounce ideas off you." The only problem was that McClure liked to get up early, and sometimes he wanted to talk to Hanscom right away. "Once he phoned me at 4.30 AM. He wanted me to meet him for a walk on the dike because he had an idea he wanted to discuss. George is a war historian. We are walking along and he's telling me a story about the Battle of Waterloo, and somehow it was an analogy about something we were going to do. I said, 'Did you really have to get me up here at 4:30 in the morning to talk about the Battle of Waterloo?' But I felt very privileged that he would talk to me and confide in me. Despite all his education, you could have a good time with him."

Hanscom's business education was also furthered by attendance at monthly management meetings of the European company. Either Harrison or Wallace usually attended these meetings, often accompanied by Mac McCarthy. Sometimes, the meetings lasted all day and into the night. One of the most memorable involved a discussion of whether McCain should operate under its own name in Germany or whether it should adopt a German name. It was a passionate debate, with most of those present adamant that "McCain" wouldn't do as a brand in Germany: it was too English for the Germans, and a Germanic name was needed instead. By 8 PM,

TOP: Harrison the horse, Mac McCarthy, Harrison the man, Herman Verloop (managing director, McCain Europa BV), and Henk van Tuyl after the purchase of the Hoofddorp factory, 1978.
BOTTOM: The Hoofddorp factory, 1978.

the matter still wasn't settled. Harrison McCain, as was often the case at such meetings, hadn't said much, preferring to listen as the conversation went back and forth and take a few notes.

Finally, he intervened. "Boys," he said, "that was a great conversation. Great. Lotta input. Now here's what we're going to do. We're going to call it McCain. We're going to call it McCain. Now let's go and eat."

Today, McCain products, bearing the McCain brand, have a strong position in Germany's retail market for frozen foods.

McClure understood from the start that, if McCain was to be a major force in Europe, much of that success would have to come from France. Along with Germany and Italy, France has one of the largest populations in western Europe, potatoes are an important part of the French diet, and the country has an important potato-growing region. In the early 1970s, McClure and Hanscom scouted France, looking for a site to build a plant. But the company decided to put the project on hold since it was planning to build a second British plant, to open at Whittlesey in 1976, that could supply the French market for the time being.

Early one morning in the mid-1970s, McClure and Harrison McCain drove up to see Henk van Tuyl, in Gameren, about an hour from the Amsterdam airport. Van Tuyl owned the largest potato business in the Netherlands and had three french fry factories. Harrison wanted to buy the business. He decided on a direct approach. "Mr. van Tuyl," he said, "I want to buy your factory, and I'll give you good money for it now. If you don't sell it to us now, we may come back later, but don't expect to get the same price."

Van Tuyl wasn't at all impressed by the overconfident Canadian in the black fedora. Van Tuyl was a proud man, and he wasn't used to being talked to in that way.

Nor was he going to do business with Harrison McCain. But in 1978, finding himself short of cash, he decided to sell his Hoofddorp french fry plant. He sent his second in command, Tony van Leersum, to the United States to look for a buyer. Cargill, the huge U.S. agriculture company, was one possibility; Simplot was another. The one company Van Leersum had been ordered not to talk to was McCain.

In the international potato business, word travels fast. Mac McCarthy had heard that Van Leersum was in the United States and suspected he might be trying to sell a french fry factory. McCarthy alerted Harrison, who phoned Van Leersum in Othello, Washington, where he was trying to interest french fry company owner Pete Taggares in the Dutch plant.

Tony van Leersum, Harrison, and George McClure, Rotterdam, 1978.

He said, "Mr. Van Leersum, we hear you are in the United States and that this is possibly about finding a partner for your business, as this is not the best year that you've had in potatoes. Why don't you come over to Boston, and I'll have somebody pick you up in our plane, and I'll put you on the next plane back home. Let's have a talk."

Van Leersum now was faced with a dilemma. Cargill and Simplot had expressed interest but neither was prepared yet to make an offer. The Van Tuyl business needed a cash infusion immediately. Van Leersum knew Harrison's earlier meeting with Van Tuyl hadn't gone well. Nevertheless, Van Leersum decided to disregard his boss's orders and go to Florenceville to see what McCain had to say. Harrison said he would have a serious offer ready in two weeks and wanted to conclude a deal quickly. So Van Leersum went home and persuaded Van Tuyl to give the Canadian company another chance.

A week later, Harrison went to Amsterdam to meet with Van Tuyl. This time, instead of bluntly making a take-it-or-leave-it offer, he raised what he knew was Van Tuyl's favourite subject: horses. Van Tuyl owned seventy-five of them. Harrison said, "If we do a deal, you have to give me one of your horses."

Van Tuyl was delighted at this. Wallace paid a quick visit, and the deal was made the next day. At a celebratory dinner, Van Tuyl presented McCain with a piece of paper, transferring ownership of the tallest horse in his stable. The horse had been renamed Harrison. "I am giving you the horse FOB," he said, meaning that the receiver would have to pay the freight.

Harrison never took delivery of Harrison the horse, but McCain Foods did take delivery of Van Leersum, who agreed to stay on at the Hoofddorp plant for a couple of months to ensure a smooth transition and instead spent the rest of his career working for McCain, in a variety of roles. When Harrison hired him, he told Van Leersum, "You work for me, but you also have to satisfy my brother. Whatever Wallace tells you to do, that is also my decision."

McClure, who had never intended to stay in Europe permanently, returned to Canada in 1975. One morning in 1978, Van Leersum got a call from Harrison, in Paris. McClure's successor had departed the night before and Harrison wanted to offer the job of managing director for Europe to Van Leersum. "We have booked you on a flight for Paris. It's leaving in an hour," he said.

TOP: Truck advertising "three-star" french fries, at the Harnes factory, 1981.
BOTTOM: Francis Dupont, managing director, McCain Alimentaire, 1981.

Van Leersum's first job as managing director was one he had little taste for. A French distributor, Pomona, had exclusive rights to McCain products in France. These products, coming from the English plants, with their more modern equipment, were superior to the product coming out of McCain's Dutch plants. Harrison had decided he wanted to supply France from the Netherlands and that Pomona would no longer have exclusive rights to McCain's fries but would have to share the McCain rights with the two French distributors for the Van Tuyl company. This decision reflected McCain's position as the company with the best potato-processing technology in Europe. It was now strong enough to insist on the most advantageous terms for itself in its arrangements with distributors.

Harrison McCain, McCarthy, and Van Leersum arrived at the Pomona office to meet with the company's officials. It was only as they were walking up the stairs that McCain told Van Leersum that it was he who would have to inform Pomona of the new arrangement. The meeting was warm and friendly until Van Leersum broke the bad news. Pomona, not surprisingly, was unhappy with the decision. Although it nominally remained a distributor, for several years afterward it made little effort to sell McCain's products. As of 2007, however, a good relationship had been re-established and Pomona was once again a valued McCain customer.

By this time, the attention of the leadership of McCain Foods was focused on France. Van Leersum's mandate was to expand the company's presence there. McCain incorporated in France as McCain Alimentaire, and Van Leersum became the first president of the French company, dividing his time between the Dutch and French offices.

After leaving Europe, George McClure headed McCain's U.S. operation, then left the company to go back into public service with the government. But in 1979, he came back as vice-president of corporate development. One of his jobs was to help McCain get established in potato processing in France. The company was growing rapidly on the continent for the same reasons it had grown in Canada and Britain – the spread of quick-service restaurants and the movement of women into the work force, which triggered greater demand for quick meal preparation at home. It needed more capacity to meet the demand; the question was where to put it. Germany was the largest market, but it was ruled out because costs were higher there. The company already had three plants in the Netherlands. France seemed the logical choice.

"France had a huge potato production that was totally untapped by processors," explains McClure, who ended up commuting for sixteen months between Canada and France in search of a site. He engaged the help of Alain Thiers, the former secretary of the French Potato Growers Association. Thiers, who had been a member of the French army's last horse-mounted cavalry operation during the war in Algeria, knew everyone in the French potato industry. With his help, McClure looked at potential sites in all the potato-growing areas but could not settle on one.

One day, McClure and Thiers were driving through Harnes, in the northwest part of the country near the Belgian border, when they spotted a large copper wire factory with a FOR SALE sign on it. McClure pulled over. The building was about the size of McCain's new plants in Canada and Great Britain, and he wanted to show Thiers, who had never seen a modern french fry factory, how big such a factory was.

The copper wire plant had high ceilings and plenty of land around it. It dawned on McClure that this might be just what he was looking for. Tim Bliss came from Florenceville to have a look, as did Wallace and Harrison McCain and Mac McCarthy. They all agreed with McClure. But they knew that doing business in France was not as easy as doing business in Canada or Britain, as the French government imposed more regulations that limit the freedom of action of private business. So McCain Foods, rather than buy the factory, bought an option to buy it. "We wanted to see what problems we would have with the French government," says McClure. "And there were lots."

TOP: The Harnes factory in 2000, a potato field in the foreground.
BOTTOM: Cor Koster, chief of operations for continental Europe, 1986.

LEFT: Gilles Lessard, Harrison, Claude Charland (then Canadian ambassador to France), Paul van der Wel, Harnes, 1989.

RIGHT: The Beaumarais factory in Bethune, France.

McClure contacted the French government's regional development agency. He explained that McCain was proposing to invest $30 million to create a manufacturing facility that would employ 120 people to process French-grown potatoes, many of which would be exported to other countries. Naturally, the officials were pleased and said they would be happy to approve the project. "The only constraint we are going to put on this," McClure was told, "is that you must have a French majority partner."

McClure replied, "That's a non-starter for us. We are family owned and we have no partners."

"I'm sorry, Mr. McClure, that's our policy. Any foreign investors must have a French majority partner."

McClure said no, and the discussion ended.

McClure and Thiers went to see the Charlie Moizard, a potato grower who was president of the Potato Growers Association in that region of France. They knew they had to get the potato growers on McCain's side if they were to budge the government's stance. They decided to take a group of French potato farmers to Britain to see McCain's operations there.

Twenty French farmers went to Scarborough, where they were hosted by Mac McCarthy. He gave them a tour of the plant and introduced them to English potato growers, who praised McCain Foods as a good customer. Once back in France, the growers began to put pressure on the government.

McClure's task was complicated by the fact that the project involved French government agencies in the fields of agriculture, energy, finance, the environment, and transportation, as well as local municipal officials. The various government agencies did not communicate among themselves, so any piece of correspondence had to be copied and hand delivered to each of them.

McClure had another meeting with the development agency. He was told there had been a change in the government's position. McCain could go ahead with its investment in France as long as it had a French minority investor. Again McClure said no.

Jean Bernou, CEO for continental Europe, with Anne-Sophie Fontaine, the sales director for France, in a French supermarket, 2006.

"We then got more and more of the French growers involved and got them to turn more and more heat on the French government. Finally, the French government agreed that we could be 100 percent foreign investment. That was very unusual, particularly in the food and agriculture sector, because they look at that as part of France."

Some of the McCain people were concerned about the local political situation. The French Communist Party was powerful in the region, and the Harnes mayor was Communist. But the mayor was as keen as any other politician would have been to get new economic development. "I will help you hire people who are not troublemakers," he promised.

McCain proceeded to convert the copper wire plant at Harnes into a state-of-the-art french fry factory. When it opened in 1981, not only was the manufacturing equipment the best available, so was the environmental technology that purified the wastewater before it left the plant. In processing, water is used in washing, transporting, and cutting the potatoes, leaving the water with bits of potato and starch in it. If it is released untreated into a river or lake, the wastewater consumes oxygen needed by the plants and wildlife in that river or lake. So the water has to be clarified, a process that releases methane gas. At Harnes, McCain employs an anaerobic system that cleans the water and recovers the methane, feeding it back into the factory to provide energy.

All the effort of getting permission to build in France turned out to be well worth it. The opening of the Harnes plant launched McCain as a major player

Paul van der Wel, CEO, Continental Europe, 1991.

in the French food industry. By 2007, France had become McCain's biggest European market, with the company holding strong positions in the retail as well as quick-service and other restaurant markets. It was worth it for the French government as well, and not just because of the economic boost to local farmers. Because the Harnes plant was the most environmentally advanced in France, it became a showpiece to which government officials proudly brought a steady stream of visitors.

Before the Harnes factory was built, André Bonduelle, president of the largest vegetable canning and freezing company in France, had warned Harrison McCain and Tony van Leersum that the French farmers could not provide raw materials as good as the Dutch potatoes McCain was used to. At first, it seemed he was right: all the potatoes McCain shipped from the Harnes area to the Hoofddorp factory for testing were rejected.

The French growers considered the contract prices McCain was offering too low and the Dutch quality conditions too strict. They put a full page ad in the local paper, *La Voix du Nord,* urging farmers not to supply McCain. As a result, no contracts were signed and the factory used potatoes from the Netherlands and Belgium. But that couldn't be a permanent solution. The company hired Michel Delaître, himself a former grower, as potato procurement manager. It also brought in its own agronomists to work with the growers. As of 2007, the potatoes supplied by the French growers were, on average, even better than those produced by their Dutch counterparts.

If you had business qualifications and experience and you came into contact with Harrison McCain and made a positive impression, the chances were good you would get a job offer. Even on purely social occasions, Harrison had business at the back of his mind, and he was always on the lookout for talent to help make McCain Foods the world's largest french fry producer. George McClure was hired after he chaired a meeting Harrison attended. Paul van der Wel became a McCain executive after attempting to sell McCain some fish processing factories.

In 1980, Van der Wel was general manager of Associated Fisheries of Canada, a New Brunswick fish processor that was selling factories in various parts of the Maritimes. He met with Harrison and Wallace McCain to try to make deal. A week later, Harrison called him and said McCain didn't want the factories but it did want Van der Wel.

In 1981, Van der Wel joined as manager of special projects, based in Florenceville. But the multilingual Van der Wel was destined to help McCain Foods in its drive to dominate Europe. Soon after joining the company, he was sent to the Netherlands to take over as managing director of McCain Foods Holland, with responsibility for the Netherlands and four other countries.

Van der Wel had been born and raised in the Netherlands, where he attended the State Agricultural College. He then completed his education in Canada, obtaining a BSc in food management from McGill and an MBA in international business from Hamilton's McMaster University. He worked for several Canadian companies before the McCain job sent him back to the Netherlands. There, Van der Wel found a European division that was "in the starting blocks" but not yet racing down the track. The main problem, in his opinion, was that McCain in Europe was "a production-driven culture, as opposed to a marketing culture."

What is the difference? In a production-driven culture, the emphasis is on selling what is produced, rather than on producing what the market tells the sales force it wants. "A marketing attitude says that you must adjust your agriculture and quality control to what the market wants," explains Van der Wel. "If you don't have the best potatoes, you have to make compromises, but in general, quality goes above production efficiency. You have to satisfy the needs of the consumer. Otherwise your reputation goes down the tubes." The problem existed, Van der Wel thought, because McCain had taken over European operations in which the production mindset was strongly imbued. This attitude was the natural result of an era in which production employees were focused on the need to keep up with demand. Van der Wel set it as his task to instill a marketing culture in his employees.

McCain at the time was based in the Netherlands, with three factories there. But the most potential for growth and profit was in Germany, and so that is where Van der Wel

The McCain booth at the 1998 Intercool food fair in Düsseldorf. The display celebrated McCain's twenty-fifth year in food service in Germany and its twentieth year in the retail market.

Opening of the Lelystad plant, 1997: Harrison; Folkert Sneep, managing director for northern Europe; and Howard Mann, president and CEO, McCain Foods Limited.

focused his attention. "There are more people and more money in Germany, and the Germans pay more for quality than the Dutch," says Van der Wel. As well, German consumers prefer to prepare their french fries in the oven.

"The value-added is higher in oven fries than in regular ones," says Van der Wel. "They are more difficult to produce, so competitors can't copy you as readily, and you have a competitive advantage, which you can market in an advertising campaign, building yourself a strong market position. In the Netherlands, we could not do that because there was not the money to advertise, and the demand for oven fries was much lower than in Germany."

To become intimately acquainted with the German market, Van der Wel spent six weeks there, travelling with each of McCain's German salespersons. This allowed him to see stores and restaurants, to meet customers, and to evaluate the strengths of the sales force. After that, he went to Germany every other week.

In 1983, Van der Wel became CEO for McCain Foods for Europe, including France, which had been under separate management before. At the same time, Tony van Leersum moved to Florenceville to take on responsibility for corporate development in Europe and the Middle East. He also served as McDonald's international account manager.

The following years were a time of rapid growth for McCain in Europe, with sales over a ten-year period ballooning from $70 million to $450 million. The growth was the result of increasing the market for french fries, introducing many new products, and acquiring new businesses. These included a frozen food company, Frima, with production facilities in Ostend and Grobbendonk, Belgium, which became McCain Frima NV; and Beaumarais, a fries and potato-flake manufacturer in Bethune, France, near Harnes. In 1988, McCain spent $33 million to double production at Harnes. And in 1991, McCain picked up its fourth french fry plant in the Netherlands, in the town of Lelystad.

Van der Wel cites several reasons for McCain's rapid growth. For one, the senior management team collaborated well and were all committed to rapid expansion. Van der Wel has worked at several major food companies but at McCain he experienced "by far the best teamwork I ever had in my career." Also, McCain was entering big markets – Germany, France, and Italy – that were underdeveloped in processed potatoes.

LEFT: The 1984 fire at the Lewedorp factory reduced the building to a burnt-out shell. The ground is littered with potatoes.
RIGHT: Jan van der Neut-Kolfschoten, chief engineer, Europe; Paul van der Wel; and Harrison at the site of the fire.

A strategic decision by Harrison and Wallace was another important factor. They differentiated McCain from competing companies by strongly supporting their own brand rather than private labels. "That requires heavy investments in marketing, which reduced short-term profitability, but it was an excellent long-term decision because it is now very profitable," says Van der Wel. "We were marketers. The competition were merchandisers."

Sometimes, however, marketing doesn't work the way it's supposed to. The selling point of oven fries is that they have less fat and less odour than their fried counterparts. In the early 1980s, an advertising agency came up with a French TV commercial that showed a poodle coming into the kitchen while fries were being prepared. The dog has its tail in the air when fries are in the oven, but when the dog comes back into the kitchen and the fryer is going, he runs away in disgust.

"It got the prize for the least effective commercial in Europe," says Van der Wel. "You don't identify human food with dogs. It was humorous, but it didn't work at all. And it was premature for France because the French weren't interested in oven fries." The advertising agency and marketing director were both fired. "We lost a lot of money. McCain was down the drain. We couldn't get listings, we couldn't get distribution. Later, we changed our whole approach to fried french fries in France."

Another miscue occurred in Germany with a new product, onion-flavoured hash browns called Rösti Ecken. The art on the package showed six triangular potato pieces. But the equipment in the plant making them couldn't be relied on to produce six per package. Although the total weight of the package contents was accurate, sometimes there were seven pieces instead of six. "The Germans are meticulous," says Van der Wel. "They want what is inside to be the same as what is shown on the bag. If the bag shows

Rolando Palazzi (right) receives the Best Partner of the Decade award from Jean Bernou, 2005.

six, that's what they want – not seven. I got thousands of complaints. When you are in the consumer marketing business, you don't make those mistakes."

An important aspect of the McCain philosophy is that problems exist to be overcome. Rather than being demoralized by setbacks, the company's founders were energized by them. Van der Wel was called at one o'clock on a Saturday morning in February 1984 by the Lewedorp plant manager, who reported that part of the factory was on fire – but that it didn't look too bad. Later, he called to say that the wind had picked up and the fire had spread to the roof. By the time Van der Wel got there, three hours later, the building was destroyed.

That afternoon, Van der Wel called Harrison McCain with the bad news. Harrison said, "Paul, make a proposal. We are going to rebuild." Van der Wel, along with John Huige and his production and engineering people, wrote up a proposal indicating what had to be done and what it would cost. He sent it by telex on Monday. Within twenty-four hours, he got a telex in reply. It read "Please proceed."

The rebuilt – and much improved – factory was running six months later. The episode, Van der Wel told *The Star* later, was "an example of McCain spirit and true cooperation and of very fast decision making," as well as an example of the confidence the company's leadership had in its regional management.

A high point of Van der Wel's McCain career was the surprising success of McCain fries in Italy, the land of pasta. McCain's sales went from four thousand metric tons of french fries a year to forty thousand metric tons during the 1980s. Some of the credit, Van der Wel believes, should go to Pope John Paul II. The Vatican owns several restaurants, which played host to thousands of potato-eating tourists from Poland after the Polish Pope was elected in 1978. "We sold the Vatican restaurants hundreds of tons of french fries," says Van der Wel. "The Vatican was our best customer."

More important than the Pope to McCain's fortunes in Italy was Rolando Palazzi, who has represented McCain there since 1976. Palazzi first met Harrison McCain in 1956, when Palazzi was a boy of fifteen. McCain Foods had been in business just a few months when Harrison decided to scout business opportunities in Europe. Palazzi's father, Nino, ran one of the best restaurants in Rome and also catered for airlines, including the now defunct Canadian Pacific Airlines. Someone at the airline suggested to Harrison that he contact Palazzi. They talked about the food business, and Palazzi introduced his young son to the Canadian visitor.

In the mid-1970s, Rolando Palazzi was working for a state-owned frozen food company that was doing business with Favorita, one of the Dutch plants purchased by McCain. Anton de Boef, who joined McCain when that factory was acquired, wanted someone to represent the company in Italy. Palazzi decided to quit his job and go into business for himself as a distributor. His first supplier was McCain.

In his first year, he sold four hundred metric tons of french fries for McCain. PomFrit, a Dutch company represented by another Italian agent, sold nine hundred metric tons. As of 2007, McCain's Italian sales were ten times those of its Dutch competitor.

Such success was the fruit of much hard labour. To help build up the Italian market, Anton de Boef and later Tony van Leersum spent eight or more days per month criss-crossing the country with Palazzi setting up a distribution network. When the weather made it too dangerous to cross the mountains at night, they slept in the car.

By 2007, McCain was selling more than thirty potato products in Italy. Its Italian business was being managed by twelve area managers and 250 distributors servicing thousands of restaurants. Italy is unusual in that the quick-service chains have not done as well as they have in most other industrialized countries. McDonald's operates in Italy, but it doesn't have many outlets and the food service industry remains dominated by independent restaurants.

The end-user system – demonstrating the advantages of McCain frozen fries to chefs – has been instrumental in cementing the company's dominant position in the Italian food service industry. This has been achieved even though competitors can offer lower prices. McCain has been able to get the message across that a small additional cost per portion is worth it for the better quality. Just as the proprietary name Kleenex has come to mean a tissue, so the McCain brand has become synonymous with french fries in the Italian food service industry. "Give me one McCain means give me one case of french fries," says Palazzi.

In an ideal world McCain would make french fries only under its own brand, but in the real world it can't avoid the private-label business entirely. Supermarkets want low-cost products bearing their own labels, and if McCain won't provide them, the competition will. The acquisition of Beaumarais in 1986 gave McCain two factories:

Alain Olivier, CFO for continental Europe, 2002.

Left to right: Folkert Sneep, CEO, northern and central Europe; Michael Figeac, CEO, southern Europe; and Gilles Lessard, CEO, continental Europe, 1996.

the one in Beaumarais, and a second, PAS, in England, producing fries for private labels. "Buying Beaumarais was very good for us," says Van der Wel, "because it allowed us to compete with the Dutch and Belgian companies with a low overhead company that could sell big contracts to private-label customers and still keep our market share."

An important contributor in organizing the financial affairs of McCain Alimentaire in France and later the European operation as a whole was Alain Olivier, who joined McCain in 1982. Olivier was working for Xerox in the Netherlands when a recruiter approached him with the news that a job as financial director of an international food company was available in his native France. Told the company's product was french fries, Olivier said he wasn't interested – he didn't think a company producing such an unsophisticated product had much of a future.

However, after hearing from his Dutch colleagues of McCain's reputation for high-quality products, he accepted an invitation to Florenceville for an interview. There, Wallace and Harrison McCain, along with Carl Ash, now vice-president of finance, changed his mind, and Olivier went to work for McCain Alimentaire. He was shocked to find no proper financial procedures in place for such basic functions as invoicing and payments. He had been told in Florenceville that McCain was an entrepreneurial company. Maybe, he now thought, it was too entrepreneurial.

But the informal management style had its advantages. Olivier recalls an occasion on which, two years after he joined, McCain Alimentaire had a cash shortage of six million French francs. Harrison told him to call Wim Broer, his counterpart at the Dutch company, and ask for the money. One phone call and the cash was transferred immediately.

Olivier later took on the job of financial director for Beaumarais while continuing to perform the same function for McCain Alimentaire. Later he became CFO for McCain, continental Europe. He retired in 2007 and was replaced by a Belgian, Erwin Pardon, who had been managing director for northern Europe.

Olivier has vivid memories of meetings with Harrison McCain, who went to France on a regular basis. Harrison would expect every manager to understand the figures in the management control report, even if they were not directly related to that manager's field. In meetings, if Olivier wanted to answer one of Harrison's questions, he was often told: "Alain, I know that you can explain this figure, but don't tell me. I want to know whether others know, because that's what we pay them for."

In another management meeting, Harrison, dissatisfied with the company's progress in penetrating the French retail market, dropped the news that he had recruited a Canadian, Gilles Lessard, to head McCain Alimentaire and that Francis Dupont, president of McCain Alimentaire, would be running Beaumarais instead. Olivier believes it was news to everybody present, including Dupont.

Lessard came to McCain from the Quebec supermarket chain Metro-Richelieu, where he had been assistant to the chief operating officer, with responsibility for frozen foods. He went for interviews at Florenceville, where Harrison told him of his frustration with two failed attempts to launch oven-prepared french fries in France's retail market. After talking with Lessard for a couple of hours, Harrison opened the door between his office and that of his brother so that Wallace could have a short meeting with Lessard. Then Harrison went into Wallace's office and shut the door, leaving Lessard alone. Five minutes later he came back and said, "Gilles, my brother and I just had a board meeting, and you should consider yourself hired as the president of McCain Alimentaire. Of course, we will speak with our managing director [Van der Wel] for continental Europe, but you should prepare yourself to go over there ASAP."

A Paris advertising agency had advised McCain that its anglophone name precluded any possibility of success in the French retail market. Harrison McCain responded that if the agency could guarantee success, he would change the brand to the non-anglophone name of McCainski. The agency declined and McCain did not use its services.

Gilles Lessard didn't think the problem was the McCain name. The reason oven-prepared french fries were a hit in the United Kingdom, the Netherlands, and Germany, and not in France was that the northern Europeans preferred to avoid deep frying, while the French liked it. The French used the deep fat fryer at home for other foods as well and did not mind the odour or fat content as much.

The northern Europe management team in 1996: (left to right) John Huige, Hans van Rouwendaal, Sylvia Patijn-Lodewijks, Cees van Rijn, Kees Oreel, Frank van Schaayk.

LEFT: Celebrating McCain's first contract with Polish potato growers.
RIGHT: The Polish sales force on a team-building rock-climbing expedition led by Edgar Thiel, a sales manager from Germany.

Lessard decided to launch a better quality frozen french fry for deep frying at home. He put them in an attractive retail package with a premium price. It worked. The new McCain fries took the French retail market by storm.

Despite the existence of a customs union and a common currency that is shared by many of its countries, Europe remains a complex market. Differences persist in cuisines, language, consumer behaviour, working habits, laws, market structures, and distribution systems. In 1989, when the Berlin Wall came down, Van der Wel's job as the head of McCain Europa became more complex still. Overnight, Communist East Germany joined capitalist West Germany. The West German retail stores McCain was supplying rushed into the former East Germany. They bought land and started building, but they couldn't wait to start selling. So they erected tents with freezers to sell frozen food supplied by McCain.

It fell upon Van der Wel to train a group of East German salespeople. Inevitably, there were culture clashes. The salespeople he hired were accustomed to driving Trabants, two-cylinder East German cars infamous for being noisy, slow, and prone to falling apart. McCain gave them brand new Volkswagen Golfs as company cars. The East Germans were thrilled by the power and speed of their new vehicles – too thrilled, as it turned out. "Within a month, most of them had driven their cars into a tree or ditch," recounts Van der Wel. "Nobody got killed, but the cars were ruined. I had to make it a rule that anybody who wrecks his car would be fired. After that, everything was fine."

LEFT: The opening of Moscow's first McDonald's, in Pushkin Square, 1990.
RIGHT: The lineup for a hamburger and fries wound around the square.

The most intriguing market for any consumer products company is the most populous. Among the former Soviet satellite countries of central Europe, that was Poland, with almost forty million people. Poland was also a potato-producing and potato-eating country and therefore of great interest to McCain. Van der Wel hired a Polish sales manager, and the two of them drove all over Poland looking for a french fry factory to buy. But the existing factories bore the same relationship to modern ones as Trabants did to cars manufactured in the West. "In every building we saw, the cafeteria was larger than the factory floor, and the equipment was from forty years ago," says Van der Wel. Worse, the Polish government imposed strict conditions on potential buyers. If McCain took over one of the existing small factories, it would be able to run it with about thirty employees. But under the existing staffing policy, the Polish factories had about four hundred employees, including quite a few idle welders, carpenters, and cleaners. The government would not allow a buyer to fire any of these employees.

Given these circumstances, Van der Wel advised McCain to delay entering Poland as a manufacturer and instead build up a market by importing from other McCain factories. After most of a decade had elapsed and capitalism was better entrenched in Poland, McCain, in 1998, spent $79 million to build a new factory in Strzelin near Wroclaw. As well as supplying Poland, it exports to neighbouring Russia and other central and eastern European markets.

A Russian potato field in the black soil region.

"If you don't get the agronomy right," Harrison McCain once said, "nothing else matters." The reason is obvious: you can't make a good french fry from a bad potato. No potato-processing company works harder on agronomy than McCain. The company employs one hundred agronomists in various parts of the world to maintain and improve the quality of the potatoes its growers produce.

An important issue for McCain in Europe was that its big customer, McDonald's, wanted potatoes of the same variety, Russet Burbank, that it used at home in the United States. The Russet Burbank is not grown at all in the Netherlands, and growers in other parts of Europe avoid it because of the risk of disease and the higher fungicide requirements than other varieties. The other problem with Russet Burbanks in Europe is that a russet-skinned potato isn't a popular table potato, as it is in North

Growing potatoes

Harrison McCain used to say, "If you don't measure it, you do not manage it." McCain's agronomists apply this principle when helping growers make the right decisions to maximize quality and yield. The agronomists pass on the knowledge gained from trials carried out in various parts of the world so that growers everywhere may implement and benefit from the best practices in growing potatoes for processing.

1. Plowing is usually done in the fall, to minimize weeds and to incorporate remainders of the previous crop.

2. French fry processors want varieties with large, long potatoes. In many regions, large seed potatoes are cut in two or more seed pieces.

3. This planter plants two rows of potatoes at a time.

4. Good soil preparation and good seed assure that the potato plants emerge from the soil evenly.

5. After the plants have fully emerged, the cultivator destroys weeds and enhances the ridges on which the potato plants grow.

6. Hilling further builds a ridge to retain moisture and maintain the right soil temperature while protecting tubers from direct sunlight.

7. Fields are scouted for diseases as part of the integrated pest management program to minimize use of artificial chemicals.

8. Sampling during the growing period provides a preview of the quality and yield of the coming crop.

9. Potatoes may be harvested while still green if they are used immediately for processing.

10. Harvesting crews wait in the early morning for the soil to warm up. Harvesting when the soil is cold can damage potatoes.

11. The windrower lifts potatoes and puts them in between the rows for the harvester to collect.

12. The harvester's movable belt carefully deposits the potatoes into an accompanying truck.

13. A grader removes excessive soil and foreign matter before the potatoes are put into storage.

14. Potatoes are transferred to a ventilated storage building, where they are piled over ducts emitting forced air to dry and cool them.

ACROSS THE CHANNEL

Potato variety and seed potato production

Although hundreds of potato varieties exist, breeders continue to search for new, hardier ones. Once a new variety is created, it takes years of experiments to find the best ways to grow it. Varieties that do well in one region may not perform as well in others. Only when the best management practices are perfected is the new variety recommended for french fry production.

1. Each potato variety has a distinctive colour and shape of flower. The sparse white flowers of the Russet Burbank are star shaped.

2. The Shepody has abundant light violet flowers with an orange-green centre.

3. Each potato variety has its own characteristic sprout, which emerges when the tuber is exposed to sunlight. Shown here is the Kennebec.

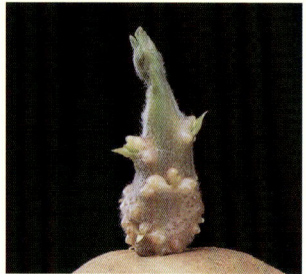

4. A Russet Burbank sprout.

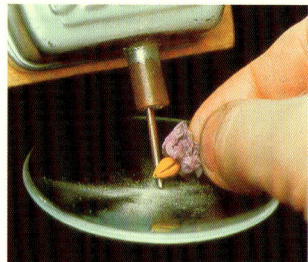

5. Pollen is extracted from the potato flower anther. Cross-pollination can produce new varieties with characteristics desirable for potato processing.

6. The berries of the potato plant contain potato seeds, or "true" seeds. Only pollinated flowers produce seed berries.

7. Each true seed in a berry resulting from cross-pollination is that of a new variety, one with characteristics of the parent plants.

8. Potato plants are grown from the tiny seeds, in a greenhouse.

9. True seeds from the same plant can produce potatoes of different colours and shapes, deriving from earlier generations.

10. New varieties are test-grown in the field for several years and in different locations to see how they respond to local environments.

11. To speed up multiplication of new plants, a tissue culture is done by cutting the stems and planting them in test tubes.

12. These test tubes are kept in a laboratory under controlled temperature and light conditions to promote rapid growth.

13. Plantlets from tissue culture are grown in an aphid-free environment to produce disease-free small tubers.

14. McCain specialists discuss performance of a new variety in the field.

America. So if a crop isn't suitable for french fries, there is less of a market for it as table stock.

McCain's agronomists have been instrumental in developing varieties that are almost equal to the Russet Burbank in length and solids while less prone to disease. These include the Santana and the Innovator, an offspring of the Canadian Shepody variety. Innovators are now grown for McCain in all the European Union countries, as well as in Australia, Argentina, and China.

No country is identified with potatoes more than Russia, with its millions of hectares of land devoted to potato production. Yet in no country is it more difficult to get the agronomy right. Any potato-processing company would be interested in a potato-eating country of 143 million people, especially when many of those people were so desperate for a taste of American-style fast food that they were willing to line up for hours in the January cold for the opening of McDonald's first Russian outlet in Moscow's Pushkin Square in 1990.

There was no french fry–processing plant in Russia, so in 1990 McDonald's Russia, a venture of McDonald's Canada, had to build its own. McDonald's was eager for McCain to build a factory, but before McCain could do that, it needed to build a market and know if satisfactory raw material would be available.

As of 2007, McCain was continuing to experiment with agronomy in Russia, growing potatoes on about two hundred hectares, in a continued effort to develop a viable agriculture program in Russia. Meanwhile, it continued to supply McDonald's and other customers from its Polish factory.

TOP LEFT: Oksana Lopyreva-Belyaeva, Pieter Toxopeus, and Erik Haasken, members of McCain's Russian team, in a trial field in Lipetzk, Russia.
TOP RIGHT: Erik Haasken and Gera Sitnik check tuber development.
BOTTOM: Ian Cameron, Dell Thornley of McDonald's, Gera Sitnik, and Oksana Lopyreva-Belyaeva en route to an island near Archangelsk, in northwestern Russia, where McCain grows seed potatoes in isolated conditions.

RIGHT: The Russia team in 2006: (left to right) Elena Pankova, Anna Kolochinskaya, Pieter Toxopeus, Irina Mokhnatkina, Erik Haasken, Irina Tishkina, Tatiana Vlasikhina, Georgiy Sitnik, Ksenia Baranova, Mikhail Aksenev, Oksana Lopyreva-Belyaeva, Elena Yulina, Dmitry Zavgorodniy, Svetlana Pronchenko, Nadia Timakova, Ekaterina Gavrish, Eldar Aleskerov, Viktoria Volkova, Olga Berkut, Sergey Mysyakov, Irina Kuznetsova, Natalia Baranova, Natalia Kulaeva, Karina Shirmazanyan, Alexander Buyanov, Svetlana Sakina.
BELOW: Russian-language packaging.

McCain almost had a french fry factory in Ukraine. It bought the plant when it was under construction but never took possession of it because the Ukrainian seller and the bank that financed the plant both went bankrupt in the wake of a severe devaluation of the Ukrainian currency.

Russia and the other republics of the former Soviet Union are designated by McCain as eastern Europe and are under the management of Nick Vermont, CEO for Britain. The former central European satellite countries, such as Poland and Hungary, are part of the territory of Jean Bernou, CEO for continental Europe. The central European countries historically had close ties to western Europe, and most of them had democratic and capitalist traditions before being forcibly attached to the Soviet bloc after World War II. Russia and other former Soviet republics are a different story: most of them were never democracies, and they lack the legal and institutional framework necessary to facilitate new business ventures.

Vermont has an odd geographical assortment under his purview – Britain, eastern Europe, and South Africa. Dale Morrison, president and CEO, McCain Foods Limited, has told him he has one developed market (Britain), one developing market (South Africa), and, in eastern Europe, one blank sheet. "Eastern Europe is a very exciting place, and it has huge long-term potential. But, culturally, it is a very different place to do business," says Vermont. "And, legally, it is a very difficult place to do business."

One Friday night in 1995, Jean Bernou, a forty-two-year-old executive in the French office of Mölnlycke, a Swedish disposable hygiene products company, was watching a documentary on French TV about a business story in Canada – the dispute between Harrison and Wallace McCain over the future management of McCain Foods. To his amazement, he received a phone call the following Monday from a recruiter, inviting him to interview for a job as managing director of Beaumarais, the French manufacturer of private-label potato products owned by McCain Foods. Bernou knew that the European division of McCain was under the supervision of Harrison McCain, whom he had just seen on TV. "The program featured a lot of interviews with Harrison," Bernou says. "I had a really good image of him."

Normally, Harrison McCain would have interviewed Bernou, but Harrison was ill. So Gilles Lessard of the European McCain office interviewed Bernou and hired him. Shortly after that, Bernou received his first phone call from Harrison. "He often repeated what he was saying. He said, 'You are the managing director? I want to see you, I want to see you. If I don't like you, I won't hire you.'"

Since Bernou had already been hired and was at work in the Beaumarais office, he was taken aback. Then Harrison said, "People have told me you are a nice guy so I don't need to interview you. So you are hired."

Bernou joined McCain because he was looking for a job with a lighter workload than the one he had at Mölnlycke. He was assured that the McCain job would take up less of his time. And it did – for one year. Then he got a call on his car phone. It was Harrison. He said, "I have a job for you. I want you to take charge of McCain Alimentaire."

Since McCain Alimentaire is the company's major enterprise in France, producing McCain-branded products for the retail market and french fries for restaurants, running it is a bigger job than running the private-label manufacturer, Beaumarais.

Bernou said, "No, thank you. I am very happy where I am. I don't want that job."

Harrison said, "Think about it, and I will call you back."

"Okay, Harrison, I'll think about it."

"You can take your time to think about it."

"Thank you, Harrison."

TOP: McCain's microwaveable fries, launched in 2004, garnered the Innovation Oscar that same year, awarded by one of France's leading retail trade publications, *LSA*.
BOTTOM: Lucille Degrave, vice-president of marketing for continental Europe, says the French consumer's reference for quality in french fries is now McCain.

ACROSS THE CHANNEL   97

The Matougues plant, 2007. This new-generation factory has McCain's biggest single production line.

Five minutes later, the car phone rang again. It was Harrison. "Okay, you've had time to think about it. I want you to start as soon as you can."

Bernou took the job. He also developed a friendship with Harrison McCain that he treasured. He particularly appreciated that Harrison offered help for certain family problems Bernou was experiencing. "He was very, very helpful opening many doors for me to get the right doctors. He would call my wife, too. This created a very strong link between Harrison and me. This is one of the reasons I am still with the company, because when you build this kind of relationship, you say, 'Okay. I have to stay.' Harrison could be very tough but he could also be a wonderful guy."

After Bernou had run the French business for two years, Harrison asked him to take over responsibility for all of southern Europe. At the time, southern and northern Europe were being run as two separate divisions. Harrison had divided the continent in two because he thought having two managers and teams looking after such a complex and large region would allow the business to grow faster than having only one. But eventually it became apparent that two captains were not better than one. So Gilles Lessard, based in Brussels, was named CEO for all of continental Europe, with the CEOs of the two continental European regions reporting to him. Then, in 2002, Bernou was given the job of merging and running the two divisions, northern and southern Europe. In 2005, central Europe was added to Bernou's responsibility. While most of the major European french fry companies are still based in the Netherlands and Germany, McCain since 2002 has maintained its continental European headquarters in France.

Although Europe, with its slow population growth, is often considered a mature market, McCain Foods is growing and thriving there. Some of the growth comes from winning consumers over to McCain products. For example, the French for many

Wallace

As a manager, Wallace McCain was famous for his mastery of detail. CFO Bruce Terry admired his ability to "talk about various cost ratios and speak about thirty years of history with absolute accuracy. I used to say he could probably still tell you what the specific gravity of peas was in 1961."

John Walsh, a crop scientist in charge of potato research, attended a meeting in St. Louis, Missouri, with Harrison McCain and representatives of Monsanto in the late 1980s to discuss genetic engineering of potatoes. When he returned, he met with Wallace, who was eager to find out everything about the meeting. Wallace had even set up a flip chart in his office so that Walsh could make drawings to explain his answers.

"I was very impressed by his knowledge of the subject and the kinds of questions he asked," recalls Walsh. "He wanted to make sure that he understood the technology properly and whether I thought the technology was viable or not. He kept me there for an hour and a half, until he was sure all his questions had been answered. I left exhausted."

(Walsh did not recommend doing a deal with Monsanto, and Wallace agreed. To date, McCain has not used genetically engineered potatoes.)

Wallace McCain understood that, in manufacturing, the winner is the company that can produce the highest possible quality at the lowest possible cost. Pennies are important because pennies add up to dollars.

"Wallace would call you into his office at ten minutes to five," recalls Jim Evans, a veteran production manager. "He might be sitting there behind a stack inches thick of purchase orders to authorize or invoices to approve for payment. He wanted to know exactly why you had to purchase this or that, why this many pieces, why it had to be of that quality and price level.

"He wanted to make sure you knew exactly what you were doing, and how you were spending the company's money. Once you knew what Wallace was looking for, you prepared for it. If anything deviated 5 percent from budget, you made sure you had all the answers before talking to Wallace."

Like his late brother Harrison, Wallace McCain is unpretentious. Both brothers had huge ambitions for their

Wallace, 1969.

company but never took themselves too seriously. Board member Paul Tellier recalls a visit in 2006 by the McCain board to France's Champagne region to see the company's Matougues plant. The Matougues factory is impressive both in its size and the attractiveness of its surrounding grounds. Tellier, who was sitting next to Wallace on the bus, expected him to be bursting with pride. After all, he had started a little company in New Brunswick and now here he was arriving at this magnificent factory that bore his family name and it was in Europe, in the country that had given the french fry its name.

Tellier said, "You must have a tremendous sense of pride looking at this."

Wallace replied curtly, "No. I'm just looking at the size of the goddamn thing and I'm wondering why it's so big. Maybe we could have made more money if it was smaller."

The continental European management team, with visitors Janice Wismer and Simon Jones, at the mid-year meeting in Chantilly, France, 2006. Front row: (left to right) Erwin Pardon, Andrzej Czudowski, Pedro Alexandre, Helga Hofmeister, Lourenço de Sottomayor, Francine Bouquillon. Second row from front: Han van den Hoek, Janice Wismer, Lucile Degrave, Laurent Ferré, Frédéric Jaubert, Michel Delaître, Furny Soerel. Third row from front: Bertrand Delannoy, George Ghonos, Jean-Louis Gilardi, Simon Jones. Back row: Alain Olivier (in black sweater), Philippe Théry, Ronald Felius, Jean Bernou, Jean-François Delage, Christophe Rigo, Jean-Claude Blaimont, Yves Roptin. Absent: Kees Oreel.

years resisted oven fries, which have long been McCain's biggest seller in Germany and Britain. But by 2006, they were quickly gaining popularity.

For the most part, however, McCain tries to adapt its product offerings to existing consumer preferences. In the Mediterranean regions, people cook most of their food, including potatoes, in an oiled pan. In northern France, Belgium, and the Netherlands, most still prefer the deep fryer for french fries. Germans prefer using the oven. Italians also use the oven, but they like to roast potatoes as part of a main dish of fish or meat. McCain has a variety of potato products to address these different culinary styles.

The decision to build a huge, state-of-the art plant at Matougues demonstrates the company's confidence that it can continue to thrive in Europe. In 2006, as McCain was celebrating its twenty-fifth anniversary in France, a third shift was added to the Matougues plant. In the same year, however, McCain closed its factory in Hoofddorp, in the Netherlands, because the company had more manufacturing capacity than was warranted given a slow-growing market for french fries.

Bernou finds that his European employees are proud of being part of a family-owned company whose practices reflect the values of honesty and trust, and respect for the individual, exemplified by its founders. They must like working for McCain, because they tend to stay a long time. The average worker at the original French plant in Harnes has worked there for thirteen years, and one-quarter of the employees have worked at Harnes for more than eighteen years.

LEFT: The French management team: (left to right) Michel Delaître, Stéphane Renault, Francis Dupont, Michel Figeac, Jean Pierre Zilinski, Jean Bernou, Alain Olivier, 2001.

RIGHT: Allison McCain with George Ghonos in an Athens supermarket.

Nowhere more than Europe, with its many different cultures, is it more obvious that McCain's global success is based on its ability to adapt to local conditions. McCain Hellas, for example, could not possibly have been successful without the leadership of George Ghonos and his team. When Harrison McCain hired Ghonos, he told him not to worry about making profits for the first five years but to concentrate on building up a market. At the time, Dutch and Belgian frozen french fry processors were unloading their lower-grade products at low prices in Greece. Paul van der Wel, then McCain's senior director for continental Europe, advised Ghonos to take on the low-cost suppliers at their own game by taking the lower-grade product from Beaumarais. Ghonos rejected that advice, deciding instead to differentiate McCain in Greece on the basis of quality. And so he imported only top-grade product.

The strategy worked brilliantly. Ghonos has "written the bible on how to succeed in an emerging market," says Jean Bernou. In a country of just eleven million people, McCain's sales volumes are as high as in some other countries with three times the population.

In Greece, the art of winemaking has been practised for four thousand years, so the McCain motto "drink the local wine" is especially appropriate. Drinking the local wine in Greece means offering an assortment that fits the local cuisine. That means heavier, thicker cut fries to go with souvlaki, for example.

Harrison and Wallace McCain were always ready to travel long distances to create local links in their global empire. Four decades ago, while Harrison McCain was expanding McCain Foods from Florenceville to Britain and continental Europe, Wallace McCain had his sights set on a much more distant market, seventeen thousand kilometres away on the other side of the world.

CHAPTER FOUR

DOWN UNDER

In 1971, Wallace McCain took a trip to Daylesford, a village about a hundred kilometres north of Melbourne, in southern Australia. Daylesford is known in Australia for its rejuvenating mineral springs, but Wallace didn't come to take the waters.

He came because Daylesford was in Australian potato country and a french fry plant there was for sale. The plant, a former woollen mill that was being used to process dehydrated potatoes, was small and dilapidated but it was going cheap. More impressive to Wallace was what he saw in the nearby fields.

He phoned his brother Harrison to tell about his remarkable discovery, something inconceivable in New Brunswick: "I was in a field today; they were planting potatoes and right across the road in another field they were harvesting potatoes."

The Daylesford plant had no potato storage facilities, but that wasn't a problem, Wallace thought, because in the temperate Australian climate potatoes could be kept in the ground until needed. It was only after he bought the plant for McCain Foods that he discovered how wrong he was.

It doesn't freeze during the Australian winter, in June, July, and August, but it rains a lot. When there are a few dry days, the farmer harvests his potatoes but by then they have too much sugar and are too low in solids to make good french fries. "We didn't understand it," Wallace says now. "We just didn't understand the agronomy."

The lack of storage at the Daylesford plant wasn't the only thing that went wrong in Australia. In the early years, not much went right. McCain was shipping product from New Brunswick, and sometimes the cardboard boxes of french fries – often called chips in Australia, as in Britain – were crushed during the voyage. The first Australian manager Wallace hired got into a dispute with the Australian government over payment of import duties. He also put his in-laws on the McCain payroll.

FACING PAGE: View of New Zealand's Heretaunga Plains, looking north toward Napier, Hawke's Bay. Gum trees, seen here in the foreground, are common in New Zealand.

The Daylesford factory, 1974.

Meanwhile, McCain was trying to carve out a place for itself in a market dominated by a well-known local company, Edgell.

McCain decided to replace the Daylesford plant with a new one in nearby Ballarat, in the heart of the Central Highlands potato farming district. The construction company hired to build it went broke in the middle of the project. Relations with the Australian labour unions were often hostile. So were relations with the farmers who claimed McCain wasn't paying enough for their potatoes. The environmental authorities threatened to close down the new plant. McDonald's decided the quality of the product coming out of the new Ballarat factory was so poor, because of inferior raw material, that it dropped McCain as a supplier, leaving it with a new plant and no business from any quick-service chain.

All of that was thirty years ago. Today Australians buy the most McCain products per capita of any market in which the company operates. McCain is the leader in frozen dinners in Australia, the only country where it is strong in that category. It also has good businesses in frozen vegetables and pizza, as well as french fries and a full array of other potato products. McCain has seven factories in Australia and New Zealand and employs sixteen hundred people in the two countries. Mention McCain to someone in Australia and chances are they will reply, "Ah, McCain, you've done it again," the catchy slogan that ends every TV commercial. "I would say 90 percent of the population in Australia know the McCain brand," estimates John Clements, the man Wallace McCain hired in 1975 to fix his Australian problems.

To those who remember the early difficulties, McCain's success in Australia is still a source of amazement. Ian Cameron, a Canadian sent by McCain to Australia shortly after the business was launched there, thinks only a privately held firm with a long-term perspective could have overcome the many early setbacks. "If it had been a public company, you'd have closed her," he says. "You had to have deep pockets to stay in and a lot of balls. It would have been easier to walk away. Australia wasn't the most sophisticated country. You had to wonder whether there was any future in it."

Certainly, it was reasonable at the time to ask why a New Brunswick–based food processor would want to start a business on the other side of the world in a country with barely half as many people as Canada.

For Wallace, who as of the mid-1970s had primary responsibility for Australia, the answer was obvious. Australia is a wealthy, potato-eating nation and one whose official language is the same as Canada's – an added advantage. Also, the quick-service chains were growing in Australia, so the market for frozen french fries would grow with them. It never occurred to him that McCain Foods, despite its early problems, would not become a major player in the food business down under.

Wallace McCain inspects an Australian potato field, 1974.

As it had been in Canada in 1956, McCain Foods was in the right place at the right time in Australia in 1968. The social trend that favoured convenience food in North America – the movement of women into the workforce – was also happening in Australia, but it had started later. So by coming to Australia in the late 1960s, McCain's timing was perfect.

McCain started by bringing in product from Florenceville in refrigerated vessels. Boxes weighing fourteen kilograms were stacked two metres high in bulk holds. If the refrigeration during the ocean trip was cold enough to keep the contents frozen, the shipment usually arrived in decent condition. But, in the beginning, the cardboard containers McCain was using weren't strong enough and sometimes arrived badly squashed.

The quality after the long voyage was poor. Fortunately for McCain, the quality of the products offered by the local competition wasn't any better. But importing was not a long-term solution. Australia was too far from the potato fields of New Brunswick, currencies were subject to unpredictable fluctuations, and the Australian government charged duties on imports.

However, the Daylesford plant turned out to be more of a problem than a solution. "If you thought the one we built in Florenceville was bad, this was a hundred times worse," says Wallace. From the outside, the plant looked like a small barn with a house attached. It produced about 2,225 kilograms of french fries an hour, compared with the 32,000 kilograms the largest modern plants produce today.

None of the effluent created in the manufacturing process was treated – wastewater went straight into the sewer system. The resulting pollution wiped out a local trout hatchery and killed a popular trout stream. (Both have since been restored.)

One manager thought he had a solution to the peel waste problem: he would feed it to his cattle. The waste contained a caustic chemical then used in the peeling process but the cattle seemed to enjoy it and ate all that was offered to them. This experiment ended when the cattle got sick.

The best that could be said about the Daylesford factory was that it was colourful. "At night, you could see stars through the roof any time you looked up," recalls Cameron, who was transferred to Australia from New Brunswick in 1975. With such a roof, it is no surprise that the plant flooded whenever it rained. On one occasion a maintenance employee went up on the roof, which was made of corrugated asbestos, to make a repair. He fell through and landed, unhurt, on the factory floor, having missed the boiling-hot fryer by just a few feet.

"We had possums," recalls Cameron. "We stored cartons there, and you'd be pulling possums out of the cardboard packaging."

The plant manager was a Canadian, Keith Thompson. Sometimes he chatted with the young man who was the vacation fill-in for the regular postman who brought the mail to Thompson's house. His name was Milton Rodda, a twenty-seven-year-old Daylesford native who earned

Milton Rodda and technical services manager Dan Dawkins, 2007.

most of his living by hunting, fishing, and doing seasonal jobs such as logging and harvesting potatoes and fruit. He had chosen this life after quitting a job as a bank teller because he wanted more freedom.

"In 1974, Keith offered me work at McCain should I ever want it, but nothing was farther from my mind," Rodda says. "At the time I was working in the forest driving a Timber Jack retrieving hardwood logs for transport to a local sawmill. My boss and good mate was killed while delivering one of these loads. And since I was suddenly without work, I contacted Keith and agreed to a one-week trial at the Daylesford plant as a labourer unloading potatoes."

That was the start of a thirty-year career with McCain Australia during which Rodda became a field manager whose expertise in potato agronomy played an important role in improving the raw materials that came out of the Australian potato fields and into McCain factories.

In a modern processing plant, truckloads of potatoes from the field are delivered directly into huge storage bins. In those days, they arrived in seventy-kilogram bags and were tipped into half-ton wooden storage crates. Rodda's job that first week was to unload the potatoes and then transfer them to the start of the production line.

"Keith and I had a discussion at the end of the first week, and I agreed to stay a little longer. Keith asked me what I thought a fair wage would be," says Rodda. "I saw a chance to end my period of poverty and suggested an amount quite a bit higher than what I had been used to as a farm labourer. Keith agreed and I was pleased with myself. Shortly after, I discovered I was getting less than the women on the production line. Another discussion with Keith solved this problem."

Because Daylesford couldn't supply all the product the market demanded, McCain continued to ship french fries from Canada. The Daylesford employees had to unload the shipments onto pallets to be placed in the cold storage unit. Unfortunately, shipboard refrigeration wasn't always reliable and the Canadian fries sometimes rotted en route.

A potato crop at D&Y Pike's farm in Gippsland, New South Wales, Australia.

"You have not lived until you've stood in front of a container of potatoes turned into five feet of slurry after a few weeks' decay at sea," observes Rodda. "And then there was the job of following the load to the local tip and scraping the lot out. We earned our pay those days."

Another of Rodda's jobs was keeping the fryer supplied with cooking fat. In a twenty-first-century french fry plant, liquid oil is pumped in at the press of a button. At Daylesford, the fat was in the form of twenty-kilogram blocks of tallow, stored in cardboard boxes. "My job was to climb onto a pallet, held by a forklift, full of these boxes. The forklift raised me above the fryer and, while taking care not to fall in, I had to unpack the blocks of tallow and slide them into the fryer while avoiding the boiling oil that splashed with each block I released." To reduce the risk, this practice was changed so that a heated rod liquefied the blocks of fat. The liquid then poured into the fryer.

Despite the plant's many defects, employees made every effort to ensure that all the food shipped from it was good. "We fried everything in boiling oil and later froze everything and to my knowledge never killed a soul," says Rodda.

Labour relations at the plant, however, were poor. Workers sometimes showed their displeasure by spraying water into the cold storage area, ruining the packages of french fries stored there. Clearly, if McCain was going to stay in Australia, it needed a better facility. The company decided to build a new factory in Ballarat, a city with a population then of about seventy thousand.

The workers were angry about losing their jobs in Daylesford, especially those whose entire family was employed at the plant, and labour relations continued to

John Clements, 1976.

deteriorate. The problems became so acute that McCain closed Daylesford early in 1975, well before the Ballarat plant was completed. The company had to rely entirely on product imported from New Brunswick until the new factory was ready. (Daylesford was reopened temporarily a few years later as a pizza plant.)

Jim Evans, an engineer, came from Canada to be project manager, working with the construction company to get Ballarat built. When the construction company went bankrupt halfway through the project, Evans took on the role of general contractor. His toughest problem was dealing with the unions. It was a period of high inflation and the unions demanded that quoted prices be adjusted in line with inflation. "It was called 'rise and fall,' says Evans, "except Wallace used to say it was always rise, never fall. If you made a deal with the bricklayers union and the plumbers got a raise, then the bricklayers had to get the same raise. It meant you could never know how much a job would cost.

"Once a building was up to two storeys, everyone got an extra twenty-five cents an hour bonus for working at a higher level even if they never left the first floor. When the site got dusty, everyone got an extra fifty cents an hour. It wasn't that the labour costs were a lot higher than in Canada, but they were less predictable."

The labourers themselves were unpredictable. Tim Bliss, who went to Australia to help oversee the construction and opening of the Ballarat plant, recalls that on Friday nights the mechanical and electrical construction crews went back home to Melbourne for the weekend, promising to return first thing Monday morning. "Monday would come and they wouldn't show up," recalls Bliss. "We spent all Monday and Tuesday calling them. The last ones would roll in sometime Wednesday."

Production at the factory was supposed to start in January 1975 but didn't until August. The final cost was twice as much as had been budgeted. And even after the plant went into production, the labour troubles continued. The McCain workers were part of a national union, so if there was a problem with an employer in another part of the country, they sometimes stopped work in solidarity. Cameron recalls arriving at the plant in the morning to find the workers outside on the street.

"What's going on?" he asked.

"We're on strike."

"Why?"

"We don't know. We were just told to come out."

John Clements took over management of the Australian operation in 1976, not long after the start of production at Ballarat. He had spent his whole career in the food industry and had previously worked for Cerebos Foods, a British company.

Before even seeing the Ballarat factory, Clements spent three months at Florenceville learning about McCain and the frozen food industry. He returned to Australia to find nothing but trouble. The labour problems – the union was staging intermittent strikes because wages were below world standards – were just one of many headaches.

The product was selling poorly, partly because of its poor quality and partly because the sales force hadn't learned McCain's end-user technique for selling to the food service industry. The company had huge stocks of french fries piled up around the country, some of it unsaleable.

The Ballarat factory, 1976.

"The potato growers were up in arms because their contract price had dropped," says Clements. "The second day I was on the job in Ballarat they marched on the factory in a group, demanding to speak to me about better prices or they would refuse to contract with us. That was the only time I have seen potato growers angry enough that they would march in a group.

"As well, we had huge environmental problems because our plant was causing bad odours over the city of Ballarat, and the Environmental Protection Agency for the state of Victoria was threatening to close us down if we didn't remedy the situation. After I had been in Ballarat about a week, I thought, 'What have I gotten myself into?'"

As engineer Neil Murdoch recalls it, there was no waste treatment at the time but, rather, waste handling. It was, he says, a matter of "What the hell do we do with this crap?"

Caustic peel waste was being dumped into lagoons on twenty hectares of land McCain had purchased about thirty kilometres from the Ballarat factory. The site was about six kilometres from the nearest town, though there were a few farmhouses nearby. "The waste treatment started quite naturally with these lagoons bubbling merrily and, of course, making quite a stink, which the neighbours didn't appreciate," Murdoch says. When there was more waste than the lagoons could handle, a student was hired to spread it on the Ballarat property.

This situation threatened the future of the plant and was demoralizing for the employees, says Clements. "We were probably the most disliked company in Ballarat."

Dennis Jesson (centre), production director in Britain, on a 1975 visit to Australia. Ian Cameron (left) was Australian plant manager and Keith Thompson (right) was manufacturing director.

Some of the employees were afraid to say where they worked because of the company's poor public image.

The problem came to a head in 1978 when the state Environmental Protection Agency gave McCain three weeks to stop dumping the peels into the lagoon or the plant would be shut down. This was an impossible demand, as a new treatment facility could not be completed in three weeks. Fortunately for the company, local politicians were on its side: they could see that McCain was going to play an important role in job creation. With their help, Clements got through to Sir Rupert Hamer, the premier of the state of Victoria. Clements promised that, given eighteen months, McCain would build a proper waste treatment plant. The premier agreed.

The treatment plant was built on schedule and performed as promised. Now the Ballarat plant's waste is fermented, producing methane, which is recycled to provide some of the energy that runs the plant's boilers.

None of McCain's problems in Australia was insurmountable. Clements tackled the problem of poor sales by dividing the sales force into separate retail and food service teams. This was done because the two markets presented different problems. This move, in tandem with proper implementation of the end-user sales technique, led to rising sales in Australia from the late 1970s and into the 1990s. For most of that period, Allen Pellat headed the food service sales force, while Mike Dawson led the retail team. "They and their sales forces deserve much of the credit for our sales success," says Clements.

As of 2007, labour relations were much improved, not just at McCain but for all unionized Australian companies, thanks to new legislation introduced in the late 1980s. "Despite what happened, the reality of today is that we enjoy excellent relationships and loyalty from our staff in Australia and New Zealand," says human resources director Derek Duncan. Many McCain employees have stayed with the company for more than twenty years. Contract negotiations can be tough, but once they are settled, the employee relations are smooth. "Our local communities view McCain as a great place to work," Duncan says.

LEFT: Ballarat trim tables, 2007.

RIGHT: Quinton Wilkinson, R&D manager; Dave Nichols, McCain Competitive Edge manager, prepared foods plant; and Gavin Lett, plant manager, french fry plant, 2006.

Milton Rodda, as field manager, was given the job of forging better relations with the growers. "For a farm kid at this time to take a job at McCain was like defecting to the enemy," says Rodda, "and looking back now, I feel that, for me, this was part of the attraction."

The farmers resented McCain because it was a foreign company offering contracts that paid them just slightly more than it cost to produce the potatoes. "In those days, potato growing was like betting on a horse," Rodda explains. "One grew potatoes in the hope that supplies for the fresh market would be limited at the time you were selling, thereby ensuring a good price. Often this was not the case, but occasionally small fortunes were made.

"Contracts were seen more as a safety net for farmers to fall back on should free market prices be lower than the contracted price. That is, you honoured the contract if free market prices were low and did all in your power to avoid delivering if market prices were higher. It was against this background that I became field manager, and a great part of my job early on was to change this culture. After a few court cases, the growers began to understand that contracts were for real and also that this new field manager – a traitor from their own ranks – was awake to their tricks.

"Things rapidly improved from then on, to the point where a McCain contract is now a valuable document. Irrigation brought about huge changes. Yields improved massively, making contract growing a better option while at the same time taking a lot of the boom and bust from the industry. Irrigation also allowed new regions to produce potatoes for the first time, thereby reducing the demand for Ballarat potatoes for the fresh market. Local growers began to understand that their futures were increasingly becoming tied to growing for processing, making my job a lot easier."

However, it got harder again in the mid-1980s when Wallace McCain made one of his regular visits to Australia and announced that he wanted Australia's potato growers to supply McCain with Russet Burbank potatoes, the variety favoured by the fast food chains, instead of the Kennebec and Sebago varieties the Australian growers were producing.

"This was a thunderbolt out of the blue to me," says Rodda. "We had previously imported some Russets and done token trials with them without any knowledge of the correct agronomy. The result was a total failure – and a strong belief that with Australian conditions, the variety would never succeed."

As it turned out, the Australian farmers converted to Russet Burbanks successfully over a few years. Rodda collected all the information he could on how to grow them, and Australian growers visited U.S. potato farms. In the mid-1990s, an American expert spent two seasons in Australia training Rodda's field crew and growers in the art of raising Russet Burbank potatoes.

Australia, in particular Tasmania, now produces one of the best Russet Burbank crops in the world, supplying most of McCain's needs in Australia. For an early season potato, the Australians use the Canadian Shepody variety. Because of the threat of water shortages in the region, McCain is gradually converting to varieties that are less susceptible to heat and water stress.

TOP: McCain bought a vegetable factory in Smithton, Tasmania, in 1984.
BOTTOM: Basil Hargrove, 1978.

Although Australia was under Wallace's supervision, Harrison made the occasional visit there, just as Wallace visited Harrison's European domain from time to time. During the 1980s, Harrison and Basil Hargrove, a native of New Brunswick who had gone to Australia in 1979 as finance director of the Australian company, met with potato growers. The farmers were complaining about how tough it was for them to make a living because the price they were getting for their potatoes was too low. McCain, a big, prosperous company, should recognize that, they said, and offer more generous contracts.

Harrison replied, "Do you know how many french fry processors there have been in the business worldwide?"

"Maybe ten or twenty," said the farmers.

"No," said Harrison. "There have been ninety-five."

Hargrove told Harrison later that the number sounded high to him.

"I'll send you a list," said Harrison, which he did. Ninety-five companies, all but a handful no longer in existence, were on the list.

Harrison's point was that it's a tough business, and if a company can't keep a tight lid on its costs, it won't survive. As the potato-processing business consolidated, high-cost producers were being absorbed by more efficient ones. McCain was a consolidator. One of the reasons it was able to expand so successfully, in Australia as elsewhere, was because it bought up competitors and integrated them into the McCain empire. This isn't an easy task. It's hard work, first to analyze the prospective purchase and decide whether it is worth buying, and then to negotiate a price that is fair to both buyer and seller.

McCain's first purchase in Australia was a potato-flake plant in Ballarat, which it bought from Unilever. Subsequently, McCain supplied Unilever with potato flakes from its own Ballarat plant, where they could be produced more cheaply as a by-product of french fries. It then converted the former Unilever facility into a pizza factory.

Premier Robin Gray turns the first sod for the McCain chip-processing plant in Tasmania, 1987. Looking on are local official Ken O'Halloran (far left) and McCain managing director John Clements.

Wallace McCain always enjoyed the hunt for new acquisitions. In 1984, he was involved in the purchase of a frozen vegetable plant in the southernmost part of the country, the island state of Tasmania. Clements and Hargrove had done the preliminary due diligence, deciding what the business was worth and what McCain could afford to pay. Now it was up to Wallace to close the deal. The problem was that Wallace had set a maximum price he was prepared to pay, and the owner, McCain's major Australian competitor, Edgell, wouldn't budge from its own higher price.

On the last day of Wallace's stay in Australia, he met again with Edgell's negotiator. It was a Friday afternoon, and Wallace's return flight to Canada was that evening. John and Wallace's son Scott, who had accompanied his father to Australia, were with him at the meeting, which was spent bickering over the price, neither side prepared to make the compromise necessary to close the deal.

Wallace recalls: "He wasn't giving in. He was a stubborn bastard like me. I said,

Plant manager Bill Goodridge and project manager Paul Andrew assess the sweet corn waiting to be processed at the Hastings factory in New Zealand.

'John, I have to get to the airport. We're leaving here in twenty minutes. Get the car; I'll meet you at the door.'"

Clements and Scott left the room, leaving Wallace and the Australian alone. "I wanted that business so bad, I was licking my chops," Wallace says. Finally, still without an agreement, he got up to leave. The Australian followed him to the corridor. Wallace pushed the elevator's down button. The elevator arrived and the door opened. Just as Wallace was about to step in, the Australian said, "It's a deal."

Ten minutes later, Wallace emerged into the parking lot, looking glum. His son turned to him and asked, "How did you make out?"

Wallace's face lit up. "We own it."

"I was there only as a bystander trying to learn from my father," says Scott McCain. "It was a great learning experience."

In 1987, McCain bought a frozen dinner business, R.M. Gow's Chalet Foods. In 1990, it expanded into New Zealand by buying a frozen vegetable business from Alpine Foods, in Timaru, on the South Island. In 1992, it bought Safries, a potato-processing business in Penola, in southeastern Australia. In 1996, it bought Griff's dinner line from Comgroup Supplies and, in 1997, another frozen vegetable business in New Zealand, Growers Foods, in Hastings. And, in 2003, it bought a frozen potato and vegetable plant from Heinz-Wattie's Ltd. in Fielding, New Zealand.

In Australia, as elsewhere, McCain turns down more deals than it accepts. An important key to the company's success has been its ability to stay focused on the businesses it understands. "You have to know what not to buy as well as what to buy," says Basil Hargrove, who in 1995 followed Clements as head of Australian operations, later becoming CEO for the Asia Pacific region and a member of Opco, McCain Foods Limited's board of directors.

While it was buying up other companies, McCain did not neglect its existing facilities. It continued to invest in upgrading them, with the objective of building McCain into a dominant player. This strategy has succeeded. Nowhere, not even in its Canadian homebase, does McCain have a more balanced market position than in Australia. This unusual balance is the result of the Australian company's strength in four separate categories: frozen potato products including fries, other frozen vegetables, pizza, and dinners.

In Britain, McCain dropped frozen dinners because it was too far behind other brands; it does not like to be a minor brand in any category. In Australia, the timing was better. When McCain acquired the frozen dinner business of R.M. Gow in 1987, the market for that category was in its early stages but on the verge of major growth. The acquisition immediately gave McCain a 20 percent market share.

Clements says much of the credit for McCain's success in the dinner category belongs to marketing director David Boyle and to Quinton Wilkinson, the research and development manager. Steve Yung also played an important role.

Aerial view of potato fields on a Tasmanian farm.

Yung was born in Vancouver and raised in Australia. During his twenty-year career with McCain, he has spent thirteen years in Australia, one in New Zealand, and six in Canada. His year in New Zealand was sandwiched between two assignments in Florenceville. "I think I'm the only one in the company who has ever been transferred to Florenceville twice," he says.

In 1987, Yung came to McCain from R.M. Gow as product manager for frozen dinners. Although he wasn't keen on moving from Queensland to the State of Victoria, he was lured by the opportunity to manage a brand that he knew the company planned to invest in – for example, through TV commercials. He also was attracted by the Ballarat plant's proximity to Melbourne, just 112 kilometres away. "It was a chance to be noticed by the Melbourne marketing community," he says. "I thought I might last two years and then move to Melbourne. Twenty years later and I'm still here."

As of 2007, Yung was managing director and CEO for Australia and New Zealand. He thinks McCain Australia has done well in frozen dinners because it "just plunged in," undaunted by the notorious difficulty of the category. Dinners are more difficult to manage than french fries, vegetables, or pizza, since each package is made up of several items. Consumers want variety, so the producer needs to offer a range of items, or what the trade calls SKUS (stock keeping units). "Every year we launched twenty to thirty SKUS," says Yung. "Sometimes we would get a little frustrated by how hard it was, but I think we've come to realize our frustration was misplaced. It was hard because the business was hard."

When McCain first entered the frozen dinner business in Australia, it was the

McCain Alfresco pesto tortellini; dinners on the Ballarat production line; Griff's curried prawns.

smallest of its retail categories. Now it's the largest, and the company works hard to maintain the category's strength. It employs a chef to create recipes. Then it's up to the food technologists to determine whether it can be profitably mass produced. Before a new dinner, or any other product, is sent to the stores, sensory testing is done by volunteer community members.

The lineup of dinners changes constantly as new ones are launched and older ones withdrawn. To cater to Australia's sizeable Asian population, there are several Asian-flavoured dinners, as well as a line of stir-fry vegetables. Hargrove points out that the advent of the microwave oven has been a big boost to McCain's continued success in both the dinner and pizza categories, and the quality of both has steadily improved.

Pizza has been a McCain strength in Australia from the beginning. Its first success in the retail market was a product called pizza subs – a french bread stick with a pizza topping. The popularity of this product also helped McCain boost sales of its french fries to supermarkets. By the late 1980s, however, sales of pizza subs had declined and the product was dropped. McCain relaunched it in 2006 to great success.

Another big success for McCain in Australia is Potato Cakes, the credit for which belongs to Boyle and Wilkinson. Boyle, who had worked with John Clements at Cerebos before joining McCain in 1984, was amazed to discover on his arrival that the marketing department consisted of one secretary, while research and development consisted of Wilkinson.

Soon after starting his new job, Boyle travelled to Florenceville, where he met Wallace McCain. He presented Wilkinson's proposal for potato cakes. A popular snack food available in every fish-and-chip shop in Australia, a potato cake is a thinly sliced piece of potato covered in tempura batter. Wilkinson's idea was to make a frozen version for the food service market with the potato bits left over from the french fry production.

"You can't be serious that people would actually want to eat this," said Wallace. "But it's your market and you know best. Good luck."

Potato Cakes quickly became McCain Australia's bestselling specialty item. They still are.

Many Australians and New Zealanders are worried about obesity and other health issues, yet the reaction against fast food has not been as widespread or intense as in the United Kingdom or the rest of Europe. Yung believes McCain pre-empted the issue by offering products that appealed to health-conscious consumers before the obesity issue came to public prominence. In the early 1990s, the company launched McCain Healthy Choice, a range of low-fat, low-cholesterol, low-calorie meals. The Healthy Choice brand has since been extended to include french fries and pizza.

In addition, McCain Australia is the retail market leader in vegetables other than potatoes. As mother always said, vegetables are good for you. "That creates a halo effect for McCain," says Yung. In other words, the company's prominence in vegetables casts all its products in a healthy light. "When I joined twenty years ago, the consumer would have thought of McCain as fast food. McCain stood for french fries and pizza. Today consumers think of McCain as an all around trusted healthy brand. So there is quite a different image of our brand, one that has been built up over the years."

The health issue is one that McCain can control to an extent by ensuring that it continues to offer wholesome products and communicates the nutritional qualities of those products to consumers. What the company cannot control is the weather. In late 2006, Australia, the driest of the world's continents, suffered the worst drought in its history. The flows of water into the major rivers that sustain the country's agriculture were at record lows, grain harvests were down sharply, and some cattle ranchers were selling their livestock because they couldn't afford feed.

Potato growers were happy to see the rains at the beginning of 2007

Basil Hargrove, CEO, Asia Pacific, 2006.

put an end to what the Australians called "the big dry." Meanwhile, McCain's agronomists were developing programs to encourage growers to adopt potato varieties less susceptible to growing disorders and early maturing caused by dry spells. The McCain agronomists were also pushing for enhanced irrigation systems. McCain employees were reminded of the drought every time they passed Lake Wendouree, site of the rowing competition in the 1956 Melbourne Olympics. The lake, in Ballarat's most prestigious residential area, was bone dry.

"The Central Highlands of Australia [where Ballarat is located] are a very good potato growing area, but these extreme drought conditions are of great concern to us," says Dan Dawkins, a New Brunswick native who, after working for McCain in Canada and Europe, became technical services manager for McCain Australia. "Water is becoming scarce, and we will have to adapt." Luckily for McCain, the water shortage is less severe in Tasmania and, as of 2007, still nonexistent in New Zealand.

The growth of quick-service chains in Australia was about ten years behind that of North America. These outlets did not start to proliferate until the late 1970s, just as the Ballarat plant had overcome its teething problems and was producing high-quality french fries. McCain had no quick-service business in the late 1970s. By 1992, it was a major supplier to almost all Australian quick-service restaurants.

Long before the U.S.–based chains came along, Australia had an abundance of individually owned takeaway restaurants and fish-and-chip shops. They don't do as much business as a McDonald's, which sells at least ten times as many chips as a fish-and-chip shop, but there are so many of them that it was worth McCain's while to try to get their business. It has succeeded.

McCain is the market leader in the Australian food service industry. It's the result, says Yung, of simple perseverance – a large sales force making thousands of cold calls on thousands of restaurants. "It's good old-fashioned hard selling, and we've kept at it," he says.

McCain's expertise in french fry technology has been a major reason for its success in Australia's diverse food service industry. In the field of french fries, one size definitely does not fit all. "There are a lot of different cuts," explains Clements. "The fast food chains all have their own specifications. McDonald's in particular is very strict about its specifications being met. But apart from the specifications of the fast food chains, there are all sorts of things you can do with french fries."

To try to appeal to as many of Australia's ten thousand takeaway and fish-and-chip shops as possible, McCain offers fries in several thicknesses, from shoestring to chunky. The shoestring chip is the crispest since its outer surface – the part that crisps – is a high percentage of the total chip. A thick chip is not as crisp since the outer surface is only a small percentage of the total chip. The thick chip, however, has a stronger potato flavour because the frying oil doesn't impregnate all of the potato, as it does with a thin chip.

Lake Wendouree suffering from "the big dry."

Another difference is the cut: crinkle or straight. "In the early days," recalls Clements, "crinkle cut was all the rage because it was different. It was something you could get with a frozen chip that you couldn't get at home. Now crinkle cuts are looked at as old-fashioned and the majority of McCain's fries are straight cut."

The off-cuts – what's left over after the fries have been cut – are also put to good use. They are mashed up, shaped, and fried into various specialty products with such names as Potato Gems, Potato Cakes, and Potato Tops, for the retail market.

New Zealand is one of the world's most beautiful countries, but Steve Yung didn't get much chance to enjoy the scenery after being assigned there by McCain Foods in 1994. He had been working in Florenceville as group product manager when he was appointed marketing manager for New Zealand.

"Our furniture had barely arrived in New Zealand when I was made vice-president of marketing for Canada back in Florenceville," Yung recalls. "In fact, our house in New Brunswick never sold, and we just put our paintings back in the same places they had been. For a time in 1994 and 1995, we lived for about thirty weeks without our household items because of moving from Canada to New Zealand and then back again. Once we were back in Canada, we had to borrow camping cots and kitchen utensils."

McCain's Timaru plant, on New Zealand's South Island.

As of 2007, Yung was managing McCain's New Zealand business as part of his job as CEO for Australia and New Zealand. "We don't call New Zealand the seventh state, as that is offensive to New Zealanders and arrogant on the part of Australians," he says. Instead, Yung borrows from the government of China: "When it took Hong Kong back, it referred to 'two countries, one system.' So here we say, 'two countries, one company.'"

The two countries are effectively run as one marketplace out of the Ballarat headquarters. Other than plant managers, the only executive based in New Zealand is the sales manager for that country. When McCain first entered the New Zealand market in the 1980s, it ran it as part of the Australia operation, but the two markets were given separate management in 1997. They were converted back to one in 2005. McCain's major customers, such as McDonald's and Woolworths, the supermarket chain that is the largest retailer in Australia, operate in the same way.

"The consumers are not different enough to not treat it as one business," Yung says. The main difference for McCain in the New Zealand retail market is that it is not the leader, as it is in Australia, but second behind Heinz-Wattie's. Wattie's, now owned by the U.S. multinational Heinz, is a well-established New Zealand brand that launched its business there much earlier than did McCain.

Obviously, a company owned by Heinz is not going to be a pushover. Neither are McCain's major competitors in Australia. Simplot, another major U.S. food company, now owns Edgell, McCain's chief competitor in french fries and vegetables. In dinners, the main competition comes from Nestlé with its brands Maggi, Findus, and Lean Cuisine. Nestlé is also a major competitor in the pizza category with its Papa Guiseppe brand. McCain is the market leader in both food service and retail in Australia and a strong second in New Zealand, but there is no room for complacency: all of its major competitors have deep pockets.

John Clements spent seventeen years with McCain, running the Australian operation and later, for a couple of years, serving as a member of the McCain Foods Limited board of directors (Opco). He has been able to observe the company's growth and success, both from a distance and close-up.

"The secret of the success in Australia and worldwide," he says, "was the way Wallace and Harrison did business. They were very good delegators, and so we had an enormous amount of autonomy in Australia. They were rushing around the world opening factories in different countries and starting new companies, and they didn't have large amounts of time to devote to Australia.

"Also, they were always more keen on expansion than on milking the company for profits in the short term. There was tremendous willingness on the part of the two McCain brothers to spend capital and allocate resources to any new project that looked promising. That suited me too because there were lots of opportunities in the frozen food business in Australia.

"For example, although we started off purely in fries, within a short time we built a pizza plant, a specialty plant, then, by acquisition, we got a full range of frozen vegetables. Then we went into frozen dinners, where we are the market leader. Then we went into New Zealand and bought companies there and built a french fry plant."

TOP: Community involvement: McCain employee Stan Brett is chief of the volunteer Hellyer, Tasmania, fire brigade.
BOTTOM: John Clements, 1990.

McCain's success in Australia is a good example of the utility of the company's "drink the local wine" philosophy, which allows it to adapt effectively to each market it enters. In Britain, consumption of french fries is greater and, consequently, McCain was able to build a strong consumer presence with that product alone, dropping other product lines where competitors were strong. Such a strategy would not have been possible in Australia where, as a result of immigration patterns, rice and pasta have greater importance in the national diet. To build a successful retail business in Australia required more diversification. McCain had no choice: it had to build strong positions in vegetables, pizza, and dinners to stay profitable.

In 1976, Clements's first year, McCain lost money in Australia. In his second year, the company turned a small profit and has been profitable ever since. During the early years, all of the profits went back into the company to pay for advertising and marketing.

Pea harvesting, 1979.

As has been the case wherever McCain has expanded, the Australian branch benefited from the expertise of McCain employees who came from other countries. In some cases, these were experienced executives bringing their knowledge and experience with them. In others, younger employees were sent to Australia to gain experience and be groomed for important jobs elsewhere. Ian Cameron, Bill Mabee, Sherry Brown, Bill Mackay, Allison McCain, Rod MacDonald, Bruce Phillips, and Dan Dawkins all came from Canada, while Paul Turner arrived from Maine and Frank van Gils came from the United Kingdom.

Other key players in building McCain Australia included Robin Cuy and Gerard Richmond in finance, Owen Porteus in manufacturing, Tony Ford in agronomy, and Ernie Jones, who for many years headed the purchasing and procurement department.

A facet of the McCain management style, much appreciated by Clements and other regional directors, was that the company's leaders were present when they were needed and absent when they weren't. "Although they gave a great deal of autonomy," continues Clements, "if there were problems – of which there were quite a few – they were only too happy to discuss them. You didn't have someone breathing down your neck all the time, but if you did have a problem, you always had a ready ear."

Long-time employees: (left to right) Peter Donovan,* Robin Cuy (seated),* John Orton, Margaret O'Brien,* Graeme (Bennie) Stewart,* Tony Ford, Ernie Jones,* Leigh-Anne Burgess,* Ian Dwyer, Steve Yung. *Asterisks indicate McCain employees with thirty years or more of service. The others have at least twenty years of service.*

Harrison and Wallace always asked their senior executives to be open about their problems. If a serious problem arose in Australia, they wanted to hear about it from the managing director for Australia, not from somebody else. Knowing that they would be kept informed, the two heads of the company felt confident delegating authority.

The McCain management style resulted in an unusually enjoyable work environment. "In most large companies there is a lot of politics going on," observes Clements. "I know because I worked in two such companies before I went to McCain. People jockeyed for positions. In McCain, it was virtually non-existent."

Milton Rodda, because of his thirty years of service, is in a good position to assess the reasons for McCain's success. "Pig-headed determination and never accepting no as an answer went a long way in the early days," he argues. "Luck backed up by hard work also helped. By 'luck' I mean that the McCain boys got into the right business at the right time and pushed hard."

Its success in Australia gave McCain a major presence in the food industry on three continents. Meanwhile, there was plenty of action back home in Canada.

CHAPTER FIVE

THE HOME FRONT

San Francisco had its "Great Fire." So did Chicago. And so did McCain. On the last day of the 1980s, Sunday, December 31, 1989, much of the Florenceville factory was destroyed by a fire that raged all day in bitterly cold temperatures.

It started at 5:45 AM. Workers were building a new freezing tunnel when a spark from a cutting torch set fire to old insulation. Smoke engulfed the site and the fire was quickly out of control. Paul Dean, a food scientist and long-time McCain employee, rushed to the scene to help, as did the town's volunteer fire department, company employees, and other Florenceville residents.

"It was twenty-five or thirty below zero, and the wind was blowing," Dean recalls. "It was so cold that by the time the firefighters got the water out of the hydrant, a lot of the hoses had frozen." Eventually, firefighters were able to use a hook and ladder truck to place hoses above the roof of the plant. They punched holes in the roof and hosed water through them, dousing much of the fire.

Because of the efforts of firefighters from fifteen communities in New Brunswick and Maine, the blaze was extinguished before it could spread to the adjacent corporate offices. But two freezing tunnels, french fry and vegetable packaging areas, and three cold storage rooms were destroyed. Although the potato processing line wasn't affected, production had to stop until the rest of the plant could be rebuilt. But McCain's customers didn't notice, since extra shifts at nearby McCain plants in Grand Falls, New Brunswick, and Easton, Maine, took up the slack. The American authorities cooperated by letting Florenceville employees cross the border to work in Maine. Those who weren't needed in the other plants worked on the cleanup and the $25 million rebuilding project in Florenceville.

About four-and-a-half-million pounds of food with a retail value of $4 million

FACING PAGE: Planting time in Alberta, in the bottomland of the Oldman River valley.

ABOVE and **LEFT**: Fire at the Florenceville factory, December 31, 1989. **BELOW**: Firefighter with volunteer firefighter Jim Bushby (right), of McCain.

couldn't be sold because of smoke damage. But it was still good to eat, so ninety-three tractor trailer loads rolled out of Florenceville to deliver it to food banks in the Atlantic provinces, Quebec, and Ontario.

The significance of the great fire is in what it revealed about the company and how far it had come since it first opened for business on that very spot thirty-two years earlier. Such a fire in the early years would have been a calamity, perhaps closing McCain Foods down for good. In 1989, however, the partial destruction and closure of the company's flagship plant was a nuisance rather than a disaster. It was merely an unfortunate end to an excellent year.

In 1989, McCain achieved $2 billion in sales for the first time in its history. This was a remarkable achievement considering that the company had passed the $1 billion mark only four years previously. By reaching $2 billion in 1989, McCain surpassed the goals it had set for itself in 1985 of doubling sales in five years. Instead, it did it in only four by increasing sales of existing products, developing new ones, and acquiring other companies.

Wallace in the lab, surveying an assortment of McCain packaging.

In the 1980s, Japan was in its heyday as the world's new economic superpower, and much was written about the management style responsible for the country's success. What it all boiled down to was an obsession with quality. The Japanese knew that the way to achieve high quality in manufacturing was through a constant flow of small improvements in the manufacturing process. Over the long term, those small improvements added up to major improvements and higher profits.

McCain's management understood that from the beginning. As Wallace McCain said in 1989, "At the same time that competition is getting tougher, we are more than meeting the challenge by increasing productivity and improving quality on a continuing basis." Or, as Harrison liked to say, "If you are standing still, you are going backwards."

Only one direction was acceptable: forward. That meant expanding to new territories and building or buying new production facilities. And it meant constant striving for improvement in the methodology of growing potatoes and processing them.

Morris and Tim Bliss, vice-president of engineering, visited the various plants

The Manufacturing Directors Council ready to sail on the Zuiderzee – what is now the IJsselmeer lake – in the Netherlands.
Front row: (left to right) Pieter van Lipzig, Ken Wilmot, Henk Jongstra, Bruce Phillips, Hans den Daas, Rob Bakker.
Back row: Maarten Stam, Rod MacDonald, Jeff Twomey, Kees Oreel, Carl Morris, Lloyd Borowski, Dave Rogers, Oscar Orbetta, Jean François Cousin, Seth Gaunch, Dale McCarthy, Peter Burman, Meindert Jan Kramer.

and passed on information from one factory to another. If, for example, a European plant came up with an improved method of blanching raw potatoes, Morris and Bliss would ensure that all the other plants in the McCain network found out about it.

In the 1980s, Morris decided the company needed more direct communication among its factories, so he initiated manufacturing conferences that took place at least once every two years. These were meetings of all McCain plant managers from around the world, convening at a different location each time. Each manager was assigned a particular subject to prepare a paper and then speak on, such as peeling or frying. His role would be to research the topic and instruct all the others about the state of the art in that particular process. Each paper was discussed and critiqued, and each manager went home with a package of papers that, as a whole, constituted the most advanced practice to that date in potato processing.

The big advantage of this system is that there is usually one person with a particular strong suit. By having that person bring everyone else up to his standard, "the whole operation is then as good as our best man on that particular subject," Morris says. And if a plant manager later has a problem, he can look at the conference paper, but he can also pick up the phone and call the manager at the other plant who is especially strong in that area.

Although the manufacturing conferences worked well, McCain eventually had too many plant managers to include them all in one meeting. In 1997, the Manufacturing Directors Council was formed, grouping together the manufacturing director from each country as well as engineering and technical people. This council meets twice a year, usually at a plant where a new improvement has recently been made. The members of the council relay what they learn to the plant managers in their home countries.

Harrison McCain had two cardboard plaques he liked to give to his managers. One said, "There is nothing a man can't achieve if he does not care who gets the credit." The other said, "If you can't measure it, you can't manage it."

Harrison put the latter slogan into practice by asking Morris to investigate Total Quality Management (TQM), a system developed by Edwards Deming, an American management expert, to help Japanese manufacturers become efficient producers of high-quality products. Morris customized TQM for McCain and in 1989 launched the McCain Quality Performance (MQP) system as a data-driven set of standards and problem-solving methods. Measuring performance was an important aspect of MQP. It allowed McCain to introduce a system of internal benchmarking by which all units were expected to match the performance of the most effective ones.

A meeting on lift truck issues during a Kaizen event, Lelystad, 2007.

Morris hired Neil D'Souza as global MQP manager, to guide the MQP managers at each factory. For many years, the program was successful at finding ways to improve the manufacturing process through employee involvement.

In 2005, a new performance enhancement system, McCain Competitive Edge (MCE), replaced MQP. Based on a continuous improvement methodology known as Lean Six Sigma, MCE's mandate is to improve safety, quality, and productivity.

Lean and Six Sigma are complementary process-improvement techniques. Lean focuses on eliminating non-value-added activities and waste from processes, while Six Sigma's aim is to reduce variation and improve quality.

"Lean makes sure we are working on the right things, while Six Sigma makes sure we are doing the right things right," explains Morris.

An important facet of MCE is the kaizen event. In Japanese, "kaizen" means "change for the better." Once a month, in every facility, teams of about ten people meet for five days to review part of the operation. During these meetings, activities are reviewed and changes implemented that transform some part of the business.

This approach depends on the contributions of the individuals who know the most about the area under review – the operators and managers who do the job every day. "This results in tremendous ownership for the identified improvements and fosters a culture of continuously reviewing and improving all aspects of the operation," says Lloyd Borowski, global vice-president of engineering and manufacturing. "It's all about continuous improvement, involving everyone – managers and operators alike – to eliminate unnecessary activities and costs throughout the system, to improve safety and quality, and to give customers 100 percent satisfaction."

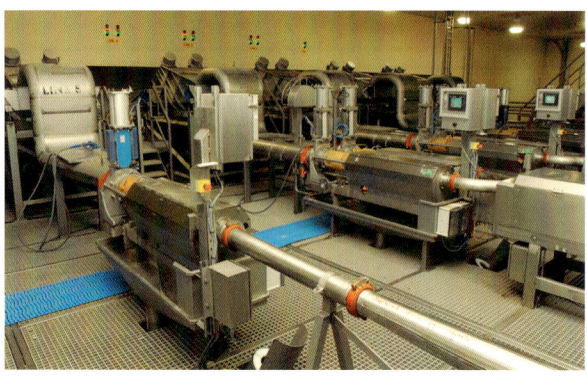

Cutter cannons.

In his 2006 webcast to McCain employees around the world, CEO Dale Morrison said that MCE will improve safety, quality, and productivity, first in individual plants and then across the entire organization. "It will make us a better company because it captures the imagination, energy, creativity, perspective, and ideas of our people."

As just one example of many, he pointed to the device developed by Ben Jenson, an employee at the Othello, Washington, plant that helps operators test the jaws on packaging equipment to make the packaging process more efficient. To honour its inventor, the machine is called a Ben-dicator.

Someone passing the parking lot of the Lamb Weston potato-processing plant in Weston, Oregon, in the late 1950s might have glimpsed an unusual sight: the owner of the plant, Gilbert Lamb, an engineer, shooting potatoes out of a fire hose. He was doing experiments that later developed into a device known as the Lamb Water Gun Knife, a major improvement over the simpler cutting devices that Lamb Weston, McCain, and other processors used when the industry was in its infancy.

The water gun knife uses high-pressure water flow to launch raw potatoes at a speed of eighty kilometres an hour through a set of steel blades that can be arranged to produce different sizes and shapes of french fries. McCain licensed the technology from its competitor, Lamb Weston, on the understanding that McCain would share any improvements it made in it.

The water gun, as originally designed, took strips out of the square centre of the potato for french fries and slabs out of the side, which were sent directly to the specialty product line. McCain wanted to increase the yield of fries from each potato. It did this by altering the gun to cut the entire potato into strips and then using the strips unsuitable for fries for the specialty products. The water gun knife handles more volume than other cutting devices. Most important, it increases yield by cutting a straight line through the longest axis of the potato, thereby getting the longest possible finished product out of it. In other words, the water gun knife makes the average potato more valuable.

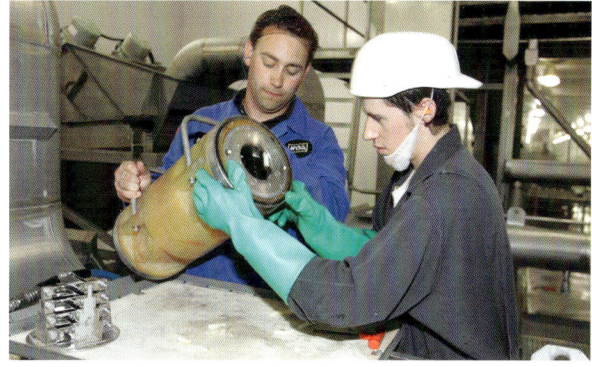

Customers expect the cones of french fries they buy in fast food restaurants to be full. "The longer the french fry, the less weight it takes to fill the container," explains Morris. If it is filled with shorter fries, four to five centimetres long, it will weigh as much or more than one filled with nine-centimetre-long fries, but it won't look as full. That's why long fries have become the norm in the quick-service restaurant industry. "Fast food is sold on the basis of appearance rather than weight, and that is the primary reason for trying to make the product longer," says Morris. Longer fries also have better "plate coverage" than shorter fries – important for sit-down restaurants.

Since the first factory began operating, in 1957, every piece of equipment in a McCain factory has evolved into something better. Automation is the reason for much of the improvement. In the early years, for example, all trimming of potato defects was done manually. During the 1970s, McCain invested in technology that uses cameras to detect the defects and automated knives to cut them out. A light is shined on the raw potato strips, which have been peeled, preheated, and cut but not yet blanched, while a bank of cameras measures the amount of reflected light. Because a defect absorbs light, the system detects when one of the strips needs attention, and a knife comes down and slices off the bad part.

In making french fries and other potato products, the raw potato is a major part of the cost. So the company has become focused on making the most of each potato that comes into its factories. In 1998, McCain launched Raw Material Utilization (RMU), a program designed by Carl Morris dedicated to that objective.

TOP: Knives are inserted into the knife box, which is similar to a cannon barrel: potatoes are fired through it.
BOTTOM: Potato strips emerge from a water cutter.

LEFT: The control room in the Matougues, France, factory.
RIGHT: State-of-the-art machinery optimizes raw material use.

Making the most of a potato means converting the highest possible amount of it into french fries. It also means that as much as possible of the rest gets converted into other saleable potato products. To give every plant a model to strive for, Morris and his team designed the perfect factory on paper. It was called Plant x. "We took in the very best of every facility we had and the very best of all the knowledge we had, and we designed this plant on paper that could give us certain recoveries and certain costs," Morris explains.

To implement the program, Morris formed a committee consisting of him, Neil D'Souza, David Rogers, and Lloyd Borowski. By comparing each existing plant with Plant x, the committee was able to come up with a capital budget to bring all of them up to state-of-the-art level. At the same time, each plant would be standardized in its processing procedures, so that all the plants around the world would receive, cut, process, and package potatoes in the same way.

Implementing RMU requires that every factory, old or new, has the latest technology and methodology. "It was basically the handling of that raw material to cut it in the most efficient way so that everything is used for finished product," says Morris. RMU didn't really include anything that wasn't already well known within the company – it was just a matter of putting it all together in one package and taking it to each factory. By giving each factory help in its areas of weakness, the average level of productivity was raised.

It's a matter of applying knowledge in a systematic and comprehensive way. "Through RMU, we upgraded the shortcomings in all our factories," says Morris. "Even though there were many changes during my time at McCain, that is probably our most rewarding operation."

How french fries are made

In the fifty years since McCain started making frozen french fries at Florenceville, the manufacturing process has been constantly improved, with the aim of producing the best french fry at the lowest cost with the greatest efficiency. In 2007, it takes one hour to transform a raw potato into frozen and packaged french fries.

1. McCain plants are located near potato farms. Here, fresh potatoes are unloaded into storage bins.

2. After stone removal, high-pressure steam loosens the skins. Automated brush peelers remove remaining skin.

3. Workers near the start of the line pick out bad potatoes and remove foreign matter.

4. Potatoes are shot by a water gun through knives that cut them into strips.

5. Automatic defect-removal machines rid the cut potatoes of any remaining imperfections.

6. Blanchers remove sugars that would cause the french fries to discolour.

7. After drying, the potato strips are put on the equilibration belt to balance the moisture within the potato strip.

8. After equilibriation, the potato strips are fried.

9. In the freezing tunnel, fries are kept for twenty minutes at a temperature of -39° Celsius.

10. The packaging machine weighs out batches of french fries and drops them into plastic bags.

11. The machine then folds, seals, and cuts the bags into packages for the food service market.

12. Machines pack the bags into cardboard boxes and then onto pallets, which are stored at -23° Celsius until shipped.

13. McCain fries being transferred from a cold storage room to a waiting delivery truck.

14. Wastewater from the french fry production process is treated behind the factory.

THE HOME FRONT

Just as McCain Foods had little expertise in food-processing technology when it started operations in 1957, so it possessed minimal expertise in agronomy. But it quickly became evident that the better the raw materials, the better the product, and the McCain brothers made it company policy to build up expertise in agronomy.

The potato is far more complex than it looks. The quality of the potato that arrives on the processing line depends on many factors, including good seed, climate, soil chemistry, pests and viruses, and the conditions in which it is stored before processing. McCain conducts agricultural research and development at its various operations. In Canada, research is carried out at the McCain Research Farm at Florenceville. McCain Foods has a global virtual breeding program for developing new potato varieties. Its specialists look at hundreds of potential new varieties each year from breeders around the world. They also do contract breeding with specialized institutes.

"If we were to start over again and travel the world to decide where we were going to start with a factory, I don't think Florenceville would be high on the list," says Ghislain Pelletier, vice-president of corporate agriculture. New Brunswick has a short growing season, which makes it difficult to grow Russet Burbanks, the potato of choice for french fries in North America. Moreover, the shorter season results in smaller yields than can be obtained in regions with longer seasons.

TOP LEFT: Trial field in Maine of organically grown potatoes.
TOP RIGHT: Don Young, creator of the Shepody variety, and grower Pablo Serra in a field of elite-grade Panda potatoes near Temuco, Chile.
FACING PAGE: A field of Shepody potatoes.

LEFT: At the research farm, across the river from the Florenceville plant. Stephen McCain of McCain Produce is front left. Also pictured are variety development specialist Gary Hawkins (fourth from left) and Yves Leclercq, chief agronomist, McCain Foods (Canada), third from right.

RIGHT: Checking out new varieties at the research farm.

Another disadvantage is that it's not practical to use irrigation in New Brunswick. For a processor, the main objective is having a reliable supply of good raw materials and an irrigated crop delivers that better than a crop dependent on rainfall.

An ideal place to grow potatoes would be one where it never rains during the growing season, the sun shines every day, and irrigation water is cheap and plentiful, says Pelletier. A potato crop needs four centimetres of water per week and, on average, that's what the skies of New Brunswick deliver. The problem is that sometimes ten centimetres falls in a single day, followed by three weeks with no rain at all. Irrigation puts four centimetres on the crop each and every week.

Of course, the Carleton County potato crop could be irrigated with water from the Saint John River, but that doesn't make economic sense. It costs too much to install an irrigation system that might be needed only once or twice a season during dry spells. Even then, it would be risky to irrigate, says Pelletier, because of Murphy's Law – "right after you irrigate, there will be a thunderstorm, resulting in too much water." That's bad, of course, because overwatered potatoes are likely to rot.

McCain eventually figured all this out. That's why there is a McCain plant in Othello, Washington, one of the best places in the world to grow potatoes. It is located in the semi-desert region east of the Cascade Mountains. Because it is so dry

LEFT: Crop rotation trial on Prince Edward Island.
RIGHT: Clarence and Eil Waldner of Brookdale, Manitoba, the 2005 McCain champion potato growers for Carberry, Manitoba.

there, growers can control, through irrigation, how much water the crop gets, and the long growing season is perfect for Russet Burbanks. Ideally, a Russet Burbank crop will get from 130 to 140 growing days, but in New Brunswick, it has only 120. Nevertheless, advances in agronomy are allowing New Brunswick farmers to grow the variety successfully.

"McCain has made a huge investment to learn how to grow and store that variety," Pelletier says. "For example, we have agronomists going into storages with CO_2 meters to see if there is enough fresh air. This was unheard of fifteen years ago. So, because of the technology, the Russet Burbank is now doing pretty well in New Brunswick." But the yield in eastern Canada can't compete with that in Washington state. In New Brunswick, the growers have to put in fewer plants per hectare to give their potatoes a chance to grow to a decent size during the short growing season. So the commercial yield in New Brunswick is about thirty metric tons per hectare, compared with Othello's sixty-five.

If Florenceville was not the easiest place to grow potatoes, it was also not the perfect location for the headquarters of a large multinational corporation. In 1988, the *Toronto Star* asked Harrison McCain to explain why McCain Foods was based in a rural village rather than a major business centre such as Toronto.

LEFT: View from the airstrip near Harrison and Wallace's houses, looking across the potato fields and river valley.
RIGHT: McCain's head office in downtown Toronto is on the thirty-sixth floor of BCE Place (centre foreground).

"I like it here," he answered. "It's nice. It doesn't make any economic sense at all. It means a huge travel bill and a lot of weariness. We're perfectly satisfied to be here and to pay a certain price for that." Part of the price is maintaining an airstrip so that company planes can shuttle McCain personnel to and from Toronto. The airstrip, which sports the McCain logo on its pavement, is not a luxury but a necessity if the company is to keep its corporate headquarters in Florenceville.

In 1995, when Howard Mann arrived as president and CEO, McCain established a global headquarters office in Toronto. As of 2007, CEO Dale Morrison and other key executives were based on the thirty-sixth floor of Toronto's BCE Place, on Bay Street, the Canadian equivalent of Wall Street. The headquarters of McCain's Canadian operations are in Florenceville, where Fred Schaeffer, CEO of McCain Foods Canada, lives. As well, some global functions, including the legal department, corporate engineering, corporate agriculture, part of corporate financing and taxation, and the data processing centre, remain in Florenceville. In 2006, the company announced a $70 million plan to rebuild the Florenceville factory. It also decided to renovate the head office, which is adjacent to the factory.

Because of the dramatic advances in communications, it may be more practical in the twenty-first century to maintain the Florenceville head office than it was in the company's earlier years. Tony van Leersum recalls that, when he joined McCain in 1978, there was no fax or email and just the occasional telex. Most communication was by ordinary post and telegram. "As managing director of continental Europe at the time I was allowed only one transatlantic phone call a week, because of the high cost. Mail from New Brunswick to Holland took twelve days. If posted in Maine, it took eight days." Today, of course, Florenceville

Air McCain

From early on, the McCain planes and airfield behind their houses made it possible for Harrison and Wallace to have a global reach while remaining based in a small village. The first plane was a little Piper Aztec (left) purchased in around 1963. A Mitsubishi MU-2 was acquired in 1970 (below left, with the Aztec on the Florenceville airfield) and used from 1970 to 1982. The Falcon 50 jet is now in use (below, at the Florenceville McCain hanger, 2002), along with the Learjet 45, pictured above preparing for its scheduled early-morning run to Toronto, 2006.

LEFT: Harrison with then prime minister Jean Chrétien and Russian president Vladimir Putin, 2000. Putin was meeting with Canadian business leaders on this, his first visit to Canada. Marilyn Strong, Harrison's companion during his latter years, is on the far left.
BELOW: Harrison mans the barbeque at a Florenceville party, along with Malcolm McLeod, then agriculture minister of New Brunswick.

Harrison

Harrison McCain liked to socialize. One of Harrison and Wallace's methods for collecting information useful to McCain Foods was simply to call up other companies and ask if they could drop by for an interview and a tour. Terry Bird, who ran Day & Ross before becoming vice-president of corporate development of McCain Foods, was often told to have a look at one or another U.S. trucking company.

Harrison would say, "Just phone them up and say you're in town, and they'll welcome you in."

To his surprise, Bird found Harrison was usually right about that: "I used to travel with Harrison, and this happened all the time. One time in Minneapolis, Harrison picked up the phone and then off we went to see the president of Pillsbury."

That's how Harrison got to know Jim Pattison, the Vancouver billionaire whose company, the Jim Pattison Group, owns an array of enterprises in food retailing, magazine distribution, and broadcasting, as well as the Ripley's Believe It or Not entertainment company.

According to Bird, one day when Harrison was in Vancouver he called Pattison and said, "I'm Harrison McCain, I've heard a lot about you, I'd like to come and see you."

They became close friends. Pattison often attended parties thrown by Harrison in New Brunswick and was also present at the opening of the Coaldale processing plant in Alberta. Billie and Harrison McCain were weekend guests at Pattison's lavish desert retreat in Palm Springs, California, a house famed for its collection of memorabilia left behind by its former owner, Frank Sinatra.

On another occasion, Harrison called Conrad Black at Black's home in Palm Beach, Florida, and was invited to visit. He later told Bird that Black seemed nervous throughout the entire meeting. "He kept waiting for the other shoe to drop – does he want to sell me something, does he want to buy something?"

There was no other shoe. Black was an interesting character, and Harrison McCain was simply curious to meet him.

is instantly connected to anywhere in McCain's global empire by telephone and internet.

Florenceville is a company town, and the ties between company and community remain strong. In a medical emergency, any local resident, whether McCain employee or not, is transported to a major hospital on a McCain plane.

McCain also covers half the cost of beautification projects, such as planting flower beds, in Florenceville and nearby towns. Beautification committees in each town were set up during the 1980s at Harrison McCain's urging and under the guidance of his wife, Billie.

Bruce Terry, who joined McCain in 1990 as CFO, recalls that Harrison McCain raised the issue of living in Florenceville when interviewing him. "He was very concerned about the way people fit the business," says Terry. "He knew not everyone was comfortable moving to a small town. He interviewed my wife for an hour to make sure she would fit. Because you need a certain maturity and a certain family relationship and character to fit in."

Some potential employees don't want to live in a rural area far from the urban amenities to which they are accustomed. On the other hand, McCain's presence in Florenceville has advantages for some, including those employees whose spouses are farmers, with no benefits, such as a prescription drug plan. The McCain job is of greater value to such employees than it would be to a family in which both spouses had benefits through their workplace.

Also, the small-town environment facilitates communication among employees. "Because people know each other and talk, you have an incredible real-time communications system that is not based on technology," Terry points out. "You have a constant communication about the business in terms of living and breathing what's going on."

David Morgan, a retired long-time McCain employee, has been mayor of Florenceville since 1995. Although McCain is the financial engine of the area, it doesn't interfere in local politics, he says. The company got a tax break when it started, but now it pays taxes at the same rate as any other business.

The hiring of Bruce Terry in 1990 as CFO signalled a shift in the way McCain Foods was run. Previously, the vice-presidents of McCain Foods Canada, the operating company in Canada, also acted as officers for the companies outside Canada. Carl

TOP: Bruce Terry, former CFO, McCain Foods Limited.
MIDDLE: Arnold Park, CEO, McCain Foods (Canada) Ltd. (retired), 2005.
BOTTOM: Michael Campbell, vice-president and general counsel, McCain Foods Limited, 2005.

TOP LEFT: Nancy Oliveira and Suzy Tremblay on the pâté line at the Tour Eiffel meat-processing plant. McCain owns Tour Eiffel's two plants, in Blainville and in Quebec City.
TOP RIGHT: The Grand Falls plant, built in 1979, makes pizza, juice, and potato products.
BOTTOM: Pizza line at Grand Falls, 2007. Carol St. Amand ensures the holder is filled with salami, ready for automated slicing onto the pizzas.

Ash had developed and implemented the Management Control Report (MCR) system around the world. His successor, Bill Mabee, had guided regional directors of finance and coordinated financial transactions and tax-related matters between them. Bliss and Morris acted more or less as corporate officers, but the task of coordinating the activities of the organization as a whole fell mainly to Harrison and Wallace.

By 1990, McCain Foods, with more than $2 billion in annual revenues, was too big to rely on such an informal structure. Terry had the job of integrating and harmonizing the financial affairs of McCain worldwide, a mandate that did not always make him popular with managing directors used to doing things their own way. "There had been other corporate people before me," Terry explains. "There was Tony van Leersum guiding people about potatoes and Tim Bliss, who was chief engineer. They were the welcome corporate interveners. But I was the one who was changing things, and that wasn't particularly welcome."

Terry's mandate was not precisely defined. "I was to become the first CFO of the company and find areas where improvements could be made," Terry says. He started out in areas where he had significantly more expertise than anyone else in the company. One was information technology, a field in which McCain could learn from other organizations of its size.

Secretaries were still using typewriters and the salesmen were taking their orders in longhand. At a meeting with a group of salesmen, Terry said, "Why wouldn't you have a portable computer with all the data about your customers on it? You could take the orders on it and transmit them automatically."

A salesman replied, "I will never take a computer into one of my customer's establishments. They will think I'm spying on them."

A few months later, Terry convened the Canadian management team to watch a film made for Frito-Lay, the snack food company, showing its sales force using handheld computers. The McCain management soon realized that it was time to enter the digital age if the company was to continue its success.

Terry's most significant initiative was to hire Anil Rastogi in 1995 as chief information officer, with a mandate to centralize information technology for the worldwide operation in Florenceville. To explain the importance of this, Terry points to a system McCain had installed across its worldwide operations, the Pansophic Resource Management System (PRMS). This is an enterprise-wide management system that allows the company to track all its order entry, distribution, production, and financial functions from start to finish. The problem was that each of twenty-five separate McCain businesses insisted that the system be modified so that none of their processes changed. No one at head office had the ability or authority to prevent PRMS being implemented in twenty-five different ways. Rastogi developed a world version of the system, and it was implemented over the objections of many of the regional offices.

Terry needed the support of Wallace and Harrison to implement his projects, and that didn't always come automatically. He recalls how he managed to change Harrison's mind about an initiative that was finding resistance with the European offices. Terry wanted to bring in a centralized finance group in Europe to take on more responsibility. The managing directors in Europe saw this as an infringement on their autonomy. Wallace supported the move, but Harrison was resisting it because of opposition from the European executives.

Over Scotch one night in Harrison's office, Terry asked, "Harrison, how long have you been running the business?"

TOP LEFT: Winnipeg mayor Bill Norrie presents Harrison and Wallace with honorary citizen's awards, 1979.
TOP RIGHT: Official opening of the Prince Edward Island plant, 1991.
BOTTOM: Anil Rastogi, chief information officer, McCain Foods Limited, 2006.

McCain's nerve centre

When one of McCain's Australian customers submits an order to McCain's Australian headquarters in Ballarat, the order and invoice are processed on the other side of the world, at the global technology centre in Florenceville, New Brunswick. The same is true for business generated by McCain's companies in the United States, Europe, South Africa, Asia, and South America.

The modern, light-filled building is the nerve centre of McCain's worldwide operations. Adjacent to the company's original offices and factory, it houses 270 information technology staff representing many nationalities – their presence makes Florenceville perhaps the most multicultural rural community in Canada.

McCain entered the information age in 1966 with a mechanical punch-card system. In 1969, it acquired its first computer which was used to process financial applications. During the early 1970s, the computer was upgraded several times to support new applications. A mainframe computer was installed in Florenceville in 1988.

Until the mid-1990s, the various McCain operations around the world ran their own information systems. In 1995, Anil Rastogi joined the company as chief information officer with the mandate of unifying IT functions in one location. Not long after his arrival, he told Harrison McCain that IT needed a new building. "Nobody thought he would approve it, but he did," Rastogi says. Harrison was not an expert in information technology but he understood its importance.

The data centre has squash courts, saunas, a state-of-the-art exercise room, a chess-playing area, and meeting rooms named after potato varieties. Its computers are used to develop and maintain business applications standardized for all regions. As of 2007, Florenceville processed about 97 percent of McCain's transactions and more than seventy thousand emails daily across a global network connecting more than eight thousand personal computers.

To attract qualified technology experts to Florenceville, McCain provides housing at low cost. The newcomers must sign a contract to stay for at least three years. Most stay longer, enjoying the friendly village environment and nearby outdoors activities such as canoeing and fishing.

For Rastogi, people are more important than technology. And his people must understand that their job is not to run computers but to facilitate the management of a multinational food-processing company. "The greatest compliment I can give to a member of my staff is, 'You understand the business,' not, 'You understand the hardware and software,'" he says.

TOP: Marion Boyer learns how to use the punch-card system.
LEFT and **BELOW:** Data processing's early days, Florenceville.
FACING PAGE: The lounge at Florenceville's data centre, 2006.

Cedric Ritchie (centre) of the Bank of Nova Scotia inducts Harrison and Wallace into the Canadian Business Hall of Fame, 1993.

"Thirty-four years."

"And you've been dealing with every aspect of it – agriculture, sales, everything?"

"Yes."

"Well, I've been doing nothing but finance for twelve years, so I guess I know a lot more about it than you, so why don't you just accept my recommendation?"

Harrison said, "Okay."

It had taken Harrison and Wallace a year to fill the CFO job, and clearly they were prepared to put a lot of trust in the person they had finally chosen. This management style was again illustrated when the brothers were approached by a Calgary-based engineering company that wanted to engineer the new McCain plant planned for Portage la Prairie, Manitoba.

"Harrison and in particular Wallace believed we should engineer the plants ourselves," says Jim Evans, a Florenceville-based engineer at the time. But the Calgarians insisted they could do a better job for less cost, and they insisted on meeting with Harrison. "Finally, Harrison agreed to see them. So they came to Florenceville, two guys in leather suits, wearing lots of jewellery. Harrison just listened.

"Then, looking over the rim of his glasses as he often did, Harrison said, 'Gentlemen, Mr. Bliss and Mr. Evans have convinced me that you will build the plant for a million dollars less. But I think the plant will then be worth more than a million dollars less. Therefore, I suggest that you go back home. We will not use your services.'"

In his efforts to centralize administrative and financial functions, Terry also had the full support of Howard Mann, McCain's first professional president and CEO, who directed the day-to-day operations of the company from 1995 until 2004. Mann also backed the work of Rastogi in reorganizing the company's information technology and encouraged Lloyd Borowski's work in standardizing factory processes.

When Mann, who grew up in London's working-class East End, first arrived at McCain, he admitted that he knew "nothing whatsoever about potatoes." But he knew plenty about the food industry, having worked in it in the United Kingdom for twenty-seven years. For his services to the industry, he was named an Officer of the Order of the British Empire (OBE) in 1994.

Mann left his mark by establishing the Toronto office and convincing Harrison McCain of the need to sell some companies that were not part of McCain's core business or which could not attain a sufficient market share or profitability. Despite selling off those assets, McCain's revenues grew from $3.5 billion to almost $6 billion during Mann's tenure. And it was Mann who persuaded Harrison McCain that, although MacFries are not a McCain brand, McDonald's should be one of the company's core businesses.

Mann established corporate vice-president positions in engineering and agriculture. He formed the senior executives council through which he promoted coordination among the regional operational CEOs and corporate vice-presidents. This paved the way for Dale Morrison's policy of developing more corporate, as opposed to regional, decision making.

Mann got along well with chairman Harrison McCain, to whom he reported until Harrison's health deteriorated.

Howard Mann speaking at the opening of the new plant in Coaldale, Alberta, 2000.

Companies grow in two ways. One way is organically, meaning that if you are producing frozen food, you produce more of it in your existing facilities or you expand those facilities or you build new ones. The second way to grow is by buying other companies.

Over the five decades of its existence, McCain has successfully used both methods: half of its growth has been organic, and the other half has come through acquisitions. By 2007, the two routes to growth had resulted in a McCain manufacturing base in North America of sixteen processing plants, nine in Canada and seven in the United States.

The two New Brunswick plants, in Florenceville and Grand Falls, had been expanded

LEFT: George McClure, 1992.
MIDDLE: (left to right) Des Doucette, John Corey, Tim Bliss, Cor Koster, Colin Richardson, and Dave Munslow attend a 1985 energy conservation conference in Europe.
RIGHT: Terry Bird, vice-president of corporate development and emerging markets, 2005.

and upgraded. As of 2007, Grand Falls was producing juice, both frozen and in aseptic packaging, as well as pizza, french fries, and other potato products. Three other french fry plants were added to the McCain chain of factories – McCain built a plant in Portage la Prairie, Manitoba, in 1979 and another in Coaldale, Alberta, in 2000. And it bought Midwest Foods in Carberry, Manitoba, in 2004. The Coaldale plant produces french fries for the Far East markets, while most of the production from the Manitoba factories goes to the United States.

In Wallace McCain's opinion, McCain Foods should also have a french fry plant on Prince Edward Island, a province famous for its large potato crop. C.M. McLean Ltd. owned a struggling frozen foods factory in New Annan, Prince Edward Island. When McLean put it up for sale in 1979, Irving, Wallace and Harrison's former employer, snapped it up. The plant was Irving's entry into the frozen french fry business; its Cavendish Farms brand remains a McCain competitor.

McCain had passed up a chance to bid on the McLean factory. "Not buying it was a mistake," Wallace admits. "We thought no one would buy it because it had almost gone broke three times." However, McCain then built a potato specialties plant in Borden-Carleton, Prince Edward Island.

George McClure, who spearheaded McCain's expansion into Europe, became the first chief buyer of companies as head of corporate development from 1979 to 1995. He played a key role in McCain's expansion by buying companies in Europe, the United States, and Canada. In 1995, McClure retired and Harrison McCain offered the job to Terry Bird, then chairman and CEO of the New Brunswick Telephone Company. Previously, Bird had been president and CEO of Day & Ross, McCain's trucking company.

Harrison

As a boss, Harrison McCain was tough but fair. He and Wallace wanted their managers to try new ideas, and they understood that new ideas don't always work out.

"Harrison told me he was always quite careful about criticizing the marketing department because he wanted it to try new product ideas and new promotions," says Allison McCain. "New ideas are expensive, and the failures are expensive. But he didn't want people to stop trying. You can't tell people we want you to be innovative but if you get it wrong we're going to drop on you like a ton of bricks – because then nothing would happen."

Harrison expected people to work hard but not at the expense of their health or family life. He didn't like to see his managers working late at night. On two occasions, Florenceville mayor David Morgan, then a McCain manager, was sent home. Once, Harrison came into the office at 10 p.m. and spotted Morgan at his desk.

"What are you doing here, David?"

"I'm working."

"I see that. That'll keep until tomorrow. Good night."

"Well, I need to …"

"Good night."

Harrison was named to *Maclean's* magazine's 1990 honour roll.

Anil Rastogi, who took over as head of information technology in 1995, was warned that Harrison had little patience for long presentations. But Rastogi had worked out a new strategy for IT that called for the centralization of some functions. It wasn't something that could be explained quickly. Rastogi decided to ignore the warnings and plunge ahead. He was right to do so. Harrison listened to him for six hours. The issues were new to him; he knew how important they were and wanted to understand. At the end, he told Rastogi, "I think you know what you are doing. I think this is important for our company and growth. You have my support."

Harrison McCain was a bundle of energy. "He was a fast walker and a fast talker," says Marilyn Strong, who was his secretary and assistant for four decades and had to learn to walk fast to keep up with him. He was extremely sociable and loved parties, but he sometimes craved solitude and quiet. After a long day at the office, he liked to relax in his book-lined den and read biographies, novels, and business books.

His interests weren't confined to business. He was a supporter of cultural institutions, especially those in New Brunswick, and was keenly interested in politics. When Pierre Trudeau ran for the leadership of the Liberal Party in 1968, Harrison McCain was one of his earliest supporters. "I'm a Liberal," he told the *Financial Post Magazine,* "a middle-of-the-road, hair-to-the-left-of-centre Liberal. I believe in social justice and taxes."

He could talk to anyone and give that person his full attention. "He was equally at ease with the Queen or Fidel Castro or the guy on the plant floor," says Strong.

Not just a fast talker and a fast walker, Harrison was also a fast driver. One morning, en route from Florenceville to Grand Falls, he was stopped for speeding. As the RCMP officer wrote out a ticket, Harrison asked if he would still be patrolling the highway that afternoon. The officer said he would.

"Then you might as well give me two tickets," said Harrison, "because that's when I'm coming back."

Bird said, "I can't do that; I've been an operator all my life, I don't know finance."

Harrison replied, "It doesn't matter, it doesn't matter. Don't worry about any of that nonsense, you can hire financial guys. Just go out and buy me some damn businesses."

On reflection, Bird decided he could do the job after all. "I had no skill in finance, but I was a good negotiator and I was diligent. Harrison felt I had good interpersonal skills and could put people at ease."

Bird has taken the lead in many acquisitions. Since 1995, he has filtered out more than five hundred potential targets. Of the twenty-two companies acquired, the most significant of these were the Anchor appetizer business and the Ore-Ida food service business, which made McCain USA a major player in the American food industry.

Corporate strategy has to adjust for changes in the marketplace. In the first decade of the twenty-first century, the growth of fast food business in the developed countries is slowing down. In addition, consumers are more health conscious. Rather than ordering a super-size french fries, the typical consumer in 2007 is more likely to ask for a regular-size portion. The result is that the total volume of french fries sold is down, while the number of servings is up. Because of more convenient and healthier options, including microwaveable and oven-prepared potato products, consumers continue to make potatoes a core part of their diets.

TOP: McCain produces an assortment of pizza products in Canada, Australia, the United Kingdom, and several European countries.
BOTTOM: Karen Basian, vice-president of corporate strategy, mergers and acquisitions, and innovation, 2006.

Karen Basian is vice-president of corporate strategy, mergers and acquisitions, and innovation. She believes changing demographics in the developed markets and the shift to healthier, more convenient products offer McCain a huge opportunity to grow through innovation. "The consumer's concern about health and convenience is a function of aging populations, increasing obesity, and busy lifestyles," she explains. "At McCain, we are part of people's everyday lives. With this new focus, we see the opportunity to provide them with better-for-you products and more accessible solutions. Our transition to healthy oils around the world is a great example of basic things we can do to help our consumers and customers."

It's an exciting time to be the head of strategy and innovation, she says. "There is so much opportunity to innovate and continue to build McCain while delivering good food that is fun, easy, and affordable. That's our magic. We like to think of it as 'creating smiles.'

"And we are excited about our emerging markets. McCain has always been ready to invest in developing markets. We think of South America, China, and India as presenting the same opportunities as Europe did in the 1970s and look forward to seeing them grow and become significant parts of the McCain family of companies."

A major win for McCain in the United States had been the appetizer business it entered via acquisitions. It is expanding this business through further acquisitions because of the growing popularity of the category, as well as its good profit margins. In Canada, McCain in 2002 bought Wong Wing Foods, the largest manufacturer in the country of frozen Chinese dinners and appetizers such as dim sum and egg rolls. The Wong Wing purchase was part of an overall strategy to build McCain's strength in appetizers, a strategy that also included the purchase of a Chinese food manufacturer in Taiwan. McCain bought Belleisle Foods, a New Brunswick company specializing in egg rolls, in 2003.

"There's no such thing today, in our perspective, as Chinese food, Indian food, or Mexican food," says Bird. These have become global foods, and McCain's marketers look for new ways to use them, perhaps combining various ethnic foods or tastes into innovative products.

At the same time, the company won't neglect its "country jewels" – product categories in which McCain has a strong presence but in one region only. So, because McCain is the market leader in frozen dinners in Australia but nowhere else, it might undertake acquisitions in that category in Australia. In Canada where, uniquely in the McCain network, the company had a strong position in frozen and aseptic juices, it acquired the Old South brand in 2000.

That McCain is a privately owned company is an advantage for its strategic planners, observes Rick Pryde, vice-president of finance: "We don't have to worry about what Bay Street or Wall Street says our quarterly earnings should be. We have the luxury, as long as we don't abuse it, of taking long-term approaches to issues."

TOP: McCain acquired Wong Wing Foods of Montreal in 2002.
BOTTOM: Fang Zhao Ce works on battered chicken ball production, Wong Wing.

McCain Foods began investing in Day & Ross in the 1960s, not because McCain was eager to expand into a different business but out of necessity. The company it had been relying on to get its goods to market, Maine Maritime, was bankrupt. McCain had to make certain that Day & Ross stayed in business because somebody's trucks had to get McCain products from New Brunswick to the rest of the continent.

Decisions based on necessity sometimes turn out better than ones based on a grand strategy. As we shall see in the next chapter, McCain got into appetizers almost by accident when it ended up owning an appetizer business as a result of a french fry acquisition. Appetizers have turned out to be a huge win, and so has Day & Ross. From a struggling regional transport firm, it has grown into a major trucking operation with 2006 sales of $600 million and recognition as one of Canada's fifty best-managed companies, an award sponsored by the national accounting firm Deloitte, CIBC Commercial Banking, the *National Post,* and the Queen's University School of Business. As of 2007, only about 10 percent of Day & Ross's business was with McCain Foods. McCain has big plans for Day & Ross. "Our ultimate goal," says Day & Ross CEO John Doucet, "is to be the brand name in transport that McCain is in french fries."

Elbert Day and Walter Ross founded Day & Ross in 1950 in Hartland, New Brunswick. At a time when the railroads dominated the transport business, they were pioneers. Their trucks hauled anything that needed hauling, from potatoes and roofing materials to fertilizer and manufactured goods. Joe Palmer, a Hartland potato farmer, was a customer and eventually bought control of the company, which he expanded rapidly, although not always profitably. McCain gradually bought Palmer out during the 1960s.

Palmer stayed on as president and, in 1977, hired Terry Bird as senior vice-president. "The company was a basket case," says Bird. Things were so bad financially that Day & Ross was delaying mailing out cheques it had already printed.

Palmer was a boss with a style of his own. While Bird was deciding whether to take the job, he and his wife went to meet Palmer at his home. "It was 10 AM on a weekday," Bird recounts. "He interviewed me in his bedroom. He was still half asleep. Afterward, my wife said, 'If you join this organization, you have to be crazier than I thought you were.'"

He did join and discovered that, although Palmer was no early riser, he was a hard worker. "He would work all afternoon, play cards all evening, and then come back and work on central dispatch through the middle of the night."

Under Palmer, Day & Ross had become one of the largest transport companies in eastern Canada. However, when the economy weakened in the early 1970s, the company got into financial trouble. It was dependent on a small number of large customers that provided small profit margins. Bird decided that targeting small shippers

TOP: Joe Palmer, president of Day & Ross, 1972.
BOTTOM: John Doucet, president and CEO, Day & Ross Transportation Group, 1999.

was the way to boost profits, and so Day & Ross became an LTL (less than truckload) specialist. An LTL transporter moves smaller shipments between terminals. At the terminal, the shipments are transferred to another truck for local delivery.

Day & Ross's rapid growth during a booming economy had hidden underlying weaknesses, including a lack of qualified managers. Bird went to the universities to recruit a stronger middle-management team. He initiated the creation of a procedural manual covering all aspects of the company's operations. He worked to improve relations with the owner-operators who drive the trucks and to improve the company's accident record, thereby lowering insurance costs.

Still, the company wasn't making money. "Day & Ross was haemorrhaging," says Bird. Harrison would call me every week. One time I told him what I planned to do and he said, 'I don't agree, but you're the boss, and if that's what you want to do, go ahead and do it.' Never once did he ever come back to me and say, 'See, I told you.' One of the things Harrison and Wallace did well was know when to give you a compliment and when to tell you to do a bit better. And it was never when you thought it would be. They were constantly motivating you to do better."

There was certainly room for improvement. When David Sanchez arrived in 1991 as CFO, he found, he says, a disaster. Day & Ross lost $20 million that year largely because of an acquisition that didn't work out, of a company in California.

In 1992, McCain hired a new CEO, John Schiller, whose mandate was to make Day & Ross profitable. He hired John Doucet, an experienced trucking executive as chief operating officer. When Schiller left in 1998, Doucet became CEO. "Transport is not that complicated," he observes. "We're only moving boxes around when you get right down to it."

TOP: Day & Ross has Canada covered coast to coast.
BOTTOM: Terry Bird, 1982, then president and CEO of Day & Ross.

The important thing is to get the boxes to their destination intact and on time. In the previous twelve months, Day & Ross's on-time delivery rate was only 60 percent. To improve on that, Doucet introduced what he calls pro-active tracking. This meant that, if a delivery was going to be late, the local terminal manager had to call the customer between 8 and 10 AM and inform him. "The terminal managers soon got the message that if they didn't want to spend the morning on the telephone, they had better get the freight delivered on time."

Doucet offered improved service for higher prices and said goodbye to the

LEFT: Harrison and Billie with their children, 1976.
Front row: (left to right) Ann, Gillian, Billie.
Back row: Peter, Harrison, Mark, Laura.

RIGHT: Family photo: Wallace and Margie (far left and right), with Eleanor, Michael, Scott, and Martha, 1979.

customers who wouldn't pay. Sales dropped, but the company became profitable. To keep the momentum going, he introduced bonus schemes for key employees based on several factors, on-time delivery and sales growth among them. Day & Ross has become one of the most successful operating companies in the McCain group. A key ingredient, Doucet says, was the financial backing McCain provided. "If we want to buy equipment and put in more terminals and infrastructure, it's always positive."

When Doucet arrived in 1992, Day & Ross was doing $180 million worth of business a year. By 2007, sales had climbed to $600 million and the goal, by 2009, is to achieve $1 billion through a combination of organic growth and acquisitions.

Day & Ross celebrated its fiftieth anniversary in 2000. The Day & Ross transport group includes such well-known companies as Sameday Right-O-Way, a courier service, and Fastrax, a truckload operator. The Day & Ross companies operate from coast to coast in Canada, as well as in the United States under the name McCain Transport. As of 2007, the group boasted a fleet of 1,500 owner-operated trucks and 2,500 company-owned trailers, operating out of forty terminals across Canada, with 4,100 employees and owner-operators.

Because the drivers are owner-operators rather than employees, they are highly motivated, says Doucet. "You've got all these people, several thousand of them, running their own business and trying to generate more business for themselves. When Day & Ross loses a customer, the driver could lose his job, so he's got to take care of those customers. They are just as much or more his customers as they are mine."

One of the industry's problems is attracting skilled and motivated long-distance drivers. "It's a hard way to make a living," Doucet says. "The driver may make an

average of $40,000 a year. And they are on the road every day." But Doucet doesn't think a driver shortage will impede his ambitious growth plans. "If you pay the right rate, if you treat your people right, you've got a better chance to attract them than the next group. That's what we try to do, treat them right and tell them they are part of the success and the winning team."

In 2007, Doucet marked his fifteenth year working for Day & Ross. He is also a member of the McCain Foods senior leadership team that advises Dale Morrison on strategy for the McCain group as a whole. But in 1992, during only his second week on the job, Doucet wasn't sure his career at McCain would be a long one.

Harrison McCain's wife, Billie, had bought some furniture in Montreal and Harrison asked Doucet to have one of his trucks pick it up. "I was worried that if anything happened to that furniture, I would only have a job for two weeks," Doucet recalls. "I got two guys to go up, take a truck, get some blankets, and get that furniture. I told them, 'Don't put it in with other stuff. You've got to take care of this furniture.'

"When they got to Florenceville, Billie wasn't there, but the maid let them in. They took the cover off the furniture, and then they called me – it seemed that the furniture had rubbed against something; it looked damaged.

"I called Fredericton, got hold of an upholsterer, and said, 'I don't care what it costs, you've got to get up here now and fix that furniture.' So he drove up. Billie was home by then. The upholsterer said, 'I'm here to fix the furniture.' She said, 'It's antique furniture, there's nothing wrong with it. It's supposed to look worn.'"

LEFT: Wallace and Margie celebrate Wallace's receipt of the Order of New Brunswick, December 3, 2003. Wallace is wearing his new Order on a ribbon under the Order of Canada; Margie wears the insignia of the Order of Canada, a Knight of the Order of St. John, and the Order of New Brunswick.
RIGHT: Harrison and Billie in Bermuda, 1985.

LEFT: Scott McCain presents an award to a Grand Falls employee.
MIDDLE: Allison McCain (centre), in Turkey, 1998. Han van den Hoek, vice-president of agriculture for continental Europe, is on the far left; beside him is Folkert Sneep, CEO for northern, central, and eastern Europe.
RIGHT: Michael McCain and Bill Boehm of Kroger at a McCain party, c.1992.

By the 1980s, the days of Wallace and Harrison pounding the pavements trying to convince restaurant chefs of the advantages of frozen french fries were long gone. The company had built up a full-time sales force, one of whose members was Wallace's son, Michael. After graduating from the University of Western Ontario with a business degree, Michael stayed in London, Ontario, to begin his McCain sales career, later moving to Hamilton.

When Michael moved to Florenceville to work in marketing, his mentor was Archie McLean, senior vice-president of marketing, who later became CEO of McCain Foods Canada. He sent Michael a note upon his arrival. "I don't care if your name is McCain," the note read. "That's not worth a cup of coffee to me. Time to get to work."

A year later, McLean gave him another piece of advice that stayed with him. Michael was complaining about not having enough responsibility to get necessary things done. McLean told him, "Don't ever forget this: responsibility is 90 percent taken and 10 percent given."

Michael wasn't the only member of the McCain family eager for responsibility. Allison McCain, chairman of McCain Foods Limited, worked his way up from draftsman in the Florenceville engineering department to coldstore manager and production manager in Florenceville, manufacturing director in Australia and then the United Kingdom, and CEO of McCain GB.

Michael's brother, Scott, started as production supervisor in the Scarborough plant in England, then had several production positions in Florenceville before becoming manufacturing director for McCain Refrigerated, a cheese business in Oakville, Ontario. He also was general manager of the Grand Falls, New Brunswick,

operation, which includes potato-processing, pizza, and juice factories. Scott and his family moved to Grand Falls, helping to cement good relationships among the McCain family and company, its employees, and the community. Scott later became vice-president of manufacturing for McCain Foods Canada.

Harrison's son Peter joined McCain Foods Canada in 1981. He took the manufacturing training program in Florenceville and then worked as a salesman. Peter had a series of management jobs before being appointed vice-president for export sales for McCain Foods Canada. In 1994 he became the first president of McCain International. Peter died in a snowmobile accident in 1997.

Harrison's other son, Mark, for many years worked as a business analyst for the corporate development department and was instrumental in launching the company's South African business, of which he is chairman.

In family-owned businesses, the issue of who will lead the company once the founding entrepreneur steps down often provokes discord. That was certainly the case for McCain Foods. The company needed to plan for a future without Harrison and Wallace. But the brothers couldn't agree on what that plan should be. Their inability to reach agreement led to an open family dispute that damaged the working relationship that had so successfully built McCain Foods into a major multinational company.

Most families avoid the problem of next-generation leadership by selling the business. According to the Business Development Bank of Canada, only 30 percent of family-owned businesses are passed on to the second generation. Only 10 percent move on to the third generation, and subsequent succession rates are less than 5 percent.

LEFT: Peter McCain on a 1989 sales trip to Japan.
RIGHT: Mark McCain (second from left), on a feasibility study trip to South Africa during the 1990s. Ponnie Marais of the West Free State Seed Growers Association is on the far right.

Kathryn McCain chairs the McCain Foundation, whose grant recipients include the Atlantic Veterinary College. At the grant presentation, in 2005, the college's dean, Timothy Ogilvie, holds a rare P.E.I. blue lobster.

But the McCain family was not interested in selling. The four brothers who had owned the company since its inception in 1957 had eighteen offspring among them. Should Wallace and Harrison McCain pass on the reins to one of them? Or should a professional manager not named McCain be hired to assume leadership of the company?

By the latter part of the 1980s, these questions were beginning to preoccupy Harrison and Wallace. Their two elder brothers were gone – Bob had died in 1977, Andrew in 1984. Wallace would turn sixty in 1990, and Harrison was three years older. Agitated by the growing disagreement between their uncles, the heirs of the older brothers were beginning to push for more involvement in the company.

During the 1980s, two members of the second generation, Allison, son of Andrew, and Wallace's son Michael, rose to hold important jobs in the McCain organization. Harrison considered Allison or perhaps one of his own sons to be a possible future CEO, while Wallace thought Michael was the best-equipped family member to assume that role.

The working arrangement between the brothers as co-CEOs was, with few exceptions, that they agreed on a course of action or they did not proceed. Unilateral actions by each of the brothers revealed the growing disagreement between them. In 1990, Harrison appointed Allison as managing director in the United Kingdom; Wallace objected but acquiesced. Later that year, Wallace appointed Michael as the CEO of U.S. operations with Harrison's apparent agreement, which he withdrew later that day.

At that point, the conflict, which had been simmering for several years, became public. It triggered lawsuits, an arbitration before a senior New Brunswick judge, more litigation in New Brunswick, an unsuccessful offer by Wallace to either buy out other shareholders or have them buy him out, and an unsuccessful attempt by Harrison to buy Wallace's shares.

In 1991, as Harrison and Wallace tried to work out their differences over succession, the governance of the company was changed. Under a plan designed by Harrison, the

At the research farm in 2006. In the background, across the river, is the Florenceville plant; the village of Florenceville lies to the right. Left to right: Don Wishart (retired),* Dick Cyr, Jim Bushby, Don Peabody (retired),* Milford Kinney (retired), Ken Cossaboom (retired), Paul Dean (retired), Murray Lovely (retired),* Marilyn Strong (retired),* Scoop Fredstrom, Paul Page (retired),* Dave Morgan (retired). *Asterisks indicate retirees with thirty-five or more years of service. The other retirees all have between twenty and thirty-five years of service.*

family holding company, McCain Foods Group Inc. (Holdco), became an active shareholders' vehicle, its board populated with second-generation McCains representing the four family groups.

Holdco gave the family members a better window on the operations of the company and provisions to protect their position as owners, without their involvement in the day-to-day management of the company. The board of McCain Foods Limited (Opco), the main operating company in the McCain Group, was restructured to include independent directors, management representatives, and a representative from Holdco.

As the dispute between the brothers continued to escalate, the families of Andrew and Bob sided with Harrison and, in 1994, the Holdco board voted to fire Wallace from his job as co-CEO of McCain Foods. However, Wallace remained as vice-chairman of Opco and retained his one-third ownership of the company.

In 2000, *Food in Canada* magazine saluted McCain Foods as Processor of the Century. The cover features Howard Mann, then president and CEO of McCain Foods Limited, and Arnold Park, president and CEO of McCain Foods Canada, with Harrison McCain and a selection of the company's top-selling potato products.

Harrison, who had suffered a heart attack in 1992, was ready to take a step back from day-to-day operations. The Opco board undertook a search for a new CEO for McCain Foods. After looking for more than a year, the board selected Howard Mann, a British food executive, who took over in 1995. Harrison remained chairman. In 1999, Allison became deputy chairman, taking over as chairman in 2002 when Harrison took the honorary position of founding chairman.

Before Wallace left active management of the company, the dispute, remarkably, did not unduly affect the management of McCain Foods, which continued to prosper. "We would have management meetings once a month, and you would never know there was a fight on," recalls Tim Bliss. "They kept the business separate from the personal fight."

"Never in a meeting would you know there was anything going on," agrees Wayne Hanscom. "They always just talked about the business issues."

Could the disagreement between the two brothers have been resolved without escalating into court battles and a public airing of hard feelings? Some who knew their older brothers, Andrew and Bob, agree that together they may have been able to prevent the escalation of the dispute or to settle it sooner. There is no way to know for certain.

Wallace McCain still had an appetite for business. In 1995, backed by the Toronto-Dominion Bank and the Ontario Teachers' Pension Plan, he bought control of Canada's largest food processor, Maple Leaf Foods, becoming chairman, while his sons Michael and Scott took senior executive positions in the same company.

The McCain feud was painful, not just for the family and the managers who worked with Wallace and Harrison but also for other employees and the residents of Florenceville, who worried that the company might be broken up or sold, depriving the village of its source of prosperity.

"When Harrison and Wallace separated, you did not know how to act or what to say," explains long-time employee Jim Evans. "It must have been an awful time for them and their families. It also was for us and for the people in the village. They were both such great guys; you loved them both."

The boards, 2007

McCain Foods has two boards of directors: the family holding company McCain Foods Group Inc. (Holdco), and the operating company McCain Foods Limited (Opco).

Holdco represents the McCain family members who are the owners of the company. Reflecting the share ownership, it has two members each from Harrison's and Wallace's families and one each from the families of the two elder brothers, Andrew and Bob.

One non-family member also sits on the Holdco board, which approves the annual operating and strategic plan, as well as capital expenditures above $25 million. The Holdco board also approves the hiring of a selection of top executives and appoints the members of the Opco board.

The Opco board oversees the business operations of McCain Foods.

The structure of the Opco board is somewhat complicated. Currently it is composed of ten members: four independent directors (representing the best of Canadian businesspeople); four family members, and two McCain executives, including the CEO. The CEO reports to Opco rather than to Holdco.

There are five committees of the Opco board: corporate governance; management resources; compensation; audit; and environment, health, and safety.

Previously, McCain had one board. Past members of that board are Andrew McCain, Robert McCain, Jed Sutherland, and Roger Wilson.

Past directors of the Holdco board are Laura McCain Jensen and Allison McCain.

Past directors of the Opco board are Arden Haynes, John Clements, David Morton, Mac McCarthy, Kendall Cork, Howard Mann, and Basil Hargrove.

The holding company board (Holdco): (left to right) George McClure, Stephen McCain, Andrew McCain, Scott McCain, Ann McCain Evans, Michael McCain, Mark McCain.

The operating company board (Opco). Front row: (seated, left to right) Mark McCain, Wallace McCain, Allison McCain, Andrew McCain, Frank van Schaayk. Back row: Victor Young, Paul Tellier, Jacques Bougie, Dale Morrison, J.P. Bisnair.

Wallace McCain   Scott McCain   Eleanor McCain   Martha McCain   Michael McCain

Allison McCain   Stephen McCain   Linda McCain   Margaret Roy   Nancy McCain   Kathryn McCain

Will Apold   Beth Apold   Mark McCain   Laura McCain Jensen   Gillian McCain   Ann McCain Evans

The shareholders, 2007

As a family-owned company, McCain's shareholders are all related to the original shareholders: Andrew, Bob, Harrison, and Wallace. Missing among these photos of the first- and second-generation shareholders are Marjorie McCain Pearson, Rosemary McCain-McMillin, Joyce McCain, Mary McCain, and Andrew McCain.

Many members of the McCain family are involved in an activity related to the company:
    Wallace McCain, vice-chairman, McCain Foods Limited (Opco)
    Scott McCain, director, McCain Foods Group Inc. (Holdco)
    Martha McCain, director, The McCain Foundation
    Michael McCain, director, McCain Foods Group Inc.
    Allison McCain, chairman, McCain Foods Limited
    Stephen McCain, director, McCain Foods Group Inc; joint managing director,
        McCain Produce Inc; chairman, McCain Fertilizer Ltd.
    Kathryn McCain, chairman, The McCain Foundation
    Beth Apold, director, The McCain Foundation
    Mark McCain, director, McCain Foods Group Inc; director, McCain Foods Limited;
        chairman, McCain South Africa (Pty) Ltd.
    Ann McCain Evans, director, McCain Foods Group Inc.
    Andrew McCain, chairman, McCain Foods Group Inc.

CHAPTER SIX

SOUTH OF THE BORDER

In a famous song about New York, Frank Sinatra sings, "If I can make it there, I'll make it anywhere." The same can be said of the United States as a whole. It is the world's largest, most competitive, and most innovative consumer market. Any company serious about being a global force in its industry must be a major player in the United States. If the company's business is convenience food, the United States is irresistible. No people has embraced fast food outside the home and convenience food inside it as enthusiastically as the Americans.

In the post–World War II era, Ray Kroc of McDonald's and other fast food pioneers built quick-service chains that have become omnipresent in the United States and household names around the world. By the turn of the twentieth century, half the meals served in the United States were eaten outside the home, and half of those were consumed in cars.

In the early years of the twenty-first century, critics of fast food branded it unhealthy and claimed it was making Americans fat. But the criticism wasn't dampening the American public's enthusiasm for the fare that the quick-service chains offered. In 2006, 34 percent of all U.S. restaurant sales were in quick-service restaurants, whose patrons spent U.S.$172 billion, up from U.S.$144 billion in 2005.

The McCain brothers had their eyes on the U.S. market from the earliest years of their company's history. And they tested it early on, exporting product into the U.S. Northeast from New Brunswick and operating french fry plants in Maine.

Wisely, they were in no hurry to make a major commitment. This typified their approach to global expansion: aggressive and cautious at the same time. Asserting that your ambition is to be the world's biggest producer of frozen french fries is aggressive. The goal could not be attained unless McCain Foods claimed a big share of all major

FACING PAGE: B.D. Grass Farm, Blaine, Maine: windrowers lift potatoes from the ground for harvesters to collect.

Fall colours in Maine.

markets, including the United States. But Wallace and Harrison McCain were also cautious, not committing to any market until they had the financial and other resources necessary to succeed.

They went first to Great Britain, then to Australia and continental Europe, because the competition in those places was weaker than in the United States. McCain had to become a major force in its other markets before it would have the clout to compete with Simplot, Lamb Weston, and Ore-Ida, the big companies that dominated the U.S. frozen potato industry.

McCain began exporting to the United States in 1969. Rather than battle the big companies for a share of the national market, Wallace and Harrison decided McCain would begin as a regional player, and so focused on the densely populated Northeast. The major processors were located in the west. McCain therefore had lower shipping costs to the Northeast than the U.S. companies and thus could offer competitive prices.

In 1975, an agricultural cooperative based in Syracuse, New York, called McCain to inquire whether the Canadian company would be interested in buying a french fry plant in Washburn, Maine. The timing couldn't have been better: McCain was ready to establish a U.S. base and, given its strategy of focusing at first on the eastern market, nearby Maine was the perfect place for it.

George McClure went to meet with the co-op officials in Syracuse. He discovered that "nobody there knew anything about the french fry factory. It was an orphan." McCain bought it and went to work upgrading all its systems. The next year, McCain bought another french fry plant in Easton, just thirty kilometres down the road from Washburn and only forty minutes from Florenceville.

Ian Cameron, a Canadian, came back from Australia to take charge of the U.S. plant operation from a base in Easton. In those early years in Maine, the company was able to operate in the black, but the return on investment was nothing to get excited about. McCain had not yet introduced its own brand. Instead, it was bidding for private-label business from supermarket chains in the region.

As usual, McCain was in it for the long haul and, with an eye to the future, made a big investment in upgrading the Easton plant. The renovated factory was more efficient than Washburn, and it made good business sense to close Washburn. Naturally, the Washburn employees, some of whom had worked at the factory for more than

LEFT: Cultivating a potato field in Maine, 2003.

RIGHT: Scouting for diseases and sampling at a trial field in Maine, 2005.

twenty years, weren't happy. McCain offered them all jobs at Easton, where a second french fry line was being installed, but ninety employees refused, considering the twenty-minute drive too onerous. "They thought it was too far away," recalls Cameron. "It was a very parochial little town. Some of the people had never been out of Maine."

When Wallace McCain learned that ninety of the Washburn workers would not go to Easton, he began to have second thoughts. "We were ready to announce the closure of the Washburn plant on a Monday morning," recalls Cameron. At eleven o'clock on Friday night, just three days before the scheduled announcement, Wallace McCain called Cameron. He said, "I've changed my mind. I don't want to do it."

Cameron was stunned. He said, "Wallace, it's all done. We've already told the state governor. Now we're just going to make it public."

Wallace said, "One of the joys I get in life is employing people. We've never shut a factory down. I really have difficulty doing it."

"Wallace, we've offered them all jobs, a lot of them are coming to Easton. The ones who aren't coming are getting a pretty good package."

After a long pause, Wallace told Cameron, "I'm going to think about it. If I don't call you back, go ahead with it. But I might be calling you back."

He didn't call back and the Washburn plant was closed. Meanwhile, production at Easton grew steadily and the factory needed labour. Most of the Washburn workers who at first had declined to work at Easton eventually took jobs there.

McCain continued to build its base in the U.S. Northeast. In 1987, it bought a large french fry plant in Presque Isle, Maine, from the J.R. Simplot Company. Three years previously, it had acquired Tater Meal, another company in the same town. Tater Meal

Wallace

Harold Durost, who worked for McCain Foods for twenty-seven years in Canada and the United States, remembers the day Wallace McCain came to Easton, Maine, for a monthly management meeting. "As was the custom, Wallace wanted a plant tour before we had lunch in the cafeteria," he recounts. "As we got to the stockroom, Wallace noticed the new McCain caps we had for sale and wanted one. As the plant manager scurried to get one for him, Wallace demanded to know the price. He made a point of paying the $5.

"This story went through the plant like wildfire the next day – that Wallace McCain was in the plant and had paid for his own McCain cap. The message was obvious: no matter who you are, you don't get treated any better or worse than the next person."

Wallace and Harrison inspired loyalty because their employees knew the brothers genuinely cared about them. When John Walsh had a serious illness in 1990, both bosses repeatedly called his wife, Sherry, to check on his condition. Says Walsh, "They told her that if we needed anything at all, to call them and it would be taken care of. There was never any question of when I was coming back to work. Their only concern was that I get better. They ended up flying us to London, Ontario, to see cardiac specialists there."

Wallace McCain became chairman of Maple Leaf Foods, Canada's largest food-processing company, in 1995. His son Michael became CEO in 1998. Wallace isn't involved in the day-to-day operations of the company and so has plenty of time for other activities, including fundraising for such favourite causes as Mount Allison University and the National Ballet School. He also serves on the boards of Brascan Corp. and Toronto's St. Michael's Hospital.

When Wallace turned seventy-six in 2006, he read that a man his age could expect to live to age eighty-four – eight more years. "So I made some changes. I booked more holidays. I don't do anything here at Maple Leaf Foods anyway. I go to meetings, I chair the board. I'm not running it day to day, so if I don't come to work, they don't miss me." In 2006 and 2007, Wallace and his wife, Margie, travelled to Europe and South America, and took a cruise on the Norwegian coast and another in the Caribbean.

But Wallace has not lost his taste for business. Most days finds him in his office at Maple Leaf Foods in midtown Toronto. "My memory isn't as good as it was. In the old days, I would know the price of potatoes in Australian dollars or in Dutch guilders. But I have to do something. As long as I've got a couple of marbles and am able to walk, I'll be coming to the office."

TOP: Wallace presents employee John Cox with a "Gold Cap" after a piece of steel slipped during construction and struck Cox's hard hat, in 1971. The New Brunswick Industrial Safety Council issued the hats at the request of a company when one of its workers had been saved by a hard hat from serious injury or death.
BOTTOM: Wallace, 2006.

made animal feed out of potato waste. Bill Mabee, who was director of finance for McCain USA at the time, says that purchase is a classic example of the management style that led to McCain's rapid growth.

Tater Meal was processing the potato waste from McCain's New Brunswick and Maine plants into animal feed. Mabee curled with the three brothers who owned the plant and he found out they were interested in selling. "We determined a fair price and I went to see Wallace about buying the business," recalls Mabee, who later went on to become vice-president of finance for the parent corporation. "We talked for ten minutes about the strategic value of that business and he said to me, 'Go buy it.'"

Ian Robinson, president of McCain USA potato division, c.1985.

McCain Foods got into the frozen juice business in Canada and the United States for very different reasons. In Canada, it had achieved a dominant position in french fries and used other frozen food categories for growth, scale with customers, and to utilize its existing distribution system. So it packed frozen juice at its plant in Grand Falls and bought the Sunny Orange juice factory in Toronto. In the United States, in contrast, its position in french fries was weak and there was no common distribution system to use. Nevertheless, since frozen juice had been a successful business at home, McCain thought it would work well south of the border as well. It seemed like a quick and easy way to grow.

Quick decision making is often lauded as a strength of the McCain management style. But sometimes decisions are made too quickly. The purchase by McCain in 1985 of Bodine's, a Chicago juice company, is a case in point. McCain, alerted by a Brazilian juice-concentrate supplier that Bodine's was for sale, had to act quickly, since ConAgra, a food industry giant, was also trying to buy the plant. Bodine's was the largest orange juice manufacturer in the Midwest. Owning it would give McCain a significant presence in the American industrial heartland, from which it could build its business, and it would give McCain much more purchasing scale with its Brazilian suppliers.

George McClure visited the plant and recommended that McCain make an offer. Although McCain knew Bodine's had been investigated by the U.S. Food and Drug Administration (FDA), it thought the problems had been resolved. Harrison flew to Chicago and made the deal quickly.

Shortly after the transaction closed, Wallace McCain toured the plant and noticed a set of water tanks. He asked what they were for and, to his amazement, the

McCain won a Supplier of the Year award from U.S. supermarket chain Kroger, c.1990; (left to right) Bob Hodge of Kroger, Michael McCain, Dick Owens of Kroger, and Richard Lan.

plant manager told him they were parts of a system used to adulterate the juice by adding artificial sugars, thereby substantially reducing the production cost. McCain found itself the new owner of a business based on outright fraud.

McCain immediately halted the adulteration, but now Bodine's was no longer profitable. The existing management was fired, and Wallace's son Michael became the president of the company, which was renamed McCain Citrus Inc.

Wayne Hanscom, who had worked for McCain in Australia, Europe, and Vancouver, had just settled in Toronto to start a new assignment when he was asked to go to Chicago to manage the financial affairs of the orange juice operation. What was supposed to be a one-year stay turned into a stay that lasted the duration of his career: Hanscom worked for McCain in Chicago until he retired in 2005.

Fixing the citrus business wasn't easy, he says. "The previous owners had put a lot of energy into being crooked. Once that had been stopped, the business's profitability didn't look so good."

"When we went to Chicago, it was immediately apparent that the entire place was totally corrupt," recalls Michael McCain. "They were adulterating the products in very sophisticated ways. The FDA was on the hunt to indict the former owners. We had to take them by the hand and show them how to accomplish this, including how to piece together the financial trail. The result was that roughly a year after Wayne and I arrived, the FDA went on air with what they described in their federal indictments as the biggest consumer fraud in American history. I remember CBS News arriving on our doorstep that day – it wasn't fun."

To help him turn around McCain Citrus, Michael relied on Hanscom and Richard Lan, who joined as vice-president of sales after McCain acquired his family's New Jersey–based juice business, Dell Products, in 1988. "We had to build an organization from scratch. It took us four years and lots of struggles to fix the business."

McCain immediately switched to producing pure orange juice that actually was pure. It bought some other juice businesses and added a line of Tetra Pak juice.

"In the tenacious McCain style, we battled on," says Hanscom. Eventually, McCain grew from being a small player to one of the biggest in the U.S. frozen private-label juice business.

The new McCain Citrus was a model of integrity. Harold Durost, who worked in senior positions for McCain USA for many years before retiring in 2005, attended a dinner during the 1980s with representatives of the insurance company managing the McCain pension. At the end of the dinner, someone from the insurance company tried to pay the bill, but Wayne Hanscom refused to let him pay for the McCain people who were present. "He was sending the message that his decision to buy services would be based on the best deal we could get, not on relationships or on perks like free meals," says Durost. "I think this was driven home by the examples Wallace and Harrison set and the code of conduct that they lived by and demanded their employees uphold."

Harold Durost, 2005.

"Our costs went way up because we were using real juice," says Hanscom. "By buying other companies and combining them, we got certain synergies. We kept working it and working it. In the end, we were good operators because we employed the high-volume, low-cost disciplines that had made the french fry businesses successful."

By the end of the 1980s, McCain Citrus had spent $31 million buying and upgrading plants, including building a new one in California. The company had won the acceptance of retailers who had once shunned it because of Bodine's tainted reputation. Major marketing campaigns were launched to establish branded retail beverages, the most successful of which were Boku and Junior Juice, in ready-to-drink Tetra Paks. In 1991, McCain Citrus made a profit for the first time and was profitable for most of the ensuing years.

The business had become "profitable and sustainable in a declining market," according to Richard Lan.

Until 1990, each of the three divisions of McCain USA – juice, pizza, and potatoes – had been reporting to Wallace directly. Harrison and Wallace agreed that there should be one head of the entire U.S. business, but Harrison did not support any of the three division presidents for the top job. After more than a year of searching, they had not found anyone from outside whom they trusted to both fit into the McCain culture and run the business. Finally, Wallace decided in the fall of 1991 to appoint Michael president and CEO of McCain USA. Richard Lan became president and CEO of McCain Citrus.

Michael McCain, 1993.

For all its efforts in the juice business, McCain never lost sight of its goal to become a big player in french fries in the United States. The original base in northern Maine had distribution advantages, but because of the agronomic limitations of the region and the processing technology of the time, french fries produced there weren't yet up to the standards of those produced in the western United States. McCain's first expansion outside the Northeast came in 1988 when it acquired potato baron Pete Taggares's French fry operations in Othello, in the prime potato-growing area of eastern Washington State, and in Clark, South Dakota. The following year, McCain spent $35 million to expand the Othello plant.

Earlier in 1988, McCain had lost out on a chance to become a major force in french fries overnight when Lamb Weston was put up for sale by its owner, Amfac. Wallace McCain, Tim Bliss, and Carl Morris toured all the Lamb Weston plants and recommended making a bid. However, Harrison did not think McCain had the management strength to absorb a company as big as Lamb Weston. And so, McCain did not make a competitive bid for Lamb Weston, and it went to ConAgra instead.

When Michael took it over in 1991, the U.S. business had just absorbed the western U.S. plants bought from Taggares. Michael was eager for more. The industry had added capacity, causing many competitors to favour volume over profit margins. Michael and his team proposed acquisitions that would have given the company the scale and product portfolio it needed to be competitive. They wanted to buy factories owned by Nestlé and another owned by Universal, which had an excellent assortment of innovative potato products. But, because of opposition from Harrison, these deals were not made.

As a result, McCain remained largely unknown in the United States, struggling to be profitable. Much of its sales were in the lower-priced private-label segments of the market. The more profitable premium market was still dominated by the big three. Michael McCain summarizes the problems in McCain's U.S. potato business at the time: "Low scale, no brand, poor product and customer mix, and many operating problems. Lamb Weston was mauling us in the marketplace. It had the brand, and it had a product mix that was giving it enormous advantage. Forty percent of its sales

LEFT: Tony Allen (centre) of Allen and Kidd Farms receives the 2004 McCain Idaho champion potato growers award; here with Laurie Jecha-Beard, vice-president of agriculture for McCain Foods USA, and Jerry Swisher, field representative for McCain Foods USA, in Burley, Idaho. RIGHT: Field manager Doug Nelson in Basset, Nebraska, 2000.

were in the new battered potato products and curly fries, with margins we believed to be exceeding 40 or 50 percent."

Lamb Weston was making so much money in the specialized segments that it could afford to be very competitive in pricing to protect its volumes in the conventional segment of the french fry market. "It had a classic mix advantage over us," says Michael. "Customer mix, product mix, and brand mix."

Michael McCain has a well-deserved reputation as a hard-driving executive who hates to lose. From McCain's U.S. headquarters outside Chicago, he and his team worked hard to build good relations with his customers. One of those customers was McDonald's. Michael established friendly relationships with members of the McDonald's management team. As Frank van Schaayk observed later, it was Michael who "turned the corner" for McCain with McDonald's for its North American business.

He also designed the landmark Argentina deal with McDonald's, that Wallace completed in 1993: an open price calculation with an agreed return on investment for McCain for a period, to entice McCain to build a plant in South America. (An open cost calculation is sometimes agreed to by a buyer and seller for a new product for which there is no historical cost of production or distribution. In this case, McCain required that all its costs plus a pre-agreed profit margin be guaranteed before it would build a plant. McDonald's thus had an incentive to buy more because a higher production volume would reduce the cost per unit.)

After almost five years at the helm of the U.S. business, Michael was fired by Harrison, in the wake of the split between the brothers, after which the Wallace McCain family acquired Maple Leaf Foods. Michael's new job was as the chief

Shepody harvest, western Idaho.

operating officer at Maple Leaf Foods, Canada's largest food company. His sixteen years at McCain Foods had prepared him for the challenge. "Most of my time at McCain was in very messy, turnaround situations," he says. "They were challenging, but also great learning experiences and opportunities to make a difference. The best part was the hundreds of committed, highly capable professional people I had the honour of working with."

When Lan followed Michael to Maple Leaf Foods, Peter Reijula, a veteran food industry executive and until then vice-president of sales of McCain Citrus Inc., took over as CEO of McCain Citrus.

In 2000, McCain, following its strategy of pursuing consolidation in the juice business, tried to buy its chief rival from a group of venture capitalists, who countered with a generous offer for McCain Citrus. That offer was accepted. In the end, McCain made a handsome return on its investment in the U.S. juice business. "We bought something that was trouble but did very well at it over time," says Hanscom.

When McCain Citrus was sold, McCain Foods, although a growing force in the United States in the french fry business, was still not a major player. This state of affairs would soon change.

One day in 1997, CEO Howard Mann was meeting with Harrison when the latter took a phone call from Wallace, who was passing on word from Michael McCain that the food service business of Ore-Ida, owned by H.J. Heinz Co., might be for sale. Both Wallace and Michael were now working for Maple Leaf Foods but, as shareholders, they continued to be interested in the well-being of McCain Foods. "Harrison promptly called Heinz chairman Tony O'Reilly, with whom he had had frequent personal contact over the years," recounts Mann. He wanted to know if Ore-Ida really was for sale.

O'Reilly said, "If you're interested, let's talk."

Harrison and Mann were soon on the McCain plane bound for Pittsburgh, world headquarters of Heinz. It was a trip that would vault McCain Foods into the major leagues of the U.S. food business. The $500 million purchase of the Ore-Ida food service business brought two major potato-processing plants and three appetizer factories into the McCain fold. The potato factories are located in Plover, Wisconsin, and in Burley, Idaho. The appetizer plants are in Fort Atkinson and Rice Lake, both in Wisconsin, and in Grand Island, Nebraska.

In 1997, Harrison McCain asked Gilles Lessard, then CEO of McCain's continental Europe operations, to go to the United States as chairman of McCain USA and supervise the integration of Ore-Ida. It was a big change for Lessard; in Europe, McCain was a strong player with a well-known brand, whereas in the United States, it was small and unknown. Fifteen other McCain executives arrived from around the world to help him.

At the time, Frank van Schaayk was global account manager for the McDonald's business, a job that Bob Cornella took over as corporate vice-president of the

TOP LEFT: Meeting of potato growers in Plover, Wisconsin, 2000.
TOP RIGHT: Bug's-eye view of Kerry Larson, McCain agronomist, in Wisconsin.
BOTTOM: Gilles Lessard, chairman McCain Foods USA, c.2000.

Mc²

In 1967, McDonald's raised its golden arches for the first time outside the United States – in the Vancouver suburb of Richmond. During one of his West Coast sales trips, Wallace McCain dropped in to have a look.

He remembers it well because customers were lined up waiting to get in. Nothing came of the visit, because all purchasing decisions at the time were made at the Chicago headquarters, and McDonald's was relying on a U.S. company to supply its french fries.

McCain's next encounter with McDonald's was even less auspicious. Wallace and Harrison met in Toronto in the early 1970s with Cal Goldstein, a McDonald's buyer, to see if McCain Foods could get some of McDonald's business. "We were cocky," says Wallace. "Harrison said, 'Give us your specifications, and we will make it.' They wanted to have a tour of the Grand Falls plant and come to see the lab. We said, 'We know how to make french fries, we don't need you to tour our plant or lab.' After that, we did not get a call for ten years."

Mac McCarthy made the first McCain sale to McDonald's, completing a deal in 1977 to supply the chain's continental European and British restaurants with McCain-made MacFries.

Howard Mann, who became CEO of McCain in 1995, worked hard to make McDonald's a core business. McCain and McDonald's have since cemented a strong global partnership. McCain supplies McDonald's restaurants in sixty-two countries and is the largest producer of MacFries.

Ray Kroc, founder of the McDonald's chain, believed in what he called the "three-legged stool," referring to McDonald's, its franchisees, and its suppliers working together as partners. "What started with a handshake has grown into a global partnership – a premier example of how a world-class supplier can enhance the strength of the three-legged foundation of the McDonald's system," said McDonald's CEO Jim Skinner and Frank Muschetto, senior vice-president and chief purchasing officer, in a joint statement to mark McCain's fiftieth anniversary.

Robert Cornella, an entrepreneur who built Good Stuff into the second-largest privately held bakery company in the United States, joined McCain in 2000 to take charge of the relationship as global vice-president of the McDonald's Worldwide Business Unit. Previously, he says, the relationship had been one of convenience: if both companies happened to be in the same place, they did business. Cornella's job is to build and maintain a worldwide partnership between the two.

McCain and McDonald's are a good fit because both are obsessive about the quality of the potatoes used to make french fries. "Identifying the right potato for the right conditions is what separates McCain from many other companies," says McDonald's agronomist Dell Thornley, who worked for Simplot before joining McDonald's in 1989. At the time, McDonald's was pushing to get Russet Burbank potatoes grown in Europe, but the growers were not enthusiastic.

Thornley recalls that two McCain experts, Han van den Hoek in the Netherlands and Tom Matthews in the United Kingdom, were instrumental in getting Russet Burbank seed production in Europe started, although both were skeptical that the variety could be successfully grown there. "Once they saw that we were not going to take no for an answer and that the only way to supply McDonald's was to grow the Russets, the program took off," says Thornley.

TOP LEFT: Bob Cornella on his Harley-Davidson in front of the Hinsdale, Illinois, McDonald's.

McDonald's business unit in 2000. In 2005, Van Schaayk took over as CEO of McCain USA when Lessard retired. Van Schaayk says it's tough to succeed in the world's biggest market unless you are big. That's why the Ore-Ida deal was pivotal. "Scale matters in the United States to a greater degree than anywhere else in the world," he says. A small player can survive if it has a unique product and is able to maintain that uniqueness or if it has some other advantage. But if your product is french fries, which are not unique, "you had better have scale so that you can hold your own against the bigger buyers and somehow equalize the leverage that will be applied against you."

The most common query after the purchase was, "Who was it that bought Ore-Ida?" Those in the food service industry who asked this question were amazed to learn that McCain Foods is the world's largest processor of frozen potato products, with factories all over the globe. Once they had digested that news, they would say, "So what are you going to do for me in the United States?"

McCain had proven itself elsewhere and now it finally had the scale to show what it could do in the United States. As Tom Albrecht, then vice-president of purchasing for McDonald's, commented, "You have now Americanized your business."

But, given the difficulties involved in absorbing a business bigger than itself, success was not going to come easily. At the time, McCain USA had annual sales of U.S.$325 million; the Ore-Ida division it had acquired had sales of U.S.$550 million. "People knew it would be the biggest integration that McCain ever did," says Van Schaayk, "but I don't think any of us really understood the challenge of an integration of that magnitude."

When the deal closed on July 1, 1997, McCain's immediate task was to extricate the Ore-Ida food service business from Heinz and into McCain's systems. "There was

TOP: Othello trim room, 1962.
BOTTOM: Frank van Schaayk, 2006.

SOUTH OF THE BORDER 177

LEFT: Randy Myles (left) vice-president of finance and CFO, McCain Foods USA, with Randy Wieland, senior vice-president, food service sales, McCain Foods USA.
RIGHT: Research and development at the Othello, Washington, plant. Bill Skorick and Sharon Nelson are on the left; Liz Jensen, research and development manager, is on the right.

great fanfare on December 1 when it came onto our system," says Van Schaayk. But the excitement quickly turned to disappointment when the service levels of the former Ore-Ida division plummeted overnight. "It was almost a catastrophe. There were so many things that had not been understood and anticipated as large issues. People were just overwhelmed."

The case fill rate fell to the mid-seventies, meaning that if a customer ordered one hundred cases of product, only about seventy-five got delivered – an unacceptably poor level of service. This was because of several problems, including information technology issues, organization of the sales force, production planning, and inadequate forecasting.

The Ore-Ida acquisition forced McCain to upgrade its entire business system to a different standard. "It made us get better in all areas of the business," says Van Schaayk. Before the acquisition, McCain was the fifth-largest potato company in the United States, points out David Sanchez, who became vice-president for integration in 1997 to supervise the integration of Ore-Ida. "Our systems and processes were extremely weak. It was an around-the-clock fight for four to five months just to do the basics of shipping product and collecting money. In the meantime, the factories got completely out of control, and we ended up with three hundred million pounds of inventory, most of it stuff we did not need." For example, McCain had a two-year supply of one product that had a shelf life of only eighteen months.

Integrating systems is hard, but integrating people and company cultures is even harder. The Ore-Ida organization, says Van Schaayk, "had a culture closer to what you would expect from a corporate food company like Heinz – it had deeper training, it was well organized, it had high expectations for personal growth, and it was dealing with a greater number of premium customers. It was a real scramble to get in front of

that sales force, to begin to paint a picture of what McCain could be with its help, to begin to try to energize that group and get it excited about helping build McCain as a premier food service business in the United States."

Randy Wieland, who as of 2007 was senior vice-president of food service sales for McCain USA, is a U.S. food industry veteran who joined McCain in 1991. He met with each Ore-Ida salesperson individually. His goal was to inform the sales force of McCain's global scale, explain how the company operated, and have it embrace the challenge of building McCain into a great U.S. food company.

To help the new arrivals to the company better grasp what McCain was all about, several of the key Ore-Ida people were brought to Florenceville for a sales planning meeting in the boardroom. Florenceville is a rural village, but the illuminated map on the wall of the boardroom impressively displays a McCain world that spans the globe. Harrison McCain spoke passionately to the group about the company and its ambitious plans for the U.S. operations. The point of the exercise was to convince the Ore-Ida people that they had joined not a small U.S. frozen food company but a major international frozen food company. "I think the people at Ore-Ida were surprised at the roll-up-your-sleeves attitude at McCain and the involvement of senior management in all aspects of the business," says Randy Myles, vice-president and chief financial officer of McCain USA.

Most of the people who came on that trip to Florenceville were still working for McCain USA in 2007, several of them in high-level positions in the food service sales force. The larger scale that came with the Ore-Ida acquisition had another important impact on McCain USA. It meant that the U.S. company could justify recruiting top personnel from other parts of the global McCain organization.

TOP LEFT: Rice Lake, Wisconsin, appetizer plant: Theresa Schultz and Sherri Becker position onions for cutting.
TOP RIGHT: Amy Christensen and Cindy Payne check product in the quality-control lab at the Grand Island, Nebraska, appetizer plant.
BOTTOM: Poppers – stuffed and breaded jalapeño peppers – are a popular Anchor finger food.

ABOVE: McCain's U.S. head-office employees work in a modern building in the Chicago suburb of Lisle.

BELOW: McCain has a wide range of speciality potato and sweet potato products.

The Ore-Ida employees who stayed with us were, in general, very happy with the change in style," reports Sanchez. "You could not ask for two more contrasting styles than us and Heinz. Heinz was slow, did not take risks, was overly analytical and fairly political. Almost everyone who came over, mainly in production and sales, thrived in the McCain culture."

As well as inheriting skeptical employees, McCain inherited skeptical customers, such as Sysco, the largest U.S. food service distributor. "The challenge over the next few years, from 1998 to 2001, was to establish ourselves in the marketplace as people who could produce good product, get it to where it needed to be, and help our customers build their business," says Van Schaayk.

McCain has succeeded brilliantly in winning the confidence of Sysco. Every year, Sysco selects the top one hundred manufacturers, whose representatives are invited to a banquet in Houston. The winners are chosen on the basis of quality, fill rates, and sales and marketing support. McCain finished among the top five in three of the years from 2002 to 2006 and is almost always in the top ten.

In addition to the Ore-Ida purchase, McCain spent $70 million in 1978 to expand the Easton plant, doubling its capacity. Between 1998 and 2005, it completely renovated all its U.S. potato facilities. As a result, McCain has become the second-largest french fry processor in the United States. And its U.S. business encompasses much more than standard french fries. The wide variety of other products includes Sweet Potato fries and Baby Cakes. The latter is a small, homestyle potato pancake made

The executive team of McCain Foods USA, 2007. Front row: (seated left to right) Chuck Gitkin, Des Doucette, Anne Linsdau, Patrick Davis, Laurie Jecha-Beard, Randy Wieland, Randy Myles. Back row: Keith Orchard, Peter Reijula, David Cowperthwait, Frank van Schaayk, Dan Dolan, Kevin Burdett.

for the restaurant industry that was given the grand prize for best new product by a chefs association in 2004. "That's a particularly pleasing award," says Van Schaayk, "because chefs, the actual users of the product, are saying, 'This is a great product.'"

Because of the sharp regional differences in the United States, some products have appeal in certain areas but not in others. Fried okra, for example, was popular in Georgia and other parts of the South but so difficult to sell anywhere else that McCain dropped it. Shredded hash browns are a bestseller in the west but a non-seller in the east. "They're a western breakfast thing," Van Schaayk explains.

"The biggest mistake people make is coming to the United States and thinking it's one culture. It's not. The Deep South is completely different from Minnesota, and Seattle is different from southern California. There are different ethnic roots, different eating styles, different consumer styles."

As chairman Allison McCain points out, McCain got into appetizers almost by accident, and yet now the category is a large and growing part of its business. When Ore-Ida decided to sell its food service potato business, it insisted that the buyer take its appetizer business as well. McCain wasn't sure it wanted to. McCain's strategy had been to grow into a major player in french fries, not to enter into a category it didn't know. Moreover, it didn't understand the economics of appetizers. The financial

ABOVE: Moore's jalapeño onion rings, and Brew City battered appetizers, acquisitions in the Ore-Ida purchase.

McCain desserts for the food service trade: Bananas Foster Cheesecake Bites, fresh-frozen fruit, and New York Style Cheesecake Bites – delicious paired with ice cream.

analyses McCain had done didn't fully reveal their strategic and financial contribution to Ore-Ida's business. As it turned out, appetizers were a great companion sale with the potato products.

The appetizer "accident" has turned into a big success for McCain that provides the company with welcome additional diversification from its potato business and excellent growth prospects. Many of McCain's appetizer and snack products are customized and thus difficult for competitors to duplicate. All this adds up to competitive advantage.

McCain quickly realized this was a business worth expanding, and it began hunting for more companies to buy. In 2001, it acquired the food service business and factories of a family-owned business, Anchor Food Products, in a three-party transaction in which Heinz bought Anchor's retail brands. Included in the deal was the main Anchor factory in Appleton, Wisconsin, which, in 2003, received an $18 million upgrade.

The Anchor acquisition was relatively easy for McCain to absorb, as by then McCain USA had developed deeper management strength. "Again, I think they were all surprised at the family culture of McCain and the willingness for all levels of management to be involved in the business," says Randy Myles.

The Anchor purchase turned McCain into the world's largest appetizer company. CEO Howard Mann asked Lessard to make the Anchor purchase part of a new company-wide strategy. "There is great potential in finger food products," Lessard said in 2003. "We are well on our way to growing this business worldwide."

Two of the former Ore-Ida appetizer plants are also located in Wisconsin. "The appetizer business started there as an offshoot of companies that battered fish out of the Great Lakes," explains Peter Reijula, who became president of McCain Snack Foods when McCain reorganized its U.S. business into snack foods and potato divisions. "When that battered fish business declined in the 1960s and 1970s, companies like Anchor started looking to extend their business. From battering fish, it wasn't a long leap to battering cheese."

While McCain often applies its brand to newly acquired businesses, the Ore-Ida brands were too well known to discard. For example, Moore's, one of the Ore-Ida brands, was recognized as the company that invented the onion ring. Another brand acquired in the Ore-Ida deal was Brew City, a line of appetizers, such as Spanish onions, jalapeño peppers, and french fries battered in a beer-flour combination, that are a staple in many U.S. bars.

Executive chefs John DaLoia and Brooke Brantley of McCain Foods USA, stay on top of consumer preferences, creating menu dishes and presentations to pass on to McCain's restaurant clients.

McCain also retained Anchor as a brand, because, says Reijula, it was so well respected in the restaurant industry. "Anchor was very much a leader in the appetizer food service business," he explains. "Their marketing practices were on the leading edge. They were a leader in the sale of value-added appetizer products. We wanted to keep that legacy alive and we wanted to lift McCain by associating with that brand. Purchasing Anchor elevated McCain Foods. All of a sudden we became much better known and much better recognized. We have won a number of industry awards that we never could have contended for before."

A research and development team at the Anchor factory in Appleton works to satisfy the restaurant chains, which have an insatiable demand for new products. As Reijula points out, "Applebee's doesn't want to sell what the other chains sell. What research and development does is customize for large chain accounts. It's hard to match our scale. And when you add customization to that scale, it's an unbeatable combination." Scale allows McCain to serve large chains and customization protects it from competition. That's why appetizers have become key to the profitability of the U.S. company.

As part of its commitment to the snack category, McCain bought two Canadian companies specializing in Asian frozen foods and, in 2002, acquired Taiwan's largest producer of frozen Chinese dumplings from Goodman Fielder International. In 2006, McCain USA bought a California-based, family-owned firm, Jon-Lin Foods. It produces a range of frozen appetizers, including sautéed, grilled, fire-roasted, and smokehouse-roasted vegetables. Jon-Lin fits neatly into McCain's business strategy of diversification.

McCain acquired the Jon-Lin appetizer business of California in 2006.

It also responds to consumers' health concerns because its products are neither breaded nor battered.

The Jon-Lin deal is also a good example of the advantages of growth through acquisition: McCain acquired intellectual capital that it could not quickly have duplicated on its own. Anyone with a barbecue can roast a red pepper. But how do you produce excellent frozen grilled red peppers in large quantities? "The owner and the other people in this company have through trial and error spent years learning how to do it," says Reijula. That's why Jon-Lin can supply such customers as the Subway restaurant chain, with its thousands of outlets.

Another 2006 addition to McCain USA's growing snack food category was Indiana-based Kempco, which makes pigs in a blanket and other snacks wrapped in dough.

Van Schaayk and Reijula, as of 2007 vice-president for corporate development for McCain USA, look for small businesses that, like Jon-Lin, have unique products based on their own intellectual capital. Typically, Reijula says, "the business is not publicly for sale. There are no prospectuses to see. There is no investment banker to spin it. It's you and the guy who has built the business with his own head and hands. You test the product and eventually he lets you look at the books."

In its early years, McCain would not have been interested in buying a roasted vegetable company in California or a Chinese-food company in Taiwan. But times – and consumers – change, and companies have to change too if they wish to grow and prosper.

"The contrasts between the typical household when Harrison and Wallace started to build the business and the typical household today are just gigantic," says Van Schaayk, who presides over the U.S. business from McCain's modern office building in Lisle, Illinois, one of Chicago's outer suburbs. "Peoples' demand for convenience because of the hectic pace of their lifestyles is greater than ever, and their knowledge about the food that they eat – what's good for them and what's not – has increased enormously."

Chef Sensations: roasted vegetables and fruits are a growing part of McCain's business.

Van Schaayk sees no contradiction between the increased health consciousness of the consumer and the continued growth of fast food chains. Because people are in a hurry, they continue to patronize these restaurants. But they expect the meals they purchase there to be good for them. In other words, the delivery mechanism – the quick-service restaurant – is here to stay. It's the food that is delivered there that is changing.

The United States, because of its wealth, size, and innovative business culture, is often where new consumer trends start. Van Schaayk remembers travelling as a teenager to the Netherlands and seeing Dutch teenagers wearing sweatshirts bearing the crests of various U.S. universities. "They were Europeans, but they aspired to certain things in American life," he says. "There is no question that the export of the American lifestyle has benefited the growth of McCain globally and still does."

By the end of the 1990s, McCain had achieved its long-standing goal of becoming a major force in the home of the modern fast food industry. McCain USA had become the largest of McCain's worldwide operations, in fiscal 2006 accounting for 32 percent of McCain's sales worldwide. Its new-found prominence in the United States gave McCain an even stronger base from which to continue its expansion around the globe. In the first decade of the new century, huge countries such as China and India were being transformed by rapid economic growth. For McCain, that meant there were more worlds to conquer.

CHAPTER SEVEN

NEW WORLDS TO CONQUER

It's not easy to sell frozen vegetables if most of your potential customers think frozen vegetables are the less desirable parts left over after fresh vegetables have been prepared.

That was just one of the problems McCain Foods had to deal with when it began doing business in South Africa in 2001. Another was that 30 percent of South Africans live in communities without electricity, so they can't operate freezers even if they could afford them.

These were problems McCain had never before encountered in four decades of expanding from its Canadian base to the rest of the world. What to do? What McCain has always done – drink the local wine.

Drinking the local wine means understanding and adapting to the circumstances of the market you are trying to enter. In the first decade of the twenty-first century, McCain is getting established in South Africa, India, China, and many other countries where cultural practices, including culinary ones, differ from those in North America and Europe. The objective is to get the local people to accept McCain as one of their own rather than view it as a foreign intruder.

One way to do that in South Africa, McCain discovered, was to offer free samples of McCain products at funerals. While this would be a poor marketing strategy in North America or Europe, it works brilliantly in South Africa. "The black community makes a huge thing of funerals," explains marketing director Heather Partner, who has played a pivotal role in introducing McCain to South Africa, a developing country of forty-four million people. She points out that as many as two thousand people might show up at a funeral in a black community such as Soweto. The bereaved family is expected to feed its guests, putting a major strain on its finances. "They prepare

FACING PAGE: Sharon Kamfer at broccoli harvest time in South Africa.

McCain helps feed mourners at a South African funeral.

feasts. It's very traditional. The women in the family spend the week before the event preparing the food. That's where McCain comes in."

A company team will arrive at the home of the deceased early on the morning of the funeral to pitch a tent displaying the black-and-yellow McCain logo. McCain provides cups and cutlery as well as frozen vegetables for the meal. Not only does the family benefit, but the women from the local community who help out are spared hours of peeling and cooking vegetables.

It's a more persuasive way of getting the McCain message out to the public than a TV ad. "We're a new brand and we need to get involved in the community," says Partner. "International visitors think it's rude to be promoting at a funeral, but in South African culture that's not the case. It's almost like a nod that you've made it if you've got McCain participating at your wedding or funeral or tombstone unveiling. It allows us to demonstrate how well our product fits into people's lives."

Owen Porteus, an Australian who came to South Africa on a temporary assignment and wound up staying on as managing director, was at first taken aback by the idea: "If anybody had told me I would be in the funeral business, I would have said, 'You're crazy.' But culture isn't so simple."

The only way to prove that McCain vegetables are not the off-cuts of fresh vegetables was to get people to try them. "We had to do one-on-one communication," explains Partner. "We go into the townships and we have tea parties. We'll get a hostess to invite twenty of her friends on a Saturday afternoon, and then we'll go in and do a cook-up. And we'll allow the consumers to cook and eat the product.

"We go to the schools as well, where we have junior chef competitions. The kids

McCain is a major contributor to school lunch programs in South Africa.

come up with recipes and menus using our product and they do a cook-up. We had the finals on national TV."

In addition, McCain gives potato flakes (dehydrated potatoes that can be reconstituted into mashed potatoes) and vegetables to charities that together provide seventy thousand free meals a month to needy children. The McCain products are combined with main dishes to make complete meals.

A good place to catch consumers in a good mood is on the beach during one of South Africa's many statutory holidays. One campaign featured a huge chip truck decorated with billboards displaying well-shaped young bodies. The point, says Partner, was that "you can be very healthy and have beautiful bodies if you eat oven-baked chips." (In South Africa, as in Britain and Australia, french fries are called chips.)

"We hit the beaches during the day. People who work for us who have magnificent bodies walk on the beaches serving chips. At night we go into the clubs and have our DJs promoting the product, giving away McCain T-shirts and beach balls."

McCain's success in South Africa is a textbook example both of the "drink the local wine" philosophy and of how the company can benefit from leveraging its global strength. McCain experts in agriculture, information technology, engineering, production, sales, and finance came from Canada, Britain, Australia, and the Netherlands. Some stayed in South Africa for a few weeks, others for a few years. And they got McCain South Africa off to a flying start.

The groundwork for McCain's South African venture was laid in the mid-1990s when George McClure's corporate development team was looking at several countries as possible sites for expansion. After some discussion in the department, Mark McCain, one of the corporate development executives at the time, was assigned South Africa as the country he would study.

It was an exciting time to go to South Africa. Nelson Mandela had been freed from prison in 1990, becoming the country's first democratically elected president in 1994.

LEFT: Mark McCain (centre) chats with Anton Haverkort (right), scientific reviewer of McCain agriculture programs around the world.

RIGHT: Andy Goodwin (left), then director of agriculture McCain South Africa, at the signing of an agreement with Technico, an Australian company, to provide pea-size micro-tubers to produce seed potatoes in South Africa.

Democracy meant the end of apartheid and, consequently, of the country's economic isolation. The result, the corporate development team believed, would be accelerated economic development. "It was the dawn of a new age," says Mark McCain, who is a son of Harrison.

Travelling around South Africa, he met with people involved in the restaurant and retail sides of the food business, as well as economic staff of the Canadian Embassy, local banks, government bodies, non-governmental organizations, and the census bureau chief for demographic information. "I was trying to get a feel for the market and the potential," he explains.

Once the corporate development team decided the market was promising, Mark began studying the all-important agricultural side. If McCain was going to open a factory to make french fries and other frozen products, it would need a steady local supply of high-quality raw materials.

South Africa grows potatoes all year round but not the preferred varieties that McCain uses in other countries to meet its international standard of french fries. So the next step was developing seed potatoes of the preferred varieties and propagating seed in different parts of the country. Like the United Kingdom, South Africa prohibits importation of potatoes except with a special permit, under quarantine, and in very small volumes. Han van den Hoek, an agriculture expert from the Netherlands, now vice-president of agriculture for continental Europe, came to help in the agricultural experiments.

The next step was to buy or build a processing facility. Irvin & Johnson, a South African conglomerate that was one of the Southern Hemisphere's largest fish companies, also owned a frozen vegetable division and a new french fry factory. But Irvin

McCain TV commercial: "Life's too short to peel a pea."

& Johnson wasn't interested in selling. "We danced around with them for about five years," says Mark. Once McCain decided it wasn't getting anywhere with Irvin & Johnson, it started looking for a building site. "When we started looking for a site, we kind of made some noise. I don't know if that scared them or if there were other factors, but they came to the table and we did a deal."

In 2000, after negotiations led by Terry Bird, who had replaced McClure as head of corporate development, McCain bought Irvin & Johnson's french fry plant, as well as two frozen vegetable plants. Then there was another important decision to make. Irvin & Johnson was well established as a frozen food brand in South Africa, whereas McCain was unknown. How to switch to the McCain brand without losing Irvin & Johnson customers?

Partner's first priority was to establish a positive image of McCain in the minds of South African consumers. The company did extensive consumer research, which revealed that homemakers would respond to a realistic depiction of their lifestyles. The message McCain got from its research, Partner says, was "Don't portray me as the paragon of virtue who is waiting for her husband with her lipstick on and the children with their hair brushed and the perfectly balanced meal on the table. Portray my life as it is and show how McCain fits into that hectic role."

So that's what McCain's first TV commercials did. They showed a woman working and trying to run a home and feed a family. At the end, the commercial said, "Life's too short to peel a pea … Think again. Think McCain." The response was overwhelmingly positive. And the catchy slogan, "Think again. Think McCain," which conveys the idea of rethinking false attitudes to frozen vegetables, has become well known in South Africa.

Yet at the beginning, McCain was nervous about too quickly abandoning the Irvin & Johnson brand, rated in an annual survey as the ninth best-known food brand in South Africa. So it decided on a one-year policy of co-branding – putting both brand

Food for Love, a South African TV series, follows the adventures of a McCain chef.

names on the package along with a message explaining that McCain had bought Irvin & Johnson's frozen food business and intended to maintain the high quality customers expected.

Partner, who is South African and had come to McCain from Irvin & Johnson, was in charge of implementing the co-branding project. "Our consumers had experienced the overnight deletion of well-known brands and the introduction of global brands without any warning, and our research showed that they found this very irritating," she says.

The co-branding was accompanied by the new McCain advertising and many new product launches, all of which sparked interest among shoppers in the frozen food category. The McCain launch was so successful that the co-branding was ended after only three months instead of twelve, as had originally been planned.

One of McCain's best marketing ploys was to buy some time on the South African national television system to carry a soap opera, *Food for Love,* about the romantic adventures of Ben, a recipe developer for McCain Foods. But McCain also got TV exposure by making news. That happened when it opened its new head office in Bedfordview, a suburb of Johannesburg. McCain wanted to put up billboards but couldn't because its building is located on a freeway. However, there were no restrictions on what could be put up above the building, so McCain erected five three-metre-high scarecrows on the roof with a wraparound on the building showing fresh vegetables.

As a result, everyone driving to and from the Johannesburg airport gets the message that McCain is taking good care of fresh vegetables. "That got us onto national TV," laughs Partner.

Mark McCain, who became chairman of McCain Foods (South Africa) Ltd. when the company was established in 1996, is optimistic because he sees the same trends occurring in South Africa in the early years of the twenty-first century that were so favourable to McCain in Canada when the company was launched in 1957. More fast food restaurants are being built, more and more people have greater disposable

Scarecrows atop McCain's office building near Johannesburg.

income, and the number of dual-income families is increasing, thereby creating new demand for convenience foods.

In addition, more homes are getting hooked up to electricity service, allowing more South Africans to own fridges, stoves, and microwaves. "The growth is coming from the people who are moving up the social ladder," says Mark McCain.

McCain did not let the absence of electricity in South Africa hold it back. "Drink the local wine" means adapting, so the company also offers small frozen vegetable packets intended to be used immediately. It's not just lack of electricity that necessitates small packages but also lack of money. Porteus points out that yogurt was not accepted by South African consumers until it was packaged in a cup and sold for one rand, the equivalent of about seventeen Canadian cents. "People have enough money for food for today, not for tomorrow, so you have to sell them just enough for today."

Irvin & Johnson had not targeted what Partner calls "the emerging markets." All of its advertising was aimed at higher income groups. "So you've got a black consumer who has never bought a frozen product before, and all of our packs are opaque. There was this question of why they were opaque and what were we trying to hide. People couldn't risk the fifteen rand to buy the product, in case it didn't perform. It has taken a lot of money and a lot of resources to communicate that we have only the best inside the bag."

Sales of the former Irvin & Johnson potato and vegetable businesses have tripled since McCain took them over and not just as a result of improved marketing. "Irvin & Johnson had good people, but those people had no access to up-to-date technology," says Porteus. "They had no access to proper management systems. They were starved of those assets. Soon after we took over, we called together all the senior management

Employees of McCain South Africa.

people from Irvin & Johnson, and it struck me that they were just dying for information. It was as if we had opened the windows and doors and let in the light."

Suddenly, they had all the knowledge of one of the world's top frozen food companies available to them. In addition to being able to learn from the various McCain specialists who travelled to South Africa, a manager could pick up the phone and call anyone in the worldwide McCain organization whenever advice was needed.

McCain now operates three South African production facilities. The Delmas potato plant and Springs vegetable-processing plant are both close to Johannesburg. The third factory, also for vegetables, is in George on the South Coast.

McCain used to operate frozen vegetable plants in Canada, Britain, the Netherlands, and Belgium but, as of 2007, the only McCain companies producing vegetables were those in Australia and South Africa. The South African operation benefits from the expertise of Porteus, who managed the frozen potato and vegetable plant in Smithton, Tasmania, before coming to South Africa.

"Australia and South Africa are very different markets," Porteus says. "South Africa has a small top-end market and a large low-end market. It is both a developed and an emerging market in one country. So it should be an excellent learning experience for McCain going into other emerging markets."

McCain's South African venture had all the ingredients for success from the beginning. It was able to buy an existing business that already had the largest market share and had good local staff. By augmenting the staff and upgrading the plant, McCain quickly created a profitable business. The South African government welcomed new investors. And because most South Africans speak English, they could easily benefit from knowledge that McCain people around the world were happy to share.

Pea harvesting.

On the downside, agriculture in South Africa is often problematic. "We've gone from extreme drought to heavy rains to very cold weather," says Porteus. "We've lost a lot of crops. If you are looking at countries that are ideal for growing potatoes, this is not one of them."

Some farms in South Africa are big, but many have too small a potato acreage to be effective suppliers, so McCain has to grow some of its potatoes and vegetables itself. McCain farms twelve hundred hectares on five farming operations around South Africa. The locations, selected for seasonal growing conditions, produce about 40 percent of the South African company's potato requirements.

In 2003, the South African government passed the Broad-Based Black Economic Empowerment Act with the aim of promoting equal opportunity and increasing the participation of the country's black majority in the economy. McCain has embraced this goal in the agricultural sector, says Tim Hedges, vice-president of agriculture for McCain South Africa. "We are able to do this by supporting newly established black farming operations. The most successful to date is the Makhatini Cotton farming project in Northern Kwazulu Natal, where we plant an average of one hundred hectares of potatoes per year in the frost-free area. The technology transfer, job creation, and skills development as a result of our involvement has been very beneficial for the community and the operation. And we are involved in four other farming operations that have been acquired through redistribution of farming land to help black agricultural empowerment."

As of 2007, black farmers were contributing 10 percent of McCain's potato needs, but the company expects their contribution to reach 40 percent by 2014. The rest of the potato supply comes from white farmers and the farms McCain operates.

Management, McCain South Africa, 2006.
Front row: (left to right) Gavin Naisby, Owen Porteus, Anthony Cripwell, Heather Partner.
Back row: S.J. de Klerk, Dan Leger, Ron Mander, Bert Weenink, Tim Hedges.

An important contributor to McCain's efforts to obtain good raw materials from South African farms was Andy Goodwin, who first travelled through the country in 1996 when McCain was searching for the best potato-growing areas. He moved to South Africa from Britain with his wife and two young children in 1997 to become chief agronomist. He played an important role in selecting the processing varieties best suited to South African conditions and worked with growers to teach them how best to grow those varieties. Goodwin became agriculture director for South Africa before returning to the United Kingdom in 2006 to become director of corporate agriculture in charge of strategic initiatives.

McCain South Africa exports to other African countries, usually in the wake of local retailers expanding there. It's not easy, as the logistics are challenging. Shipping companies and customers don't always understand that frozen food has to stay frozen. The result is sometimes what Porteus calls "thermally abused" product that has been left on a dock in the hot sun, rendering it inedible.

Sub-Saharan Africa has 650 million people, a potential market too large for McCain to ignore. The solid base it has built in South Africa will help it penetrate more of that market if and when more African countries enjoy political stability and economic development. It may take years until the rest of Africa is ready for McCain. What's certain is that McCain will be ready for Africa.

The "drink the local wine" philosophy is fundamental to the worldwide success of McCain Foods. George McClure explains it this way: "We didn't have an ego when we went into a country. Whether it was Great Britain, the Netherlands, or South America, we didn't go in with the attitude, 'Well, we know more about growing potatoes, we know more about processing potatoes then anybody else.' We went in and said, 'Let's just watch and learn and see what they're doing.' So we watched them grow the potatoes and we watched them process them and we then said, 'Well, here is an area where we can make some improvements.' We went in with an open mind, and I think that's primarily what Harrison and Wallace meant when they spoke about drinking the local wine."

Traditional potato growing in Argentina: rows of corn are grown in between potatoes so the stalks can be used at harvest time to cover the potatoes, which are stored in the field in piles.

"To drink the local wine literally was not hard in Argentina," says Ghislain Pelletier, who went there in 1992 to help McCain establish a potato-processing business in South America. "And the people were warm and welcoming. It was an opportunity to learn about another culture and another language. My wife and I and our two kids have become fluent in Spanish."

Pelletier, a native of Grand Falls, New Brunswick, worked for that province's agriculture department as a potato specialist before accepting a two-year posting to Jordan for a seed potato project sponsored by the Canadian International Development Agency. When the Gulf War broke out, the project was shelved. But Pelletier and his wife, Suzanne, were determined to see the world before their two young children went into school. Also, Pelletier knew there was plenty to learn about agriculture that he couldn't learn in New Brunswick. So he decided to explore the opportunities at McCain Foods.

He went to see Wallace McCain, who told him that the company was eyeing three regions for future growth: East Germany, New Zealand, and South America. Wallace told Pelletier, "I am going to send you there, young guy. You are going to travel the world. But first I am going to send you to Nebraska."

McCain was considering setting up a factory in Nebraska, and it also had a study in progress on growing potatoes under irrigation on four hundred hectares of farmland it had rented. "You measure the water in the soil, and when the soil reaches a

Manual harvesting and bagging seed potatoes in a field near Balcarce.

certain level of water content, you irrigate," explains Pelletier. "That was my apprenticeship in the science of irrigation."

From Nebraska, Pelletier moved on to Othello, Washington, where McCain did have a factory. One day, he received a phone call from Wallace. He said, "Ghislain, when you and I talked last year, you told me you wanted to see the world. Well, I have something for you today."

Pelletier asked, "Where?"

Wallace replied, "Argentina. You talk to your wife tonight and give me a call tomorrow."

Pelletier, eager for travel, accepted the assignment. His task would be to report on where McCain should locate a South American plant. First, Pelletier went to Florenceville to be briefed by Bob Coston, an executive who had been hired from Nestlé to manage the South America program in its initial stages, and by Tony van Leersum, who had years of experience in South America. Then the Pelletier family, with eleven suitcases and a couple of Spanish dictionaries, left for Argentina.

He wasn't the first McCain employee to explore South America. George McClure had investigated the business and economic environment of the continent, assisted by Don Young, who looked at the agricultural side. Also, McCain Produce for some years had barter arrangements with South American companies in which it exchanged seed potatoes for fresh fruit and vegetables. As for Van Leersum, he had travelled there on sales trips when working for a Dutch company before joining McCain. He was acquainted with some South American growers, including the largest farm co-operative in Brazil. Both Van Leersum and McCain agronomist Han van den Hoek had made many trips to Brazil and Argentina to

help McDonald's obtain better fresh potatoes when the chain was still producing fries in its restaurants.

The issue for McCain was which of the two major markets in South America to choose as the site for a plant: Brazil or Argentina. McDonald's favoured Brazil because it has more customers – a population of 180 million, compared with Argentina's 40 million. The consensus of McCain's experts, including Pelletier, was that Brazil is a better place for growing oranges than potatoes. The climate is too hot for potatoes, there are more pests, and the yields aren't as good as those of Argentina, which has better soil conditions and cooler nights.

McCain settled on Balcarce, a city of forty thousand people about five hundred kilometres south of Buenos Aires, as the site for its new plant. Not only is Balcarce on the outer circle of the area Pelletier had identified as good potato-growing country, it has an agriculture faculty. "The city is home to many agronomists," says Pelletier. "Even the mayor is an agronomist."

Pelletier hired local talent to work on McCain's agricultural program, which involved visiting growers and persuading them to grow good processing potatoes. Gustavo Scioli, one of the agronomists hired, was the son of a local grower.

The most popular locally grown variety was the Spunta, a high-yielding table potato that isn't much good for processing. "It's a bag of water," says Pelletier. He encouraged the farmers to grow the Shepody and Russet Burbank varieties and ran trials with the help of the local research station. Then he began recruiting growers to work with McCain. By the time he left, in 1996, McCain was processing the second crop in its new factory. The first year, McCain bought twenty thousand metric tons of local potatoes and, in the second year, twice that amount.

TOP LEFT: Unloading fifty-kilogram bags of potatoes at the Balcarce plant during the Argentina plant's early years.
TOP RIGHT: Bulk body trucks are now used to transport potatoes from the fields to the storage facilities.
BOTTOM: Grower Sergio Scioli and Ghislain Pelletier, 1995.

TOP LEFT: Harrison, Balcarce mayor Jose Luis Perez, and Stephen McCain at the opening of the Argentina plant, 1995.
TOP RIGHT: Potato trial field across the road from McCain's Balcarce factory.
BOTTOM: Argentina president Carlos Menem presents an export award to Adolfo Lopez Rouger, CEO of McCain South America, 2002.

Getting the growers to produce good raw materials for the factory was not easy. They were used to getting paid by the bag without the bag being weighed. But McCain used a scale, reducing the payout for soil and for low-quality potatoes. The price for good potatoes remained the same, but the amount of soil was now deducted from the total weight and a lesser amount was paid for potatoes that didn't meet the quality standards specified in the contract.

"It was quite a learning experience for growers to adapt to the higher standards we had," says Pelletier. On the other hand, growers selling to the fresh market in Argentina often had trouble getting paid. "Part of their costs was all the phone calls they had to make to get a cheque. At McCain, once your crop is accepted at the factory, you knew you would get your money."

The McCain name was already known to many of the growers, as Van Leersum discovered when he visited some of them during construction of the Balcarce plant. "I found potato bags with the McCain Produce logo that they had saved from imports from Canada in the 1970s," he recalls. In those days, the growers imported Canadian seed or table potatoes from McCain Produce when their own crops were small and local potato prices were high. They exported in good years, partly to reduce the local supply and influence the domestic price upward.

When McCain launched its Balcarce operation, potatoes in the region were still harvested by hand, the potatoes dumped in pyramidal piles in the field and covered with stalks of corn that were grown in strips in between the potatoes for that purpose. None of the growers had climate-controlled indoor storage.

The supply from the fields came in fifty-kilogram jute bags on flatbed trucks. Each bag had to be emptied onto a conveyer belt, to be transferred to McCain's storage

LEFT: Enrique Sanchez Acosta, managing director of McCain Argentina (far right) with McCain production employees, at the start-up of Balcarce's second flake drum.
RIGHT: The second flake drum at Balcarce.

buildings at the factory. McCain employed seventy-five workers to do this job, day and night. Since then, specialized transport and unloading systems have been developed.

The Balcarce factory, which supplies both Argentina and Brazil and neighbouring countries, including Chile and Uruguay, is one of the biggest in the McCain network. As well as relying on local farmers for supply, McCain has developed twenty-four circles of fifty hectares each on a farm of twenty-three thousand hectares. It grows potatoes there in a four-year rotation. The farm is located in Patagonia, where the climate is better suited for growing and long-term storage of Russet Burbank potatoes. McCain, with Gustavo Scioli as director of agriculture, also grows potatoes on leased land in the Balcarce area.

Andrew Green, an engineer from Florenceville, came from Canada to be project manager for the construction of the Balcarce plant. His most vivid recollection is of his encounter with a troublesome Argentinian cat. When the construction was almost finished, McDonald's, whose presence in South America was McCain's reason for building the factory, announced it was sending representatives for an inspection tour. Green decided it was time to get rid of a cat that had taken up residence on the site.

"I kept telling the guys to get rid of that cat, but they couldn't catch it. One day I was walking through the factory and right in front of me I saw this nice little cat nobody could catch. I walked gently up behind it and grabbed it around its body for fear it would scamper off.

"Apparently cats in Argentina are part cat, part mountain lion. The cat spun around in my hands and attacked me. But I did not want to let go because McDonald's was coming. After the cat had shredded my hands and had a fang embedded in my knuckle, I decided maybe McDonald's would understand that sometimes cats

LEFT: Adolfo Lopez Rouger with Eduardo Hadad, chief engineer, next to the potato specialty line at Balcarce.
RIGHT: Gustavo Martin, quality-assurance supervisor at Balcarce, with an array of packaging, including those for french fries and potato specialties.

get into factories during construction. I let the cat go and went to the hospital and was bandaged up like a mummy for a week."

Dennis Jesson, who had been a key player in launching McCain's first foreign plant, in Scarborough, England, came out of retirement to start up the factory's operations. Importing expertise was necessary because in Balcarce McCain faced a situation similar to that Wallace and Harrison confronted when they started the Florenceville factory in 1957: the local area lacked the infrastructure and personnel to support a major manufacturing operation.

Demand was strong enough that McCain expanded the plant in 1996, 1997, and again in 2000. The total cost, including the two expansions, was U.S.$160 million. However, the sharp devaluation of the Argentinean peso in 2002 severely diminished the market for McCain's products, and it took several years to recover. A Brazilian currency crisis three years previously also had a severe impact on McCain's South American business. "A lot of companies would have just shut down," says Terry Bird, vice-president of corporate development and emerging markets. "But we stuck with our South American plant, and it has become a valuable contributor."

In 1996, Adolfo Lopez Rouger, an executive with the international manufacturer Unilever, got a call from a recruiter to inquire whether he would be interested in a job as managing director of McCain Argentina. CEO Howard Mann had told Tony van Leersum, then president of McCain Argentina, to look for an experienced marketing person for that position. But Van Leersum thought that, to serve the McDonald's account well, the managing director needed manufacturing experience.

Rouger was hesitant to make the move. It seemed risky to leave a huge company like Unilever for a smaller company that was not yet well established in South America. It took several meetings to convince him that it would not be a great risk for him and his family, because McCain does not walk away from its investments, even if the results are poor in the short term.

Adolfo Lopez Rouger at the output end of the dryer on the fifteen-metric-ton-per-hour french fry line.

Mann had asked for at least three candidates, but Van Leersum convinced him and Harrison to meet Rouger in Toronto. During the meeting, Rouger asked about the company's bonus scheme. Harrison said, "Adolfo, we really love to pay good bonuses." Rouger got the message: McCain pays good bonuses when it makes money – and it likes to make money.

Rouger took the job. Based in Buenos Aires, he oversees McCain's operations in Argentina, Brazil, Chile, Uruguay, Paraguay, and Colombia. "We have a big market share in the region because McCain had the guts to come to a non-developed region well in advance of other companies," says Rouger. "And that has been the tradition of Wallace and Harrison."

McCain International, the sales and marketing division responsible for areas of the world where McCain has not set up a separate operation, was active in South America for many years before McCain decided to build a plant there. It had been selling its products through exclusive deals with local distributors. This system worked especially well in Brazil, where McCain's distributor had built up a substantial food service business for the McCain brand. Once McCain had its own factory in Argentina, however, it wanted to build up its own sales and marketing organization, rather than be restricted to exclusive agreements with distributors. The distributors weren't pleased about losing their exclusivity. The Argentine distributor sued McCain, while the Brazilian one stopped its payments, forcing the company to take the distributor to court.

McCain didn't want to rely on just one distributor, especially in Buenos Aires, where 70 percent of its Argentine business is and where there are thousands of restaurants. Instead, it made arrangements with many small distributors, some of them table-potato distributors and others individuals new to the food industry who were

McCain employees at the tenth-anniversary party of McCain Argentina, in Balcarce.

The beginning of all

By Gustavo Scioli
Field Department Manager, McCain Argentina

We were awaiting a visit from Harrison McCain. This was important: one of the owners of the company was coming, and we wanted to make a good impression.

As the date came closer, our nerves increased. The day would start with field visits, followed by a barbecue lunch with some of the farmers. In the afternoon, Harrison would visit the plant.

I was responsible for the field visits. I made sure our agronomy vehicles were clean and I organized the walkie-talkies. Nothing could fail. One of my worries was the weather – rain would complicate things. I checked the forecasts but all indicated good conditions.

The day finally came. We picked up Harrison at the airport early in the morning. The weather was good, the vehicles looked bright, everything seemed perfect.

The first field we visited was one surrounded by hills, making the vista especially beautiful. It was potato-planting season and the farmer was conditioning and planting the seed. Seagulls flew about the seeder. The sun shined. Looking at the passing seeder, I had a moment of poetic inspiration. "Look, Mr. Harrison," I said, "the beginning of all."

He turned to me with a serious expression on his face and answered without hesitation. "This is not the

Harrison's 1998 visit to McCain Argentina: Harrison (in white shirt) is standing behind the pile of potatoes, with Adolfo Lopez Rouger (left) and Tony van Leersum (right). The workers in the foreground are hand-cutting the seed potatoes.

beginning of all. The beginning is when a child asks for a cone of french fries in a restaurant."

That ended the conversation, and he walked away to join the rest of the group. I was perplexed by his response. I had never thought about it in that way. For me, an agronomist, the beginning was always the planting.

But the old sea wolf was absolutely right. If a child doesn't ask for french fries in the restaurant, planting is not necessary. It was a good lesson, one I will never forget.

eager to be their own boss and build up a business themselves. McCain helped them lease small vehicles, paid for painting their vehicles in McCain colours and decorating them with the McCain logo, and trained them to sell frozen french fries. The same system of demonstrating the virtues of frozen fries to chefs that had worked elsewhere was successfully used in Argentina, although with one difference: often the new customers would take only a few bags of frozen fries – not even a full carton.

McCain also helped distributors choose other frozen products to sell, products compatible with and of a quality comparable to McCain's products. Selling more products helps the distributor cover overheads faster than if it sold only McCain products. "This strategy in Argentina was 'drink the local wine' and that has proven very successful," says Van Leersum. As of 2007, McCain had 120 distributors covering Buenos Aires and the rest of the country. In Brazil, McCain worked with existing food service distributors to develop a network to cover that vast country.

The McCain approach to South America was the same one it used in other parts of the world: export first, build when a beachhead has been established, and keep spreading the word to the food service industry that frozen french fries have several advantages over fresh. Of course, it didn't hurt that McDonald's was expanding in the region and needed McCain to supply its famous MacFries. In the early years, McDonald's was 90 percent of McCain South America's sales. By 2007, McDonald's accounted for only 30 percent of McCain's business. The non-McDonald's market was growing faster in part because of the success of McCain salespeople in persuading small chains, independent restaurants, and school cafeterias to switch to a frozen product.

The major difference between the North American and South American markets, from McCain's point of view, is in the degree to which there is room for growth in

LEFT and **MIDDLE**: Potato Smiles are a favourite with kids: TV commercial auditions for the potato specialty.
RIGHT: A puppet show in school educates kids about nutrition.

LEFT: McCain Argentina management, 2007. Front row: (left to right) Néstor Zanolli, Carlos Becerra, Pedro Lelkes (retired), Graciela Parafita. Back row: Javier Montenegro, Adolfo Lopez Rouger, Juan Manuel Fluguerto Martí (retired), Fabián Bojalil.

RIGHT: Management, sales and administrative staff of the Buenos Aires office, 2003.

sales of the company's primary product, french fries. In North America, most of the people who would be interested in buying frozen french fries to prepare at home are already doing so. Not so in South America, where many people can't afford what is, for most North Americans, a low-cost food option.

"People living in a developed country like England, France, or Canada, where income per capita is high, can afford to pay for a convenience product," explains Rouger. "When income per capita is low, there is not a big market for these products, and there is less retail business. This makes us much more focused on the quick-service chains, which is why we came here hand in hand with McDonald's."

Per capita consumption of frozen french fries in South America is one-tenth that in the United States. Because there is so much room to grow in that category, the company has chosen not to expand yet into other product lines. French fries account for 90 percent of what McCain sells in South America; the remaining 10 percent consists mostly of other potato products.

When Rouger says it took guts for McCain to make a major commitment to South America, he means that the company was placing a bet on a region prone to political unrest and economic crisis. Beginning in 1999, the entire region suffered from a series of bank and currency crises, accompanied by political unrest that often spilled into the streets. As of 2007, the economy was growing again and so were the quick-service chains. But, because of the bad years, McCain South America in 2007 was two years behind where it thought it would be by then.

Meanwhile, the town of Balcarce has benefited from McCain's presence. When McCain first arrived, employees did not have bank accounts and their wages had to be paid in cash under the supervision of armed guards. Since then, retail banking has

Argentina management, Balcarce, 2007: (left to right) Gustavo Scioli, Marcelo Aguirre, Carlos Becerra, Patricio Gonzalez Roelants, Juan Andrade, Maria Echeverria, Ana Alanis, Adolfo Lopez Rouger, Ana Sudan, Enrique Sanchez Acosta, Alejandra Ibarra, Fernando Mendoza.

become common, a giant supermarket has opened, and hotel accommodation is much improved. The growth in Balcarce is typical of what happens whenever McCain opens a factory in a rural area. The multiplier is 3.5, meaning that for every dollar invested by McCain, 3.5 dollars are invested by service industries, fertilizer and agrichemical companies, farm equipment suppliers, supermarkets, banks, transport companies, car dealerships, clothing stores, and others.

Once the factory was up and running smoothly, the group Dennis Jesson had dubbed the "foreign legion" – McCain people from Canada, Australia, Great Britain, the Netherlands, and France who came to get the Argentina operation off the ground – went home and left local management in charge. Like the other McCain operations, McCain South America makes no effort to stress its Canadian nationality, preferring instead to blend in with the community. Indeed, on one occasion, being Canadian was a distinct disadvantage for McCain in Brazil. That was during the 1990s, when the Canadian aircraft manufacturer Bombardier was embroiled in a dispute with its Brazilian competitor, Embraer, each company claiming the other benefited from illegal government subsidies. Opponents of Bombardier in Brazil urged a boycott of McCain since it is a Canadian company. "It didn't affect the business; it was only a couple of leaflets," says Rouger. "That's in the past now."

LEFT: Dave Morgan with Japanese colleagues at a food expo sampling booth in Tokyo, 1998.
RIGHT: Carl Morris (left) launched and managed McCain's Japan business; here in 1996 with George Suzuki, national sales manager for Japan, and Yon Yamaguchi, country manager.

One day in 1974, Wallace McCain called David Morgan, a veteran McCain employee who was working at production planning in the Florenceville plant. He said, "David, I've got a customer I want you to look after. He calls most every day, and I want you to look after him."

The customer worked for Nichirei, a Japanese food distributor. Wallace McCain had made contact with Nichirei during a trip to Japan as part of a Canadian trade mission. The distributor had already sold one container of retail product, and it was obvious that this was a promising opportunity for McCain.

Japan had emerged from wartime devastation to become, by the mid-1970s, an important industrial power. It was a populous, wealthy country and getting wealthier all the time. The Japanese are traditionally rice eaters, not potato eaters, but they were receptive to Western influences, and the American fast food chains were beginning to make inroads. So David Morgan became the scheduler for exports to Japan and Korea, with Nichirei continuing as McCain's agent in Japan.

Because many of the boxes in that first shipment had arrived broken, Wallace decided he needed a trusted employee on the spot to look after this potentially lucrative new business. Carl Morris, looking for a change after many years on the production side, got the assignment and made the first of many day-long trips from Florenceville to Tokyo. From 1974 to 1989, he made two to five trips per year. From 1989 to 1994, he spent six months of each year based in Tokyo, as president of McCain Japan.

It soon became apparent that the Japanese market deserved a full-time McCain presence, so Morris hired Yon Yamaguchi, a Japanese who had lived in Canada for twelve years, to head the Tokyo office. Morgan, in Florenceville, reported to Morris as export manager.

LEFT: McCain's Japan team, 2006.
RIGHT: McCain's Taiwan team, 2006.

A South Korean office was opened in Seoul in 1990, with Mike Cho as country manager, a position he still held in 2007. By 1995, McCain had fifty full-time employees in Japan, most based in Tokyo, with a few in Osaka. McCain employees tend to stay McCain employees, which turned out to be a major competitive advantage for McCain – the other foreign companies competing with McCain in the Japanese market tended to have rapid turnover among their sales representatives. "There would be different people every two years representing a company," says Morris. "It got to the point where some of my customers told me they had been visited in the same year by the same person representing two different companies."

It's common for a Japanese to remain with one company throughout his or her working career, and Morris found that his Japanese customers were favourably impressed that the McCain representatives stayed put. "It showed them that we were there to stay." In addition, the Japanese tend to have a positive attitude toward Canada. "The average Japanese thinks of the United States as smokestacks in Pittsburgh. When he thinks of Canada, he thinks of clean air and Niagara Falls."

Although the big U.S. fast food chains are present, the main business for McCain in Japan has turned out to be what Morris calls "street business" – restaurants other than the quick-service chains. Japan has thousands upon thousands of restaurants, many of them tiny. They don't have much room for storing frozen products, so the wholesaler distributing McCain french fries often makes daily or twice-daily deliveries.

"It's a tough market," says Morris, "though a lot of people think it's a lot tougher than it is. Most people hear about all the difficulties of entering Japan. And it is very difficult to do it by telephone and emails if you don't speak the language. You have to go there. A lot of companies haven't done that, so they say it's difficult."

LEFT: A McDonald's on a busy Shanghai street.
RIGHT: Ronald Muller, project coordinator, at the start-up of the Harbin factory, 2006.

The typical McCain policy in any large market, such as France, Poland, China, or India, is first to build demand by exporting and then to build a factory. In this sense, Japan is unusual because no matter how much sales grow, McCain is most unlikely ever to build a potato-processing factory there. Morris did look into acquiring a factory in Japan but decided it didn't make economic sense because land is too expensive, as would be the price of locally grown potatoes. It's cheaper to ship product in from North America, Australia, or New Zealand and store it in rented warehouses.

McCain's business in Japan has risen steadily since it began in the 1970s, and Morris expects this growth to continue. "It's a good market for McCain, and the Japanese are wonderful people to work with. I worked there for thirty years and I don't think I ever signed a contract. It has been all verbal agreements, and everything anyone told me they were going to do, they have done. And we have tried to do the same."

Every new territory presents a new opportunity for McCain, but none is more glittering than China. With 1.3 billion people, it is the world's largest market. Its economy is growing at a ferocious pace, and people are migrating en masse into the cities. The Chinese welcome Western ways, including U.S.-style quick-service restaurants, which is why, as of 2007, KFC was opening a store in China every day. McDonald's has also targeted China as one of its major growth markets. Taiwan, with its dynamic capitalist economy and affluent population of twenty-three million, is also an important market for McCain.

Most North Americans associate China with rice, not potatoes. Therefore, it may be surprising to learn that China produces more potatoes than any other country.

According to the UN Food and Agriculture Organization (FAO), China grew 73 million metric tons of potatoes in 2005, twice as much as the 36.4 million produced by Russia. India came third with 25 million, followed by Ukraine (19.5 million) and the United States (19.1 million). About half the Chinese crop is used as table potatoes and 15 percent is processed into flakes, starch, or alcohol. The rest is lost to disease, exported, or used as animal feed and seed.

With opportunity comes challenge, and no country has been more challenging for McCain than China. When McCain went to South Africa, it was easy for its personnel from Canada, Australia, and Britain to help train South Africans because they spoke the same language. No such luck in China. Perhaps most challenging of all is that the noodles and rice Chinese people have eaten for centuries are cheaper than french fries – important in a country where average incomes remain low. A Shanghai office worker might try KFC occasionally, but if she can eat lunch in a Chinese restaurant for one dollar, that's where she'll take most of her meals.

Still, even a small percentage of 1.3 billion people is a lot of potential customers, which is why McCain began sending agricultural experts to China during the 1990s. There was plenty of work to be done.

Ghislain Pelletier recalls his first visit in 1999 when McCain agronomist Wang Rengui showed him a plot of land that was supposed to be growing Russet Burbank potatoes. "I scratched my head and said, 'These don't look like Russet Burbank.' The foliage looked all spindly. I was wondering if we had the right variety or if it would grow there. They were full of disease."

The problem was that there was no good seed in China of the varieties McCain wanted to test. "The seed harbours the diseases," Pelletier explains. "That was why we

LEFT: Tony Ford (left), agriculture director for McCain Australia, headed the company's project to develop reliable raw material supplies in China; here with agronomist Wang Rengui (far right), chief agronomist of McCain China; and Liu Wenlong (centre), also a McCain agronomist.
RIGHT: A KFC in Shanghai.

needed clean seed to do the trials, to see if it would grow at all." But China, like all countries, is protective of its agriculture and reluctant to allow the import of foreign seed. Allison McCain contacted government officials and told them that McCain would not invest unless it was able to test with good-quality seed. Finally, the Chinese authorities agreed to allow McCain to import a very small amount of Canadian high-grade seed potatoes.

The China agriculture project was the responsibility of Tony Ford, agriculture director for McCain Australia. The company spent seven years looking for a good location in China to grow processing potatoes, a decision that would in turn determine where the first factory would be built. The south of the country was too warm. The temperatures were better in the far north, but the soils there were too heavy. Finally, McCain's experts settled on the area around Harbin, in northeast China. In 2005, a state-of-the-art french fry factory, built at a cost of $50 million, opened in that city of ten million people.

Since there were no potato farms near the new factory, McCain has had to train growers, as well as rent land to grow its own potatoes. Just as when the company first began processing operations in New Brunswick in 1957, the quality of the potatoes in China at first was not good. Potatoes were damaged during harvesting and while being transported to the plant. Consequently, the plant's early products were not up to the standards of KFC and McDonald's, the major customers for french fries in China.

As of 2007, McCain was not making money in China. However, Kai Bockmann, managing director of the Chinese operation, predicts that of all the start-ups in recent company history, it will be the one to break even the fastest. The only local competitor is the U.S. company Simplot, which built a french fry line in a vegetable factory as a joint venture with a Chinese company in 1990.

KFC is a huge success in China, and McDonald's is also growing quickly. The only other important chain is Dicos Fried Chicken, owned by a Taiwan company. "The big problem in China is to get people to eat french fries outside of KFC, McDonald's, and Dicos," says Bockmann. For example, there are more than thirty restaurants in the food court of the Shanghai office building that has housed McCain's Chinese sales office since 1996 but not one of them sells french fries. Typically, the market for french fries in countries without a french fry tradition evolves from international quick-service chains to local chains to independent restaurants and then to the retail stores. As of 2007 in China, however, the three major chains were still 80 percent of the market. As always, McCain is in it for the long haul.

The people of northern China, where the McCain factory is located, are potato eaters, but they eat their potatoes in stews and soups, not as french fries. Eventually, McCain hopes, they will enjoy the same fries they ordered at KFC and McDonald's in their homes. On the package they will see the same McCain brand and logo that is familiar in much of the world, but they will also see the Chinese letters that are as phonetically close as the company is able to come to reproducing the word McCain in Chinese. It's pronounced "Mei Kang." In Chinese, that means "perfect health."

ABOVE: The China team at the new plant at Harbin, 2006. Kai Bockmann and Ian Robinson are front row, second and third from the left.
FACING PAGE, TOP: Chinese workers cutting seed potatoes, 2004.
MIDDLE: Liu Zhenbao, McCain seed potato manager, in Keshan, China, proudly displaying high-class seed potatoes, a pile of Russet Burbank seed potatoes behind him, 2005.
BOTTOM: Traditional harvesting of potatoes in China, 2005.

McCain India: In the middle row, fifth from the left, is agriculture manager Devendra Kumar, the longest serving member of McCain's India team. Engineering manager Dominic Rush is sixth from the left in the back row, finance director Rajeev Chauhan is fifth from the left, and country manager Jaideep Mukherji is fourth from the left. John Allan, factory manager, is fourth from the right in the second row from the back.

China is not the only country that's home to over one billion people. Like China, the other member of the exclusive billion-population club is undergoing rapid economic development and creating a vast, newly affluent middle class.

In one important way, India is even more attractive than China as a market for McCain Foods: unlike the Chinese, Indians already have a taste for potato specialties. And so, the McCain plant in India's Gujarat province produces a variety of potato products, including savoury wedges, spicy wedges, rösti fingers, rösti rounds, and pom poms. "In India, potatoes are an almost daily staple food," explains Terry Bird. "They are cooked in a wok-like pan called a karahi. The wedges and crunchy potato specialties we produce in a frozen format are similar to what Indians traditionally eat as snacks."

On the other hand, almost nobody in India eats french fries. The challenge for McCain will be to increase the market for french fries. If it succeeds, the rewards will be great. "In North America," says Bird, "the average person eats almost fifteen kilograms of french fries a year. What if we could get the average consumer in India to eat just half a kilo?"

As elsewhere, McCain started its business in India by shipping in its product. Then it began to produce McCain products at a Mumbai factory partly owned by McDonald's. Finally, it decided to build a plant of its own.

As in Argentina and China, it was Ghislain Pelletier's job to travel the country and analyze the suitability of various areas for growing potatoes to supply a large processing plant. Before McCain invests millions in a plant, it needs to have a good understanding of the risks involved. The better the market, the more risk McCain can afford to take. If business can be established beyond quick-service restaurants, in the broader food service market and in retail, then perhaps construction of a plant is warranted. If not, it might be too risky. Another major issue is the likelihood of drought or some other weather disaster that could lead to a potato shortage. If McCain is going to invest $50 million in a factory, it needs to be sure it will have enough raw materials to fill it.

In India, potatoes are a winter crop, as the summers are too hot to grow them successfully. They are planted in November and harvested in March. Pelletier travelled around India with Jaideep Mukherji, the country manager; agronomist Devandra Kumar; and business development officer Dan Singer. Eventually, they settled on the province of Gujarat as the right place to build a factory.

Although Gujarat produces potatoes that so far are smaller than McCain would like, the quality is good in terms of both solids and colour. "There are always some trade-offs," says Pelletier.

As in China, introducing to India the potato varieties McCain favours was a long process. The company imported tissue culture, which had to remain in quarantine for more than a year before being released as plantlets. It then had to set up a seed program to multiply the plantlets for three years before they were ready for the local growers to plant.

TOP LEFT: Indian street vendors offer a range of deep-fried potatoes and other snacks.
TOP MIDDLE: An insulated minivan for short-distance deliveries in Pune, a city in the western Indian province of Maharashtra. The van can hold twenty cases of french fries.
TOP RIGHT: A McDonald's in Mumbai.
BOTTOM: Taking part in the groundbreaking ceremony for the Gujarat factory on August 28, 2005: (left to right) Simon Jones, Terry Bird, Derrick MacDougall, Devendra Kumar, Robert Martin, Larry Derrah, Tom Kaszas, Lloyd Borowski, Rajeev Chauhan.

As of 2007, the growers were producing crops from these seed potatoes to their great advantage: yields had doubled, yet they were using only one-third as much water as before. This was the result of irrigation technology McCain introduced to replace flood irrigation, the inefficient and wasteful method previously used. The Gujarat farmers are eager to learn all they can. When McCain announces a seminar on some potato-growing topic, several hundred farmers inevitably show up.

It's expected that the Gujarat area can reliably produce potatoes from irrigated fields every year. Although it is dry during the growing season, the monsoon rains during the summer ensure there is plenty of underground water to use for irrigation.

McCain has also investigated the possibilities in the Middle East. In the late 1990s, McCain considered building a factory there to supply McDonald's restaurants in Israel and Jordan. It would have been a joint venture with an Israeli company that was processing french fries for McDonald's. Israel has a highly developed agricultural sector and grows good potatoes. However, the market potential is not great enough to offset major risks in the region, including water shortages, political instability, and the ever-present possibility of war.

TOP: Agriculture manager Devendra Kumar (in striped shirt) with Gujarati farmers and the McCain-designed flatbed planter, which can plant 3.2 hectares a day. A traditional planter can plant only 1.2 hectares.
MIDDLE: Harvesting in Pune, July 2001.
BOTTOM: Pune farmer, 2002.

"Join the army, see the world" was a famous recruiting slogan used by the U.S. military. "Join McCain, see the world" might be almost as appropriate.

Because it is a global company, McCain attracts people who want to experience living in other countries. "McCain people loved going to South Africa," Mark McCain recalls. "You could work in a young, charged company that was embracing change, and on the weekend you could tour a game farm. There wasn't anyone that we asked to go for a week or three months who didn't want to go."

Dan Leger, from Florenceville, went to South Africa and stayed. He married a South African woman, developed a South African accent, and has had family members, some of whom had never left New Brunswick before, come to visit.

Ian Robinson left Britain to be plant manager in Hoofddorp, in the Netherlands. Then he moved to Poland as the first plant manager of the new McCain factory there. Next stop was Delmas, South Africa, where he managed the french fry plant. He then spent some time back home in Britain before moving to China to manage McCain's plant in Harbin.

Employees of McCain International and McDonald's visit the Coaldale, Alberta, plant 2001.
Front row: (left to right) Mark MacPhail, Emmanuel Araya.
Back row: Richard Bartlett; Lisa Yee, McDonald's Central America; Alvaro Cofino, McDonald's Guatemala; Marco Gordon, McDonald's Guatemala; Paul Tol.

Perhaps the best-travelled McCain employee is Kai Bockmann, managing director for China, whose travels began long before he joined the company. When he was seven, attending grade school in Vancouver, his parents decided his education wasn't broad enough. So they bought a camper and hit the road. They soon ditched the camper and spent the next six years hitchhiking around the world, through 120 countries.

After university, Bockmann joined the Canadian foreign affairs department and was assigned to Colombia. In 1996, while on vacation in Vancouver, he got a call from McCain Foods, which was looking for a Spanish speaker with knowledge of Latin America. He met with Terry Bird in Florenceville the next day and joined McCain's corporate development department. On his first day on the job, Bird told him: "You're going to Chile tomorrow. I want you to go there for a month, visit all the frozen food companies, do a feasibility study, identify acquisition targets, and come back with your recommendations."

For someone who had been working in a government bureaucracy, McCain was a culture shock. "I came from foreign affairs, where you've got a manual on how to fill out an expense report, to an environment where you're expected to learn by doing. There was no training program. I didn't even know what McCain was making at that time other than french fries. I was only twenty-six. Yet on the second day on

A McCain International group on a 1996 whitewater rafting excursion in Penobscot, Maine, to celebrate a record year. Rafters are David Sanchez, Debbie Demerchant, Alex Scholten, Chris Wishart, Marie Smith, Dale Perley, and Keith McGlone. The guide (far left) was not a McCain employee.

the job, they shipped me down to Chile. That's pretty amazing."

Bockmann has been travelling the world for McCain ever since. "I am just continuing what was instilled in me as a kid," he says. "Travel has always been in my blood." At the age of thirty-one, Bockmann, who speaks four languages, became head of McCain International, the Florenceville-based division responsible for sales and marketing in all the countries not assigned to a regional management team or factory source. McCain International covers Mexico, Central America, the Caribbean, parts of South America, the Middle East, southeast Asia, most of Africa, Iceland, and small Mediterranean states, including Malta. Sales representatives represent McCain in each location.

McCain International was created from the export division of McCain Foods (Canada) in 1994, when the company increased its focus on market development. Its first president was Harrison's son, Peter, who was ideally suited to the job. He loved to travel and was fascinated by foreign cultures and languages. He had worked as a salesman in France for Pomona, one of McCain's distributors. In addition to French, he spoke Portuguese and some Spanish. He had been a salesman for Day & Ross and served in the sales, finance, marketing, and export sales departments of McCain before assuming the job of vice-president of export sales for McCain Foods Canada. He was, therefore, well prepared to launch McCain International.

"Peter was probably smarter than Harrison, which is hard to believe," says David Sanchez, who helped Peter get McCain International established and who later became CFO for McCain Foods Limited. "He had the same mix of raw intellect, curiosity, focus on the important aspects of business, and an incredible market sense."

As of 2007, McCain International had a staff of about one hundred people, some based in Florenceville, the rest sprinkled around the globe. "McCain International is able to try out new ideas that the rest of the group can latch on to," says Bockmann, who ran the division for four years until he was appointed to the China job in 2006. "For example, you can try out a marketing idea in one small country. If it fails, it only cost $50,000. If you were to try it in Canada or the United States, it might cost $1 million."

A McCain sales trip
By Paul Tol

In 1999, Douglas Henderson, area manager for the Caribbean, and I visited Guyana, Suriname, and French Guiana on a sales trip for McCain International. At our first appointment, in Guyana's Georgetown, on the north coast of South America, we took an order from a KFC franchise owner. However, the only store in the area with freezers was the Texaco Minimart, and it needed them for ice cream: so much for the retail market and Harrison McCain's goal of a McCain Foods bag in every household freezer in the region.

Our flight to the Suriname capital of Paramaribo had been bumped by two days so we looked for alternate transportation. Told that a taxi would take eight hours, we left at noon, expecting to dine in Suriname that evening. Nobody mentioned we would have to cross three rivers by ferry, finding a new taxi after each crossing. The first two went smoothly, though two guys with laptops looked a bit out of place on the ferry amid the farmers, field workers, and other locals.

We arrived at the Suriname river border crossing to learn that the last ferry of the day had left and the next was not until morning. For $20, the customs officer was willing to find someone to transport us – illegally – the two kilometres across the river. His neighbour had a handmade wooden canoe with an outboard motor; the fare was $40.

Halfway across the river, it started raining, but we made it. It was now five o'clock. We found someone who would drive us the four hours to Paramaribo, first stopping to have our passports stamped, to ensure a trouble-free departure. The officer was not happy to see us: he knew we hadn't been on that last ferry. He told us to go back to Guyana the way we had come. Debate ensued. But it was dinnertime, and he decided he would rather eat than argue. He relented, and we were on our way.

Three hours later and sixty kilometres from our destination, the taxi had mechanical problems. Fortunately, the driver's cousin lived nearby, and we borrowed his minivan. The vehicle had no side windows, the windshield was cracked, and the rear door hung loose. Still, we arrived at our hotel at 10:30 p.m.

After our appointments the next day, we went to the airport for our flight to Cayenne, capital of French Guiana, a French overseas department. At the airline counter, the

Paul Tol speaking at a distributor-appreciation night in 2004, as Allison McCain and Kai Bockmann look on.

clerk refused to check us in, as we couldn't prove we had had our yellow fever shots. But the pilot agreed to take us if we stayed in the Cayenne airport's transit area and took the next flight out. However, on arrival, French customs let us in.

The next morning we met with the local McDonald's owner and visited stores. Then we flew to Martinique, another French overseas department. We enjoyed a fine bottle of wine with dinner and went to sleep early. The next day we headed to the airport for our short flight to St. Lucia.

Because of a strike, the airport road was blocked. But by this time we had learned there is usually more than one route. We took a ferry across the bay: we would approach the airport by taxi from another direction. But the second road was blockaded also. A boat owner said he could get us within two kilometres of the airport for $100. He did, and a fisherman then got us through to the airport in his pickup truck.

Because of the blockades, no check-in or immigration staff was on duty. We walked to the departure gate, gave the captain our tickets, and away we went.

In St. Lucia, for once, everything went smoothly, including our meetings with KFC and the J.Q. Charles supermarket chain. I returned to Florida, mission accomplished. I had arrived home in one piece and with new orders – although after I turned in my expense account, I had some explaining to do.

Peter McCain and David Sanchez, McCain International, 1996.

Bockmann's predecessor as head of McCain International was Richard Bartlett. His successor was Richard Efting, who had previously been sales manager in Canada and South Africa. Efting is responsible for McCain's business in small countries such as Iceland as well as big ones such as Mexico, where McCain not only sells potato products but is a market leader in desserts and appetizers.

McCain companies have not always done well at borrowing good ideas from other McCain companies, but that is something at which McCain International has excelled. "We don't care where an idea originated," Efting says. "Why not pick the best of the experiences from around the world?"

In fact, it was precisely because many of McCain International's markets were small that it pursued non-potato business. If there wasn't enough demand for french fries to fill a shipping container, McCain International filled it with desserts and juices. As a result, in many small markets, McCain is seen not just as a french fry company but as a general frozen food company, just as it is in Canada and Australia.

McCain International allows McCain to make the most of its fifty-seven manufacturing facilities around the world. If, for example, the Coaldale, Alberta, plant has excess supply, McCain International can ship that supply anywhere in the world it can find customers for it.

"McCain International's job," says Efting, "is to get into markets early and create brand awareness. Even if the sales are very small at first, eventually those markets are going to fuel the growth of the company."

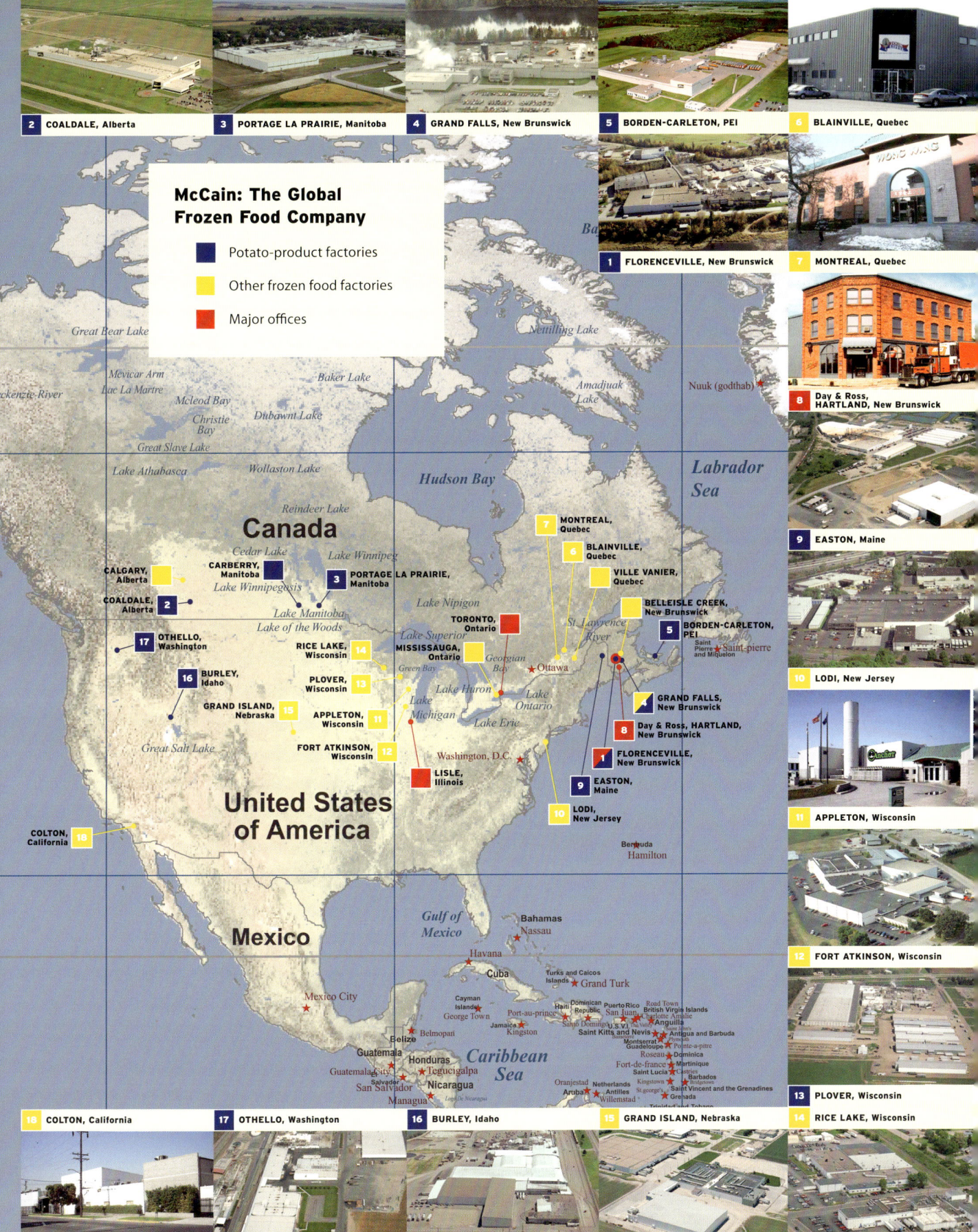

CHAPTER EIGHT

A WORLD OF CHANGE

The McCain brothers were ambitious from the start. But even they could not have imagined, back in 1957, that McCain Foods would one day own fifty-seven factories around the world, including one in China. In 1957, when they launched the company, China was a closed society and a declared enemy of Western capitalism.

The opening of China and its rapid economic growth is just one of the dramatic changes that have transformed the world since production began in Florenceville fifty years ago. As the world has changed, so has McCain Foods. Not only has it expanded globally but, in the global village of 2007, the world has come to it, which is why McCain Foods in Canada produces Asian specialities and pizza, a dish that was unknown in most of North America in 1957.

No one can predict the future with certainty. The only certainty is that change will continue to occur and at a faster pace than ever. Companies that can adapt to change will succeed, while those that can't will fail.

Economic development in China, India, and other parts of the developing world present huge opportunities for McCain Foods, as millions more people will want – and be able to afford – the convenience of frozen foods.

But while some changes present opportunities to exploit, others offer challenges to overcome. Like all food companies, McCain has to respond to the greater concern and sophistication among consumers about issues of health and nutrition. As the thinking of consumers evolves, so do their product preferences. In addition, the worldwide phenomenon of population aging is transforming consumer behaviour. As the eldest members of the North American baby boom approach retirement age, that trend will intensify. Consolidation within the food industry presents yet another challenge. Finally, McCain's agronomists have to anticipate the possible impact of climate change, especially as it may affect crops in some regions.

FACING PAGE: Irrigating a potato field in western Canada. McCain's agronomists help growers use water as efficiently as possible.

Dale Morrison exchanges ideas with Don Butterfield (left), Murray Holmes, and Michel Lacroix at the Portage la Prairie plant, which in 2006 won the McCain North American MacFry Plant of the Year award.

"The world is moving much faster today than it was even ten years ago," says Dale Morrison, the company's president and CEO, and, he says, success in a changing world requires perpetual renewal. Morrison insists that all McCain employees understand this essential fact: "If the rate of change outside a company is faster than inside the company, there is big trouble ahead."

Morrison joined McCain as CEO in 2004, the same year Harrison McCain died. He is the second professional manager to head the company and possibly one of the few executives ever recruited to McCain Foods who failed to be taken aback by the smallness of Florenceville, New Brunswick. Perhaps that is because Florenceville is three times bigger than Milton, North Dakota, was when Morrison was growing up there. (The population of this farming community has since shrunk from two hundred to eighty.) He worked on his family's farm, which produced barley, wheat, oats, and cattle. One year, he harvested potatoes on another farm in the Red River Valley. The metropolis of the region was north of the border – Winnipeg, a city Morrison then considered monstrous in size. His high school graduating class consisted of thirteen people. "I graduated in the top ten," he boasts.

After obtaining a business degree from the University of North Dakota, Morrison landed a job with General Foods in sales and marketing. Ten years later, he joined PepsiCo, where he held a variety of positions, including CEO of Frito-Lay UK and Toronto-based president of Frito-Lay for Canada and part of the United States. After relocating seven times in fourteen years with PepsiCo, Morrison promised his family their moving days were over and, in 1995, he accepted a job in Princeton, New Jersey, with the Campbell Soup Company, first as head of Pepperidge Farms, the bakery division, and then as CEO.

For his next job, Morrison decided he needed a change from the food business and so joined a New York–based private equity company managing $1.6 billion in investments. "I assumed it was the last job I would do," he says. That was before he received a call from a recruiter helping McCain in its search for a new CEO. The search committee wanted to meet Morrison. One of the committee members was Wallace McCain.

Morrison had turned down several job opportunities since leaving Campbell. He didn't want a new job, but he did want to meet Wallace McCain. He thought, "I'm not going to do this, but how many chances do you get to meet somebody who has helped create a $6 billion company? It's like getting a chance to meet Sam Walton [the founder of Wal-Mart]."

After a series of meetings with the committee and members of the board, Morrison was no longer sure that he wasn't interested. "While it may not seem totally logical or rational, there are times in life when you run into a career opportunity and you conclude that it is the perfect fit for you. That was the case for me with McCain; I concluded that the company was right for me. I liked the family and the board, I liked the governance structure, and, most importantly, I felt I could really embrace and build on the McCain culture and the McCain business. It seemed to be the best of two worlds: a private company with a corporate governance structure close to that of a public company."

Morrison says his job is similar to that of a public company CEO reporting to a "progressive, contemporary board." While he doesn't have to answer to Bay Street analysts, he does have to answer to the family. "That's really the only difference. Having run a public company and now running McCain, I feel as much weight with twenty-four shareholders as I did with thousands of shareholders. I would say I feel the weight even more because I know the shareholders personally."

Morrison says, "We build on the shoulders of those who came before us. We have such a solid foundation to build on." The first fifty years of McCain Foods were more about keeping up with demand. But, since then, the marketplace in which McCain operates has evolved, and, in the twenty-first century, the company must focus more on creating demand.

In 1957, the newborn McCain Foods had perfect timing. The Canadian, U.S. and Australian baby booms all started in the 1940s after the war, and women were flocking into the workforce. This combination of rapid population growth and greater need for convenience translated into steadily increasing demand for McCain's products. At the same time, the technology for a frozen food industry was being perfected and the fast food industry was just beginning. For years, McCain was able to grow at rates of 10 to 15 percent per year simply by responding to ever rising demand created naturally by the social and economic environment. Wallace McCain used to tell new recruits: "This train is going to fly by, and your job is to grab it and hold on for the ride."

Today's McCain logo (second from the top) was stylized from the original McCain Produce logo (top). The Russian logo (second from bottom) is a phonetic rendering in Cyrillic letters of "McCain." At the bottom is the Chinese version; the English transliteration of the Chinese characters is "Mei Kang," meaning "perfect health."

In 2001, Canada Post honoured McCain by featuring it on one of its stamps.

ABOVE: packages of McCain potato products inform consumers that the contents are trans fat–free.

FACING PAGE: McCain ads comparing the nutritional information of a serving portion of Superfries to that of a small potato.

But the market for processed potato products is now well developed in North America, the United Kingdom, Europe, and Australia. Most potential french fry consumers are already consuming them. Moreover, the populations of the industrialized nations are aging. Older people eat fewer french fries than younger people or eat french fries less frequently, and they need fewer calories in general.

Morrison's goal is to take McCain deeper into the world by winning over new populations while at the same time taking it deeper into the food marketplace of the developed world by broadening its product line. And he emphasizes that this does not imply neglecting potato products. "Potatoes are our core business and will continue to be," he says. "I think there is enormous growth potential in that category."

If your major product is french fries and public opinion adopts the idea that french fries are unhealthy, you've got a problem.

First the food industry had to contend with the low-carbohydrate craze promulgated by the Atkins and other diets that claim carbohydrates such as potatoes cause obesity. By the turn of the twentieth century, nutritional common sense – that carbohydrates are an essential part of a balanced diet – had prevailed. However, a new nutritional villain had been identified: bad fats. It was no longer the potatoes that were bad for you but the oil they were fried in.

This argument had merit. In restaurants, frozen fries are refried in cooking oil that may contain unhealthy fats. Animal fats and the tropical oils that were commonly used in the industry contain about 50 percent saturated fatty acids. These saturated fats can raise blood cholesterol, thereby increasing the risk of heart attacks and strokes. During the 1980s, the restaurant industry in North America switched to oils much lower in saturated fats, such as soybean (15 percent) and canola (7 percent). To stabilize them, these oils were partially hydrogenated, resulting in better texture, longer shelf life, and greater ease of use in processing. However, during the 1990s, it became evident that the trans fatty acids created by the hydrogenation process also boosted cholesterol levels and increased the risk of heart attacks.

McCain's goal is to remove as much of the saturated fats as possible from its french fries. Better factory fryers and other improvements in processing have made it possible to use non-hydrogenated oils, thereby ensuring that the finished product is free of trans fat. As of June 2007, all McCain branded retail and food-service frozen french fries and other potato products are fried in oils that are low in saturated fats and have zero trans fats.

Consumers are thus reassured that the occasional serving of french fries can be part of a healthy diet. As Nancy Schwartz, a nutrition expert and former professor at the University of British Columbia points out, "Potatoes are a wonderful vegetable. They are low in calories, are fat-free, and are a source of potassium, vitamin C, iron, and fibre."

French fries are one of many ways to prepare a vegetable that was discovered seven thousand years ago in the Andes mountains of Peru and has since become the world's fourth most important crop, after maize, wheat, and rice. Potatoes are rich in carbohydrates and thus a good source of energy. They also contain protein. In recognition of the importance of the potato, the consumption of which is growing steadily in the developing countries, the United Nations declared 2008 the International Year of the Potato.

Once the health concerns about french fries are alleviated, says Morrison, "we are going to give people who have left the category permission to come back. And we are going to give people who were buying french fries once a week and reduced that to once every three weeks permission to increase their frequency." There is, says Morrison, a psychic benefit to eating french fries that few other foods can offer. He knows it's the reason french fries will always be McCain's core product.

Sustainability is another area that McCain Foods will focus on in the years ahead. In 1987, the report of the Brundtland Commission, convened by the United Nations, defined sustainable development as that which "meets the needs of the present without compromising the ability of future generations to meet their own needs." "At McCain, we describe this as responsibility and trust," says Janice Wismer, global vice-president of human resources. "We must develop our people and drive sustainable, profitable growth while caring for the environment and being a responsible corporate citizen."

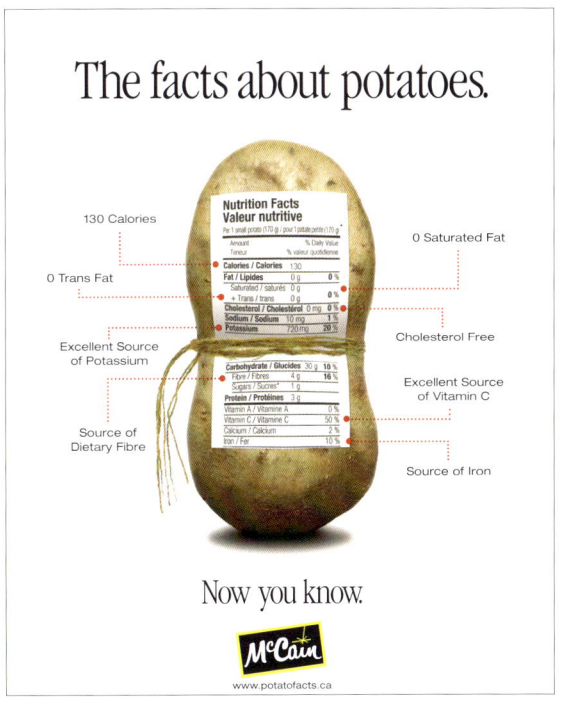

TOP LEFT: Barb Corey of the McCain Canada marketing group and Peter Reijula at a McCain-sponsored one-week course at the Culinary Institute of America in Hyde Park, New York, 2006.

TOP RIGHT: McCain means much more than just french fries.

BOTTOM: Tony van Leersum, corporate vice-president of agriculture in 2002.

For a food company, sustainable development begins with sustainable agriculture. McCain Foods, along with Unilever, Nestlé, Danone, Coca-Cola, Kraft, McDonald's, and others, is a member of the Sustainable Agriculture Initiative Platform. Members of the platform commit themselves to promoting sustainable agriculture in their supply chain.

Some nations, including Great Britain, France, the Netherlands, Canada, and the United States, have programs that comply with sustainable agriculture guidelines, and these are reflected in McCain's contracts with growers. Integrated pest management and integrated crop management programs aim to reduce the use of agrochemicals, improve soil, and reduce disease pressures through crop rotation. In these farming systems, principles such as sustainability and food safety take precedence over maximizing yield. With the help of McCain agronomists, farmers make these principles an integral part of their growing practices and decision making.

Climate change may also challenge McCain's growers as the twenty-first century unfolds. In several regions, changes in weather patterns may require changes in agricultural practices to reduce the risks of crop failure and to maintain potato quality.

The increasing importance of biofuels is likely to trigger more competition for land and water among crops for food, animal feed, fibre, and fuel. As growers alter their crop rotations to maximize profits, commodities such as potatoes may become scarcer in some regions and consequently more expensive. If this occurs, the food industry would likely pass on the higher costs to consumers.

Says Tony van Leersum: "McCain has a very extensive agricultural program, second to none in our industry. It includes new variety development and research to understand the most water-efficient irrigation systems. Also, we already operate in different climates. I expect that our near global experience and collective knowledge will give us a competitive edge in regions where climate change will become evident."

In the face of such uncertainty, McCain's international scale is an advantage. For example, restaurant chains and grocery store owners in Australia know that if the Australian crop is inadequate because of drought, McCain will be able to ship in product from elsewhere in its global network, which has happened more than once.

Yet another part of the sustainability agenda is energy efficiency. Making french fries is an energy-intensive process that first uses heat to remove water from the potatoes and then refrigeration to freeze them. The company spends a lot of money each year on energy. According to Lloyd Borowski, global vice-president of engineering and manufacturing, McCain improved its energy efficiency by 16 percent in the three years between 2004 and 2006 and intends to continue improving it. McCain uses methods ranging from the mundane, such as being more vigilant about turning off lights, to taking such initiatives as adopting alternate energy sources. In Whittlesey, England, three windmills will provide 80 percent of McCain's energy needs when installation is complete by the end of 2007. For many years, McCain has used biogas recouped from wastewater treatment as an energy source.

Des Doucette, senior director of engineering for McCain USA, aims to reduce energy costs by 30 percent through conservation and improved efficiency. This makes both environmental and economic sense. Part of the savings will come from better equipment and making sure equipment is turned off when not in use. And part of it comes from catching up to what the Europeans, who have had to cope with high energy costs for many years, are already doing.

"When you fry french fries, you are evaporating water," explains Doucette. "A lot of energy goes up the smoke stack. Europeans have had energy reclaim systems on the smoke stacks for many years. We are going to implement those systems in all our factories in the United States and Canada." In this case, McCain's American operation is learning from its European counterpart. It's an example, according to Morrison, of a necessary shift in how the company operates. Under the management of Harrison and Wallace, the company was highly decentralized. The head of each regional company focused solely on success in that region, "drinking the local wine," while at the same time working closely with Wallace or Harrison.

"Our biggest competitive advantage today is our global scale," asserts Morrison. "While we need to continue to drink the local wine, we must at the same time take advantage of the power that comes from our global footprint. We have to be better at taking a big productivity or product idea from Australia and moving that idea to the

TOP: Lloyd Borowski, global vice-president of engineering and manufacturing.
BOTTOM: Bruce Phillips, vice-president of global quality systems.

LEFT: A computer rendering of one of three wind turbines that together will provide 80 percent of the energy for the Whittlesey, England, plant once installed, in 2007.

RIGHT: Solid set irrigation, as at this farm in Chile, is a system of irrigation sprinklers and piping placed in the field. A more efficient use of water than flooding, it is becoming the predominant irrigation method in India and elsewhere.

other regions around the world swiftly." Morrison's focus is on ensuring that people at all levels of the organization are leading and that decisions are being taken at the closest level to the customer, while at the same time taking full advantage of the best ideas around the globe. He calls this "distributed and networked leadership," and it is a key feature of the Growing Together strategy.

For example, if it happens that McCain USA has developed an excellent product, or a quality or cost-saving idea with global potential, then it is U.S. CEO Frank van Schaayk's job, not just Morrison's, to play an active role in spreading that product to the rest of the world and the responsibility of the other CEOs to adapt that product quickly to their respective markets.

Van Schaayk sees the Growing Together strategy as an excellent platform for McCain's continued push to be a major presence in the American food industry. Growing Together emphasizes operations excellence in McCain's core potato business while also stimulating innovation in other areas that appeal to consumers, Van Schaayk says. "Most importantly, the plan sits on a foundation of people and values – no different from when Harrison and Wallace were building the company."

Through the years, McCain has developed the managerial talent to take on additional responsibility and leadership. Janice Wismer points out that 44 percent of the company's more than one hundred senior managers have worked in another region or function, 93 percent have degrees, and almost half have master's degrees or professional certification. "Not a lot of companies can boast that kind of experience and education," she says. McCain's senior leadership team includes both McCain veterans and new recruits with wide-ranging experience. "This team is totally focused on taking McCain to the next level of performance," says Wismer.

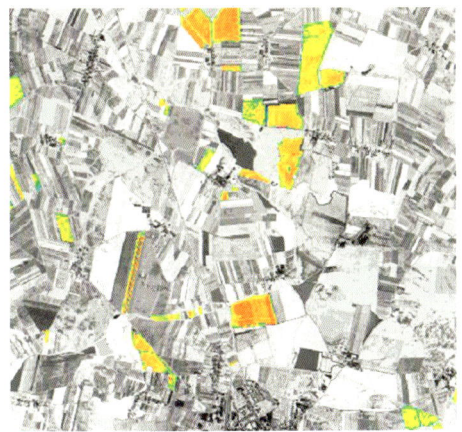 

As part of the implementation of the Growing Together strategy, McCain has established several global councils, bringing together McCain people from around the world to share their expertise in different areas. As of 2007, global councils were operating in agriculture, supply chain, human resources, food service sales and marketing, retail sales and marketing, quality, manufacturing, and safety. Each council has a sponsor from a high level of management, either a CEO or vice-president. In addition to the global councils, McCain has a health and wellness advisory board.

Morrison is a believer in big ideas. He says he would rather fail to reach a bold goal than succeed in meeting a modest one. It's better to aim to increase sales from $6 billion to $10 billion and fail, reaching only $8 billion, than to try to go from $6 billion to $7 billion and succeed. Real success, he says, requires a willingness to "embrace the art of the possible."

Says Morrison: "I think Harrison and Wallace always embraced the art of the possible. For the first ten years, they bet the company every year. That's courage. It's having your sights set very high. They could easily have stayed in Canada and had a wonderful food business in Canada. Instead, they were talking global food company before most of the food multinationals were even thinking about it."

Andrew McCain, chairman of Holdco, says the Growing Together plan continues to build the company for the long term, and the family is particularly proud that the values established in the company over the past fifty years remain the same. Allison

LEFT: Fields are monitored with the help of satellite imagery. The yellow areas in this image are the McCain fields outside Strzelin, Poland. The more red a field shows, the higher the potato yield per hectare.

RIGHT: The cab of a tractor in a modern farming system is a high-tech environment.

TOP: Paul Tellier, an Opco board member since 1996.
BOTTOM: Victor Young, an Opco board member since 1992.

McCain, chairman of Opco, agrees, adding that the consistent long-term commitment underpins the strategy going forward.

In his 2006 webcast to McCain employees all over the world, Dale Morrison emphasized that McCain is a values-driven company: "We believe in honesty, integrity, and fair dealing, and we believe they're integral to our success. Harrison said it: 'Good ethics is good business.' We are multicultural and care about our people, our families, and the communities we operate in. We take pride in being a family business.

"We value continuous improvement in our people, our products, in our business. That's how we win long term. We cherish the can-do spirit. Trying but failing is okay, but failing to try is not okay.

"We dare to be different – new ideas, innovation, and differentiation matter."

Just as the values of Harrison and Wallace McCain remain in place, so does the tradition of a lean management structure. Given its current size and growth ambitions, the company is focused on disciplined global management, which is vital to ensure that risks are well identified and managed and that it gains an advantage from the ideas and efficiencies generated through its global scale. Nevertheless, McCain Foods is both leaner and quicker than most companies of its size.

Paul Tellier, a veteran McCain Opco board member, marvelled at Harrison's unpretentious style. Tellier knows how large corporations work because he was CEO and president of both CN Rail and Bombardier. Unlike the heads of most corporations the size of McCain, Harrison McCain did not travel with a team of assistants. Tellier recalls attending a McCain board meeting in Coeur d'Alene, Idaho. "There is a lake there, and one evening we were going to have dinner on a boat. I came out of the board meeting and heard Harrison himself on the phone checking about the dinner reservations. Here was the chairman of the board who owns a third of the stock, checking on restaurant reservations."

Conventional wisdom has it that Harrison was the visionary while Wallace was the nuts-and-bolts mechanic who made sure things worked. Tellier doesn't buy that. "Wallace also had strong views about the long term, and Harrison was a very hands-on manager. I remember that one day there was a request before the board for approving capital expenditures for a cold storage. They started exchanging among themselves very detailed accounts of other cold storages. Both of them knew the most minute details."

Vic Young, another veteran board member, is the former chairman and CEO of Fishery Products International (FPI) of St. John's, Newfoundland, Canada's largest seafood harvesting and processing company. He says McCain Foods has been successful for a simple reason: it was founded by two brilliant entrepreneurs. "They

were fabulous risk takers with gut instincts for doing business. And they understood all of the potato business, including the farmers. Can you grow potatoes? That's where they always started: can you grow potatoes here? Then they understood how to produce them.

"And their Canadian experience had shown them how to market it. If you review financially the history of every country – they went in there for two, three, four years and lost a bundle of money, but they understood that if they kept at it, they would bring it around and have a successful business in the United Kingdom and the Netherlands and France and all over the world. They just had a natural instinct for doing business and making money."

During a period of turmoil in the Atlantic fishing industry in the early 1990s, plant workers and trawlermen staged frequent demonstrations outside Young's office. The fish were disappearing, FPI was laying off workers, and Young himself was the target of the protestors' anger. Harrison McCain saw a protest on the news one night and called Young. They had a conversation Young has never forgotten. Harrison said, "I know all these people are picking on you and I know they are saying all these things about you and I know that your temptation is to push back, but just remember that they are fighting for their livelihood. If you were in their position, you'd be doing exactly the same thing. So even if everything they are saying about you is untrue, be careful about pushing back."

Then he compared the fishing industry to the potato-processing industry. McCain has thirty-five hundred contract growers around the world, whose annual potato production ranges from fifty metric tons to five thousand metric tons. Harrison told

LEFT: Brian Ruff, Paul Dean, Tony van Leersum, and Ramesh Manoharan at the Potato Processing Technology Centre in Florenceville, 2006.
RIGHT: The Potato Processing Technology Centre.

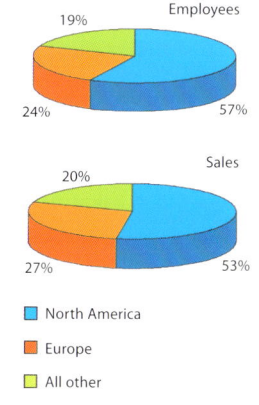

ABOVE: These charts show the geographical distribution of McCain Foods Limited employees and sales as of 2006.

A WORLD OF CHANGE

Harrison and Wallace, 1988.

Young: "My industry can be nothing and go nowhere without the farmers. And your industry can be nothing and go nowhere without the fishermen. So if you don't feel it in your heart to try to treat the fishermen with respect, then you're in the wrong industry. You've got to find a way to keep that relationship of respect."

Young concludes: "Harrison and Wallace were great marketers and producers, but they never forgot that they had to treat the primary producers of the potato with the respect they deserved, and I think that was why they were so successful. Lots of people can be entrepreneurial and brilliant, but if one of their core values is not treating people at all levels – customer, employee, or farmer – with respect, then they won't build a $6 billion international company."

Both brothers knew that people, not nuts and bolts, were their greatest asset. They were tough bosses, yet they inspired loyalty. Many key managers and other employees stayed with the company for decades, in the process accumulating priceless knowledge which they then distributed to McCain operations throughout the world.

In an interview, Harrison McCain said that, while seeing McCain grow into the world's largest french fry manufacturer was satisfying, "I think the thing I'm most proud of is seeing young people rise to the top of the ladder and develop into top McCain executives."

Although the company grew too large for the brothers to know everyone, they did know hundreds of employees by name. "Even in 1990 when they employed around twelve thousand people, they would walk up to workers at the various factories and ask them about their children," recalls Bruce Terry, former CFO.

Jim Evans, a long-time employee whose main contact of the two brothers was with Wallace McCain, concurs that strong employee relations were fundamental to McCain's success. "You had a distinct feeling that you were part of the organization, of the family. It was different from other companies and that was because of the personal contact with the owners. You were treated as a person, often as a friend."

Everyone who worked with Harrison and Wallace during the first three decades of

McCain Foods remembers them in their adjacent offices calling out to each other through the open door between the two rooms. Later, to everyone's chagrin, the door was shut because of the break between the brothers.

In later years, the brotherly affection reasserted itself. In his eulogy at Harrison McCain's funeral in 2004, then New Brunswick premier Frank McKenna recalled his amazement, the previous Christmas, at being invited to vacation with Harrison. When McKenna asked where, Harrison replied, "We're staying at Wallace's down in Jamaica." McKenna told the mourners that the pair had "left their business differences aside … Harrison and Wallace talked or visited each other almost on a daily basis."

In 1957, Harrison and Wallace decided to make a product, french fries, that almost everyone likes, and they found a better way of doing it. That, plus good timing, good luck, and incredibly hard work, made McCain Foods a huge success. A measure of that phenomenal success was that, fifty years after McCain Foods was founded at one small factory in the rural village of Florenceville, a New York consulting firm, the Reputation Institute, named it one of the world's most respected companies.

In March 2007, Harrison and Wallace McCain were chosen as the greatest Canadian entrepreneurs ever in an online poll conducted by Roynat Capital. They finished ahead of a long list of business giants, including Jim Pattison, K.C. Irving, Ken Thomson, Alexander Graham Bell, Frank Stronach, and Joseph-Armand Bombardier. The McCain brothers were both proud men, but they never overestimated themselves. "We didn't know anything about the business in 1957," Harrison told an interviewer. "We had to live and learn just the same as everybody else."

They had great capacity for enjoyment, of work, and of life. Repeating himself as he always did, Harrison told another interviewer in 2001, "We've had a pretty good run, we've had a pretty good run."

Adds Wallace: "We had a lot of fun. Raised a lot of hell."

Harrison at his front door, Christmas 2000.

A WORLD OF CHANGE

Adolfo Lopez Rouger, CEO McCain South America

Fred Schaeffer, President & CEO McCain Foods (Canada)

Frank van Schaayk, CEO McCain Foods USA

Nick Vermont, CEO McCain Foods GB, Eastern Europe, South Africa

Jean Bernou, CEO McCain Continental Europe

Dale Morrison, President & CEO McCain Foods Limited

The Senior Leadership Team, 2007

The Senior Leadership Team (SLT) brings together senior McCain executives representing various regional businesses and diverse functions within the company. Its members thus play dual roles: their primary role in their own region or function and a global role in helping to set a strategic course for the worldwide McCain organization. Not shown here: Rick Ciccone, Global Supply Chain Officer.

John Doucet,
President & CEO, Day & Ross
Transportation Group

Steve Yung,
Managing Director, McCain
Australia/NZ

Janice Wismer,
VP Human Resources,
McCain Foods Limited

David Sanchez,
Chief Financial Officer, McCain
Foods Limited

Anil Rastogi,
Chief Information Officer,
McCain Foods Limited

Lloyd Borowski,
VP Global Engineering
and Manufacturing,
McCain Foods Limited

Bob Cornella,
Corporate VP, McDonald's
Worldwide Business Unit,
McCain Foods Limited

Ghislain Pelletier,
Corporate VP, Agriculture,
McCain Foods Limited

Terry Bird,
VP Corporate Development
and Emerging Markets,
McCain Foods Limited

Michael Campbell,
VP and General Counsel,
McCain Foods Limited

A WORLD OF CHANGE

DALE MORRISON

AFTERWORD

Dale Morrison at the McCain offices at BCE Place in Toronto, Canada, 2005.

Seizing opportunities to meet demand marked the first fifty years of McCain Foods growth. Our challenge today is to create demand in an ever changing marketplace.

To meet our challenges we must harness the same strength of character that has made McCain the success story it is today. Nothing happens without responsible, talented, and high-performing people. Our people have been, and will continue to be, our greatest strength. So it should be no surprise that at the very core of our strategic direction – Growing Together – is our commitment to the continuous development of each and every person on our team. We will be more powerful as a team – and more successful as a business – when each of us is empowered to be the very best we can be.

Our goal is to become a market-facing company that consistently wins with customers and consumers by making them smile. We will be working hard and creatively to introduce value-added products in our developed markets in order to create new demand, and we will be looking for ways to reach hundreds of millions of people in the emerging markets of Asia, Africa, and South America who are not yet consumers of our products. That's over 60 percent of the world's population to win over!

It's a tall order. Competition has increased. Food preferences have changed. The state of the world's environment dictates only the most responsible and sustainable means of growth.

We will grow and win in this marketplace by focusing the entire team on our priorities: Enablers, Quality, and Innovation. *Enablers*, quite simply, are all of us working together to improve efficiency and productivity, thereby eliminating waste. The savings from our collective efforts provide the resources to reinvest in our business and our people. *Quality* must be a defining characteristic of the McCain brand. Every box, every bag, and every bite of every product we make must be the best, every time. *Innovation* will be the magic in our success formula. Constantly developing new products and searching for new and better ways of doing things is the key to our short- and long-term growth.

We will win by leveraging our global scale while remaining a decentralized company that responds to local issues and needs with those people who understand them best. But we're not going to miss taking advantage of big, powerful global initiatives and practices that can make us all stronger and better able to meet the needs of our customers and consumers. By linking together the functions in each of our businesses and sharing the best ideas among us swiftly, we create a powerful web and a significant competitive advantage.

I have every confidence that our global, multicultural family business will continue to grow together and succeed. I am very excited about our future. Thanks to Wallace, to Harrison, and to those employees who came before us, we have a solid foundation on which to build.

Dale Morrison
President and CEO
McCain Foods Limited
Toronto, Canada
May 2007

ACKNOWLEDGEMENTS

From Dale Morrison
McCain is filled with many stars … one of those stars deserves a special mention here. It was the tireless efforts of Tony van Leersum that provided remarkable illumination to tell this tale. Semi-retired after leading our agriculture division, Tony continues to be at the forefront of McCain's development. He deserves enormous credit for building the bridges to bring the right people together on this project, including the author Daniel Stoffman, who has done an excellent job in bringing life to the McCain story. In doing so, Tony has honoured the founders and those people chosen by them to build the company.

From Daniel Stoffman
This book exists because Dale Morrison, CEO of McCain Foods, decided that the company's colourful history should be captured and preserved in book form as part of the celebration of McCain's fiftieth anniversary. Wisely, he assigned the project to quasi-retired McCain executive Tony van Leersum, confident that Tony would not rest until the idea of a book became reality.

Tony was my invaluable collaborator in researching *From the Ground Up*. He located retired McCain people and persuaded them to be interviewed, conducted interviews himself, and shared his knowledge of all aspects of McCain's business. After the text was completed, he spent countless hours checking facts to ensure accuracy, helping to obtain and select photos and other illustrations, and providing information for captions.

Janice Wismer, in her capacity as head of the McCain Learning Centre, backed the project from start to finish. Her enthusiastic support was indispensable. And her son, Kyle Wismer, deserves credit for coming up with the title.

Linda Gustafson, book designer extraordinaire, thinks a book should be a work of art. She worked tirelessly to design the pages into a seamless combination of text and image. She searched the globe to find the best illustrations available to help bring the story of a great international company to life. In her role as book producer, Linda expertly co-ordinated the project right up until delivery of the finished product from the printers.

Editor Judy Phillips was relentless in exposing points that needed further explanation or elaboration. She helped to clarify a complex story.

This book would not exist without the cooperation of dozens of McCain employees, past and present, who gave their time and knowledge to help us tell the company's remarkable story. Their generous cooperation is greatly appreciated. I would also like to thank Nina Colangelo of the Toronto office who was always ready to find a phone number or email address and Darlene Koenings for arranging my interviews in Lisle, Illinois.

Assembling the illustrations to document a history that spans five decades and six continents was a huge task. Linda Gustafson is especially grateful to the following for their help: Dawn Shaw, Edwina McBrine, Scoop Fredstrom, Donna McCarthy, Pam Procter, Shona Adams, Heather Partner, Francine Bouquillon, Erik Haasken, John Walsh, Christine Alexander, Sarah Zilik, and the staff of Alethio BV.

Finally, the author would like to thank his in-house editor, Judy Stoffman, for her advice, support and encouragement.

INDEX

Page numbers in italic refer to illustrations and photographs

A.C. Neilson, 5
ACD (darkening, potatoes), 12, 13
Adams, Bill, 26, *26*
advertising, 43, 51, 53, 57, 58, 62, 78, 85, 189, 228, *229* (*See also* commercials; It's All Good campaign; slogans)
aging population, 150, 225, 228
Agriculture Canada Research Centre (NB), 13
agrochemicals, 207, 230
agronomy, 13, 92–95, *93–94*, 118, 135–37, *136, 137,* 195–96, 199, 225 (*See also* sustainable agriculture)
Aguirre, Marcelo, *207*
Ahmadabad (India) plant, *223* (*See also* Gujarat [India] plant)
air pollution, 109
AirVac harvester, *7*
Aksenev, Mikhail, *96*
Alanis, Ana, *207*
Albrecht, Tom, *177*
Aleskerov, Eldar, *96*
Alexandre, Pedro, *100*
Allan, John, *214*
Allen and Kidd Farms (ID), *173*
Allen, Tony, *173*
Alpine Foods (NZ), 114
Amfac, 172
Anchor Food Products, 150, 182–83
Andrade, Juan, *207*
Andrews, Paul, *114*
Antworth, Clarence, 48, *48*
Antworth, Elaine, *48*
Antworth, Ken, 37
apartheid, 190
Apold, Beth (daughter, Bob McCain), 163
Apold, Will, 163
appetizers, 60, 150, 151, 175, *179,* 181–85, *184, 185,* 220 (*See also* snack products)
Appleton (WI) plant, 182, 183, *221*
Araya, Emmanuel, *217*
Arbeau, Dwight, 37
Archangelsk (Russia), 95
Archer, Gussie, 37
Argentina, 19, 49, 95, 173, 197 (*See also* McCain Argentina)
Aroostook County (ME), 12
Ars, Rinus, 37
aseptic packaging, 148, 151
Ash, Carl, 27–30, *30,* 31, 88, 141–42
Asian frozen foods, 151, 183–84, 225
Associated Fisheries of Canada, 82–83
Atkins diet, 228
Atlantic Veterinary College, 158
Australia, 20, 27, 31, 32, 37, 44, 57, 58, 62, 64, 72, 74, 95, 200 (*See also* McCain Australia)
Austria, 74
automation, 62, 131
A&W, 22

baby boom, 5, 225, 227
Baby Cakes, 180–81, *180*
Baddley, Mick, *63*
Bakker, Rob, *128*
Balcarce (Argentina) plant, 198–207, *198, 199, 201, 204, 206, 207, 222*
Ballarat (Australia) plant, 107, 108–10, *109, 111,* 115–18, 120, 145, *223*
Baranova, Ksenia, *96*
Baranova, Natalia, *96*
Bartlett, Richard, *217,* 220
Basian, Karen, 150–51, *150*
Batten, Robin, 37
Baxter, John, 7, 9, 12
BCE Place (Toronto), 138, *138*
B.D. Grass Farm (ME), 164
Beaulieu, Camile, 37
Beaumarais (manufacturer), 80, 84, 87–87, 97, 101
beautification committees, 141
Becerra, Carlos, *206, 207*
Becker, Sherri, *179*
Bedfordview (Johannesburg) HQ, 192, *193*
Belgium, 69, 71, 72, 73, 82, 83, 84, 194
Bell, Alberta, 37
Bell, Alexander Graham, 237
Belleisle Creek (NB) plant, *221*
Belleisle Foods, 151
Benton and Bowles, 74
Berkut, Olga, *96*
Berlin Wall, 90
Bernier, Nelson, 37
Bernou, Jean, 69, *81, 86,* 96–98, *100, 100, 101,* 238
Best Partner of the Decade Award (2005), 86
Beswick, Peter, 37
Bethune (France) plant, *80,* 84, *222*
Betts, Betty, 14–15, *14*
Bintje potatoes, 73
biofuels, 230, 231
Bird, Terry, 14, 140, 148, *148,* 150, 151, 152–53, *153,* 191, 202, 214, *215, 217,* 239
Birds Eye, 59
Birds Eye (ME) plant, 6, 11, 17–18
Birdseye, Clarence, 6
Birdseye Seafoods, 6
Bisnair, J.P., *161*
Black, Conrad, 140
Blackburn, John, *63*
Blaimont, Jean-Claude, *100*
Blainville (QC) (Tour Eiffel) plant, 142, *221*
Blake, Warner, 37
Bliss, Connie, 25
Bliss, Tim, 20–21, *20,* 22, 23, 26, *26,* 31, 72–73, 79, 108, 127–28, 142, 146, *148,* 160, 172
Bobcat (company), 60
Bockmann, Kai, 212, *213, 217*–18, 219, *219*

Bodine's (company), 169–70
Boehm, Bill, 156
Boesch, Hartmut, *74*
Bojalil, Fabián, *206*
Boku (beverage), 171
Bombardier (company), 207, 234
Bombardier, Joseph-Armand, 237
Bonduelle, André, 82
Borden-Carleton (PE) plant, *143,* 148, *221*
Borowski, Lloyd, *128, 130, 132, 146, 215, 231, 231,* 239
Bougie, Jacques, *161*
Bouquillon, Francine, *100*
Bourgoin, George, 37
Boyer, Marion, *145*
Boyle, David, *115, 116*–17
brand autonomy, 66
brand recognition, 87, 183, 220
brand uniformity, 52
Brantley, Brooke, *183*
Brascan Corp., 168
Brazil, 169, 198, 199, 201, 203, 207 (*See also* McCain South America)
breakfast meals, 59
Brett, Stan, *121*
Brew City (brand), *181,* 183
Briggs, Bob, *63*
Britfish, 59–60
British Rail, 54
Broad-Based Black Economic Empowerment Act, 195
Broer, Wim, 37, 88
Brown, Bob, 37
Brown, Ken, 37
Brown, Sherry, *122*
Brundtland Commission, 229
Buenos Aires, 199, 205 (*See also* McCain Argentina)
bulk body trucks, *199*
Bullock, Steve, 48–49, 54, *63*
Bulmer, Gene, 13
Burdett, Kevin, *181*

244 FROM THE GROUND UP

Burger King, 51
Burgess, Leigh-Anne, *123*
Burgos (Spain), 62
Burley (ID) plant, *221*
Burman, Peter, 62, *63*, 128
Bushby, Jim, *126*, *159*
Business Development Bank of Canada, 157
Butterfield, Don, *226*
Buurma, Rob, *37*
Buyanov, Alexander, *96*

Calgary (AB) plant, *221*
Cameron, Ian, 26, 62–63, *63*, *95*, 104, 106, *110*, 122, 166–67
Campbell, Ken, 63
Campbell, Michael, *141*, *239*
Campbell Soup Company, 24, 226
Canada Post, 228
Canadian Business Hall of Fame, *146*
Canadian Business magazine, 34
Canadian High Commission, 41
Canadian International Development Agency (CIDA), 197
Carberry (MB) plant, *221*
carbohydrates, 228, 229
Cargill (company), 77
car ownership, 5
Caribbean, 1, 2, 27, 218, 219
Carleton County Council, 8
Carter, Mabel, *19*
Caterpac (food distributor), 25, 43, 50
Cavendish Farms, 148
CBS News, 170
Central America, 218
Cerebos Foods, 108
Chalet Foods, 114
Chamas, Pierre, *37*
Charland, Claude, *80*
Charles, prince of Wales, 66
Chartier, Dan, *37*
Chauhan, Rajeev, *214*, *215*
cheese, 30, 156
Chef Sensations, *185*
chefs, 23, 24, 43, 60, 72, 87, 116, 181, *183*, 189–90, 192, *192*, 205
Chelley, Dave, *73*
Chernecki, Bob, *37*
chicken, frozen, 41
Chile, *135*, 201, 203, 217, 232
China, 14, 95, 151, 185, 187, 225 (*See also* McCain China)
Chinese frozen foods, 151, 183–84

Cho, Mike, 209
cholesterol, 228
Chrétien, Jean, *140*
Christensen, Amy, *179*
CIBC Commercial Banking, 152
Ciccone, Rick, 238
Clark (SD) plant, 172
Clements, John, 104, 108, *108–10*, 113–14, *113*, 115, 118, 121, 122, 161
climate change, 225, 230–31
C.M. McLean Ltd., 148
CN Rail, 234
Coaldale (AB) plant, 148, *217*, 220, 221
Coca-Cola, 1, 29, 230
Cofino, Alvaro, *217*
cold storage facilities, 8, 12, 15, 48
Collins, John, *37*
Colombia, 203, 217
Colton (CA) plant, *221*
Comgroup Supplies, 114
commercials, 191, *191*, 205
computerization, 43, 62, 142–43
ConAgra, 169
continuous improvement, xii–xiii, 129–30
Corey, Barb, *230*
Corey, John, *148*
Corinna (ME) plant, *7*, *9*
Cork, Kendall, 161
Cornella, Bob, 175, 176, *176*, 239
Cossaboom, Ken, 27, *159*
Coston, Bob, 198
"country jewels" categories, 151
Cousin, Jean François, *37*, *128*
Cowperthwait, David, *181*
Cox, John, *168*
Cox, Lester "Bud," *15*, *15*, *17*
Cox, Sherdon, *15*
Cox, Tony, *17*
Cripwell, Anthony, *196*
crop rotation, 137, 230
cross-pollination, *94*
Culinary Institute of America, *230*
currency crises, 202, 206
cutter cannons, *130*
Cuy, Robin, 122, *123*
Cyr, Dick, *159*
Czudowski, Andrzej, *100*

DaLoia, John, *183*
Danone, 230
Davis, Patrick, *181*
Dawkins, Dan, *106*, 118, 122
Dawson, Mike, 110

Day, Elbert, 33, 152
Day & Ross Transportation Group, 16, 26, 33, *33*, 62, 70, 71, 148, 151–55, 218
Daylesford (Australia), plant, 103–8, *104*
Davidson, Tom, *37*
Davis, Patrick, *181*
Dean, Paul, 16, 29–30, 31, *125*, *159*, *235*
de Boef, Anton, *73*, *87*
de Klerk, S.J., *196*
de Kok, Bram, *37*
de Sottomayor, Lourenço, *100*
deep frying, 59, *59*, 60, 89
defect removal systems, 51, 62, 131, *133*
Degrave, Lucille, *97*, *100*
Deiting, Leo, *74*
Delage, Jean-François, *100*
Delaître, Michel, 82, *100*, *101*
Delannoy, Bertrand, *100*
Dell Products (juice company), 170
Delmas (South Africa) plant, 194, *217*, *222*
Deloitte (accounting firm), 152
Deming, Edwards, 129
den Daas, Hans, 128
Denmark, *70*, 71
Dent, Geoff, *37*
Derrah, Larry, *215*
desserts, 59, *182*, 220
Devine, Wayne, *37*
Dicos Fried Chicken, 213
Dolan, Dan, *181*
Dominion Bridge Company, 27, 28
Donovan, Peter, *123*
Doucet, John, 152, *152*, 153–55, *239*
Doucette, Des, *148*, *181*, *231*
Dowbiggin, Steve, *37*
Downey, James, 25
"drink the local wine" philosophy. *See* McCain Foods Limited, philosophy
drought, 117–18, *119*, *215*, 231
Drummond, Pat, *37*
Drury, Alan, *63*
D'Souza, Neil, 129, 132
Duncan, Derek, 110
Dunlap, Ray, 7
Dupont, Francis, *78*, *101*
Durost, Harold, 168, 171, *171*
Dwyer, Ian, *123*
D&Y Pike's farm (Australia), *107*

eastern Europe, 54 (*See also* specific countries)
Easton (ME) plant, 125, 166–68, 180, *221*
Echeverria, Maria, *207*
Eddleston, Peter, *37*
Edgell (company), 104, 113–14, 120
Efting, Richard, 220
Elizabeth, queen of England, 65, *65*
Elliott, Dave, *63*
Embraer (company), 207
end-user sales technique, 22–24, 44, 87, 109, 110
energy conservation, 231
Engineering Consultants Inc., 20
England, 31, 34, 43, 50–51, 230 (*See also* McCain Britain)
Environmental Protection Agency (Australia), 10–9, 110
environmental technology, 81
equilibriation, *133*
Erickson, Arthur, 25
Eskimo Foods, 41, 42
Esquimalt (BC), 20
Europe. *See* McCain Europa; McCain in Europe; specific countries under McCain
European Economic Community (EEC), 47, 71
Evans, Jim, 49–51, 99, 108, 146, 160, 236
Executive magazine, 34, 67

Fang Zhao Ce, *151*
Far East, 148 (*See also* specific countries)
fast food restaurants. *See* quick-service chains
Fastrax (truckload operator), 154
Favorita, 50, 72, 73, 87
FDA. *See* U.S. Food and Drug Administration
Felius, Ronald, *100*
Ferguson, Bob, *18*
Ferrar, Dave, *37*
Ferré, Laurent, *100*
fertilizers, 2, 3
FFA (free fatty acid), 55
Figeac, Michel, *88*, *101*
Findus (brand), 59, 120
Finn, Graham, 55, *55*, 58
fires, plants, 11, 85, 86, 125–27, *126*
fish and chips, 22, 118, 119
fish, frozen, 41, 59

Fishery Products International (FPI), 234, 235
flake drum, *201*
flame extinguishing systems, 11
flatbed planters, *216*
Flemming, Hugh John, 10, *10*, 11
Flor, Richard, *74*
Florenceville (NB), 3, *3*, 138, 141
   data processing centre, *67*, *144*, *145*
   plant, vii–ix, *3*, 10–33, *10*, *32*, 62, 66, 125–27, *126*, 138, 147–48, 203, 221
   Potato Processing Technology Centre, 235
   research farm, 135, *159*
Fontaine, Anne Sophie, *81*
Food and Agriculture Organization (FAO), 211
Food for Love (TV series), 192, *192*
Food in Canada magazine, 160
food processing technology, 130–33, *130*, *131*, *132*, *133*
Ford, Tony, 122, *123*, 211, 212
Fort Atkinson (WI) plant, 175, *221*
France, 19, 62, 71, 73, 74, 76, 210, 230 (*See also* McCain Alimentaire)
Fraser Vale (company), 22
Fredstrom, Scoop, *159*
freezers, 6, 43
freezing food, 6
freezing tunnel, *17*
French Communist Party, 81
french fries
   cuts/off-cuts, 119
   early McCain, 12–13
   frozen vs. fresh, 23, *43*
   growth of market for, 21–22, 62
   and health concerns. *See* health consciousness
   invention of, 69
   longer vs. shorter, 131
   McCain grades, 50
   manufacturing process, *51*, *133*
   microwaveable, 97
   optimal potato for, 12–13
   oven-baked. *See* oven-baked fries
   –potato ratio, 14
   thicknesses, *119*
French Guiana, 219
French, John, 26
French Potato Growers Association, 79
Frima (company), 84
Frito-Lay, 143, 226
frozen dinners, 6, 104, 114, 115–16, *116*, 120, 121, 151

fryers, 11, 228
funerals (South Africa), 187–89, *180*

Gaunch, Seth, *128*
Gavrish, Ekaterina, *96*
General Foods, 6, 17, 18, 34, 226
genetic engineering, 99
George (South Africa) plant, *194*, 222
Germany, 71, 73, 74, 75–76, *74*, 79, 83–84, 90, 98
Ghonos, George, 100, *101*, *101*
Giberson, Marie, 37
Gilardi, Jean-Louis, *100*
Gitkin, Chuck, *181*
global councils, 233
global foods, 151, 225
global locations map, 221–23
globalization, 60–61
Goenner, Johanna Christine, *74*
Goldstein, Cal, *176*
Good Stuff (company), 176
Goodman Fielder International, 183
Goodridge, Bill, *114*
Goodwin, Andy, *190*, *196*
Gordon, Marco, *217*
graders, *93*
Grand Falls (NB) plant, 19, 57, 125, *142*, 147–48, 156–57, 169, *221*
Grand Island (NE) plant, 175, *179*, *221*
Grantham (UK) plant, *222*
Gray, Robin, *113*
Great Britain. *See* McCain Britain
Greece. *See* McCain Hellas
Green, Andrew, *201*
Green Cross (company), 3
Gregg, Milton, 10, *10*, 11
Griff's dinner line, 114, *116*
Grobbendonk (Belgium) plant, 84, *222*
Growers Foods, 114
Growing Together strategy, 231–33, 240–41
Guatemala, *217*
Gujarat (India) plant, 214, 215–16, *215* (*See also* Ahmadabad)
Guyana, 219

Haasken, Erik, *95*, *96*
Hadad, Eduardo, *202*
Hague, Doug, *63*
Hallett, Helen, *19*
Hamer, Sir Rupert, 110
Hanscom, Margaret, *74*
Hanscom, Wayne, 73, 74–75, *76*, 160, 170–71

Harbin (China) plant, *210*, 212, *213*, *217*, 223
Harbo, Annemarie Oosterhoff, *70*
Hargrove, Basil, 112–13, *112*, 114, *118*, 161
Harnes (France) plant, 62, 79–82, *80*, 84, 100, 222
Harris, Richard, *63*
Harrison (horse), *76*, 68
Harrison, A., *74*
Harrison, Harry, 44
Hartland (NB) (Day & Ross) head office, 221
Harvesters, 60, *93*
hash browns, 85–86, *181*
Hastings (NZ) plant, 114, *114*, *223*
Haverkort, Anton, *190*
Hawaii, 20, 70
Hawkins, Gary, *136*
Haynes, Arden, 161
health consciousness, 60, 150, 184, 185, 189, 225, 228–29, *228*
Hedges, Tim, *195*, *196*
Heinz. *See* H.J. Heinz Co.
Heinz-Wattie's Ltd., 114, 120
Henderson, Douglas, 219
Heretaunga Plains (NZ), *102*
Hickling, Frank, 11, *13*, 34
H.J. Heinz Co., 34, 120, 175, *178*, *180*, 182
HMCS *Ontario*, 20
hockey, 26, *26*
Hodge, Bob, *170*
Hofmeister, Helga, *100*
Holdco (holding company board), 7, 159, 160, *161*, 163, 233 (*See also* Opco)
Holmes, Murray, 226
Home Fries, 60
Hood, Derek, *63*
Hoofddorp (Netherlands) plant, 62, 77–78, *77*, 82, 100, 217
hot air drying, 62
Howatt, Doug, 37
Howes, Malcolm, *63*
Huige, John, 73, *74*, *75*, 86, 89
Hull (UK) plant, 59–60, *222*
Hume, Pat, 37
Hungary, 96
Hurst, Bob, 37
Huzo (french fry processor), 72, 73
hydrogenation, 228

Ibarra, Alejandra, *207*
Iceland, 218, 220
Idaho, 6, 7, 13, 52, *173*
IJsselmeer lake (Netherlands), *128*
IKEA, 66
Imasco, 34
India, 14, 151, 185, 187, 210, 211, 225, 232 (*See also* McCain India)
industrial safety, *168* (*See also* fires)
information technology, 138, 141–45, *144*, *145*, 149
Inman, Burt, 37
Inman, Horace, 8–9
Innovation Oscar (2004), 97
Innovator potato, 95
Intercool food fair (Düsseldorf, 1998), 83
International Food Show (1976, London), 21
International Year of the Potato (2008), 229
Inuit, 6
Ireland, 3, 43, 54
Irish potato famine, 58
Irons, John, 49
irrigation, 111, 118, 136–37, 197–98, 216, 225, 230, 232
Irvin & Johnson, 190–94
Irving (company), 7, 20, 148
Irving, K.C., 1, 237
Irving Oil, 1
Israel, 216
Italy, 74, 76, 84, 86–87
It's All Good campaign, 59, *61*, 62

Jamaica, 31, 237
"Jamie's School Dinners" campaign, 60
Japan, 20, 127, *128*, *157* (*See also* McCain Japan)
Jar, Pierre, 72
Jaubert, Frédéric, *100*
Jecha-Beard, Laurie, *173*, *181*
Jefferson, Sue, *61*
Jenkinson, Colin, 37
Jensen, Liz, *178*
Jenson, Ben, *130*
Jesson, Dennis, 48–49, *48*, *49*, 110, 202, 207
Jesson, Esme, *48*
Jim Pattison Group, 140, 237
Johannesburg (South Africa), *192*
John Paul II, pope, 86
Johnson, Fred, *63*
Johnson, Patrick, 55

Johnson, Eleanor (McCain) (sister, Harrison, Wallace), 16, 55
Johnston, Eion, 63
Jones, Ernie, 122, 123
Jones, Simon, 100, 215
Jon-Lin Foods, 183–84, 185
Jongstra, Henk, 128
Jordan, 197, 216
J.Q. Charles (supermarkets), 219
J.R. Simplot Dehydrating Company, 6–7, 13, 40, 77, 120, 166, 167, 176, 212
juice, frozen, 6, 59, 142, 148, 151, 157, 169–71, 174, 220
Junior Juice, 171
Just Au Four (french fries), 31

kaizen, 127, 128–29, 128
Kamfer, Sharon, 187
Kaohsiung (Taiwan) plant, 223
Kaszas, Tom, 215
Katahdin potato, 12
Kellogg, 23, 24
Kempco, 184
Kennebec potato, 12, 94, 112
Kentucky Fried Chicken, 4, 5, 22, 51 (*See also* KFC)
Kentville (NS) food research station, 29
KFC, 4, 51, 210, 211, 211, 212, 213, 219 (*See also* Kentucky Fried Chicken)
Kilfoil, Harold, 37
Kinder, Hal, 44–45, 63
Kinney, Harry, 15
Kinney, Margaret, 48
Kinney, Milford, 47–48, 48, 159
Kolochinskaya, Anna, 96
Korea, 208
Koster, Cor, 79, 148
Kraft Foods, 24, 230
Kramer, Meindert Jan, 128
Kroc, Ray, 5, 165, 176
Kroger (supermarkets), 170
Kuenemann, Ray, 7
Kulaeva, Natalia, 96
Kumar, Devandra, 214, 215, 215, 216
Kuznetsova, Irina, 96

labour unions, 52, 107, 108–9, 110
Lacroix, Michel, 226
Laforge, Gilles, 37
Lamb, Gilbert "Gib," 40, 130
Lamb Water Gun Knife, 130

Lamb Weston, 13, 40, 130, 166, 172–73
Lan, Richard, 170, 170, 174
Larson, Kerry, 175
Latin America, 1, 2 (*See also* Central America; South America)
Laurie, Peter, 24
La Voix du Nord (paper), 82
Lawler, Jean, 14
Lean Cuisine, 120
Lean Six Sigma, 129
Leclercq, Yves, 136
Leger, Dan, 196, 217
Leivers, Julie, 37
Lelievre, Kevin, 37
Lelkes, Pedro, 206
Lelystad (Netherlands) plant, 84, 84, 222
Lessard, Gilles, 80, 88, 89–90, 97, 98, 175, 175, 182
Lett, Gavin, 111
Lewedorp (Netherlands) plant, 72, 73, 75, 85, 86, 222
Liberal Party of Canada, 149
Lillyman, Roger, 58
Linsdau, Anne, 181
Lipetzk (Russia), 95
Lisle (IL), McCain US HQ, 180, 184, 221
Liu Wenlong, 211
Liu Zhenbao, 212
Lodi (NJ) plant, 221
Lopez Rouger, Adolfo, 200, 202, 202, 203, 204, 206, 206, 207, 207, 238
Lopyreva-Belyaeva, Oksana, 95, 96
Lord, Claude, 37
Lovely, Beatrice, 48
Lovely, Murray, 48, 48, 159
LSA (trade publication), 97
LTL (less than truckload) transporter, 153
Lunn, Alden, 37
Lunn, Bertha, 15
Lyall, Angus "Gus," 37

Mabee, Bill, 28, 122, 142, 169
Mabee, Peter, 37
McCain, A.D. (father, Harrison, Wallace), 1, 2, 7, 9, 16, 34
McCain, Allison (son, Andrew Sr.), 14, 15, 16, 41, 53–54, 57, 64, 65, 101, 122, 149, 156, 156, 160, 161, 162, 181–82, 212, 219, 233–34
McCain, Andrew (Sr., brother, Wallace, Harrison), 2, 7–8, 7, 8, 9, 16, 31, 158, 159, 160,

McCain, Andrew (son, Bob), 16, 161, 163, 233–34
McCain, Billie (Marion) (wife, Harrison), 9, 10, 55, 140, 141, 154, 155, 155
McCain, Bob (Robert) (brother, Wallace, Harrison), 1, 2, 7–8, 7, 8, 9, 16, 31, 158, 159, 160, 161
McCain, Eleanor (daughter, Wallace), 154, 162
McCain, Gillian (daughter, Harrison), 154, 163
McCain, Harrison, 6
  family background, 2, 3, 16
  and founding of McCain Foods, 1–33
  funeral, 237
  interests, 140, 140, 149
  management style, 48, 56, 57, 149, 234–36
  personality, 25, 54, 99, 149, 237
  political beliefs, 149
  relationship with Wallace, x–xi, 3, 160, 237
  residence, 3, 10
  salary, 33–34
  sales trips, 22, 32, 41
  and succession dispute, 158–60
  visit to Argentina, 204, 204
McCain, Joyce (wife, Peter), 163
McCain, Kathryn (daughter, Andrew Sr.), 158, 162
McCain, Laura ("Mrs. A.D.") (mother, Harrison, Wallace), 2, 9, 16, 16, 46, 46
McCain, Linda (daughter, Andrew Sr.), 162
McCain, Margie (Margaret) (wife, Wallace), 9, 10, 26, 47, 55, 154, 155, 168
McCain, Mark (son, Harrison), 154, 157, 157, 161, 163, 189, 190–91, 190, 192, 217
McCain, Martha (daughter, Wallace), 154, 162
McCain, Mary (daughter, Bob), 163
McCain, Michael (son, Wallace), 15, 32, 154, 156, 158, 160, 161, 162, 168, 170, 172–74, 172, 175
McCain, Nancy (daughter, Andrew Sr.), 162
McCain, Peter (son, Harrison), 15, 154, 157, 157, 218, 220
McCain, Scott (son, Wallace), 15,

26, 113–14, 154, 156–57, 156, 160, 161, 162
McCain, Stephen (son, Andrew), 2, 136, 161, 162, 200
McCain, Wallace F., x, 6
  education, 20
  family background, 2, 3, 26
  and founding of McCain Foods, 1–33
  honours, 155
  interests, 26
  management style, 48, 57, 234–36
  personality, 26, 54, 99, 237
  relationship with Harrison, x–xi, 3, 160, 237
  residence, 3, 10
  salary, 33–34
  sales trips, 22
  succession dispute, 158–60
McCain Evans, Ann (daughter, Harrison), 154, 161, 163
McCain Jensen, Laura (daughter, Harrison), 154, 161, 163
McCain-McMillin, Rosemary (wife, Bob), 9, 163
McCain Pearson, Marjorie (wife, Andrew Sr.), 9, 163
McCain airfield, 138, 139
McCain Alimentaire (France), 62, 78–82, 84, 88–90, 97–98, 99
McCain Argentina, 198–207, 198, 199, 201, 206, 207, 215
McCain Australia, 103–23, 145, 151, 156, 166, 194, 211, 212, 220, 228, 231
McCain Britain, 39–67, 156, 166, 288
McCain China, 210–13, 225
McCain Citrus Inc., 171–72, 174, 175
McCain Competitive Edge (MCE), 129–30, 129
McCain Europa, 70, 90
McCain in Europe, 69–101
McCain Fertilizer, 2, 163
McCain Foods Canada Ltd., 20, 30, 65, 138, 141, 156, 157, 218
McCain Foods (GB) Ltd. *See* McCain Britain
McCain Foods Group Inc. *See* Holdco
McCain Foods Holland, 62, 69, 70, 71–78, 83, 84, 88
McCain Foods Limited, 28, 156
  acquisitions/corporate development, 32, 33, 43, 49, 54, 55, 59,

72–73, 76–77, 79–82, 84, 87–88, 113, 114, 121, 147–51, 160, 169–71, 172, 174–75, 177–79, 182, 183–84
agricultural program, 229–33
awards and honours, 61–62, *61*, 65, 72, *97*, *143*, *146*, *149*, *155*, *160*, *170*, *180*, *181*, *183*, *200*, *226*, *228*, 237
boards of directors, 161, *161*
business growth formula, 58
celebrations, 3, *24*, *25*, *30*, *35*, *45*, *204*
competitors, 22, 40, 41, 59, 113, 120, 148, 160, 212–13
corporate culture/values, 14–15, 17, 19, 31, 34, 35, 41, 54, 55, 57, 64, 86, 100, 234–36, 240–41
and emerging markets, 14–15, 101, 150–51, 193, 194, 240 (See also specific countries)
employee relations, xii, 14–15, 17, 27, 51, 100, 110, 123, 141, 145, *159*, 167, 168, 179, 209, 232, 235–36, *235*, 240
environmental initiatives, 229–33
farm equipment. *See* Thomas Equipment
future of, 240–41
global reach, 19–20, 27, 29, 31, 34, 37, 39–40, 49, 53, 65, 67, 73, 74, 84, 101, 165–66, 179, 185, 217, 221–23, 231–33, 241
Growing Together strategy, 231–33, 240–41
logo, *227*
management style, 47–48, 54, 55, 57, 58, 63, 88–89, 99, 122–23, 127–30, 147, 169, 179, 180, 182, 227
manufacturing conferences, 128–29
manufacturing culture, 62, 83
marketing culture, 83, 85, 235
philanthropies, 168, 189
philosophy, 56, 86, 121, 129, 187–88, 193, 197, 205, 231
revenues/sales, 3, 27–28, 33, 53, 59, 69, 70, 84, 87, 101, 121, 127, 142, 147, 177, 185, 193, 205, 235
Senior Leadership Team (SLT), 238–39
setbacks, 18–19, 50, 58, 74, 85–86, 103–4, 107, 108–10, 125–27
shareholders (2007), 162–63
succession planning, 157–60
McCain Foods (South Africa) Ltd. *See* McCain South Africa

McCain Foundation, *158*, 163
McCain Frima NV, 84
McCain Healthy Choice, 117
McCain Hellas, 101
McCain Home Fries, 59, *60*, 61–62
McCain India, 214–16
McCain International Ltd., 54, 157, 203, 217–20, *217*, *218*, 220 (See also McCain Foods Limited, global reach)
McCain Japan, 20, 208–10, *208*
McCain Learning Centre, xii–xiii
McCain Potatoes, 53
McCain Produce, 2, *2*, 7, 8, *12*, *136*, 163, 198, 200
McCain Quality Performance (MQP) system, 129, *129*
McCain Refrigerated, 156
McCain Research Farm (Florenceville), 135, *159*
McCain Snack Foods, 182–83
McCain South Africa, 163, 187–96, *196*, 217, 220
McCain South America, 197–205
McCain Stadium (UK), 65
McCain Transport, 154
McCain USA, 62, 79, 150, 151, 165–85, 231
McCarthy, Dale, *128*
McCarthy, James, 48
McCarthy, Mac, 31, 39, 41–47, *46*, *47*, 51–52, 53, *54*, 55–56, 63, *63*, 64–65, *65*, 66, *66*, 67, *67*, 75, 77, 79, 80, 176, 180
McCarthy, Sheila, 43, *47*, 54
McCarthy, Wanda, 37
McCarthy, Wilfred, 37
McClure, Donna, 69, 71–72, *71*
McClure, George, 34, *34*, 35, 69, 70–71, *71*, 73, 74, 75, *75*, 79–81, 82, 148, *148*, 161, 166, 169, 189, 191, 197, 198
McDonald, Dick, 5
McDonald, Mac, 5
MacDonald, Rod, 122, *128*
McDonald's, 4, 5, 51–52, 53, 61, 66, 84, 87, *91*, 92, 95, 118, 119, 120, 147, 165, 173, 176–77, *176*, 199, 201–2, 203, 205, 210, 212, 213, 215, 216, 219, 230
McDonald's Central America, 217
McDonald's Guatemala, 217
MacDougall, Derrick, 215
MacFries, 52, 176, 205

machinery, 62, 78, 131–32, *132*
McInroy, Dave, 37
McIntosh, Les, 20
Mackay, Bill, 122
McKenna, Frank, 66, 237
McLean, Archie, 24, 30, *31*, 156
Maclean's magazine, 149
McLeod, Malcolm, 140
MacPhail, Mark, 217
McWhirter, Dick, *22*, 23, 24, *24*, 27
Maggi (brand), 120
Maine, 2–3, 12, 62
Maine Maritime (company), 151
Makhatini Cotton project (South Africa), 195
Malta, 218
management control report (MCR), 28, 142
Mandela, Nelson, 189
Mander, Ron, 196
Mann, Howard, 65, *84*, 138, 146–47, *147*, 160, *160*, 161, 175, 176, 182, 202–3
Manoharan, Ramesh, 235
Manufacturing Directors Council, *128*, 129
Maple Leaf Foods, 160, 158, 173–74, 175
Marais, Ponnie, 157
Maris Piper potato, 61
Marti, Juan Manuel Fluguerto, 206
Martin, Gustavo, 202
Martin, Robert, 215
Martinique, 219
Matougues (France) plant, 69–70, *98*, *99*, 100, *132*, 222
Matthews, Tom, 176
Medallion d'Or, *72*
Mendoza, Fernando, 207
Menem, Carlos, 200
methane, 81, 110
Metro-Richelieu (supermarkets), 89
Mexico, 218, 220
Micro Chips, 59
microwave, 79, *97*, 116, 150
Middle East, 37, 84, 216, 218
Midwest Foods, 148
Mieth, Stefan, *74*
Milton, Allan, 37
Minty, Roy, 37
Mississauga (ON) plant, 221
Mokhnatkina, Irina, 96
Mölnlycke (company), 97
Monsanto, 99

Montenegro, Javier, 206
Montreal (QC) plant, 221
Montrose (Scotland), 53
Moore's (brand), *181*, 183
Morgan, Dave, 141, 149, *159*, 208, *208*
Morrell, Alton, 37
Morris, Carl, 17–18, *17*, 19–20, 22, 23, 24, 28, 29, 31, 127–28, *128*, 129, 131–32, 141, 142, 172, 208–10, *208*
Morris, Don, 37
Morris, Shirley, 25
Morrison, Dale, 65, 96, 131, 147, 155, *161*, 226–28, *226*, 229, 231–33, 234, 238, 240–41, *240*
Morton, David, 161
Moscow, *91*, 95
Muenker, Gisela, *74*
Mukherji, Jaideep, 214, 215
Muller, Ronald, 210
Mumbai, 215
Munslow, Dave, 148
Murdoch, Neil, 109
Muschetto, Frank, 176
Myles, Randy, *178*, 179, *181*, 182
Mysyakov, Sergey, 96

Naisby, Gavin, 196
National Ballet School, 168
National Post, 152
Nebraska, 197–98
Negus, Robin, 63
Nelson, Doug, 173
Nelson, Sharon, *178*
Nestlé, 120, 172, 198, 230
Netherlands, 7 (See also McCain Foods Holland)
New Brunswick Industrial Safety Council, 168
New Brunswick Telephone Company, 148
New Zealand, 37, *102*, 104, 110, 114, 115, 118, 119–20, 197, 210
Nichirei (food distributor), 208
Nichols, Dave, *111*
Nichols, Ken, 37
Norrie, Bill, *143*
Northern Ireland, 43
Northern Kwazulu Natal (South Africa), 195
Norton, Elaine, 37

obesity, 60, 117, 150, 165, 228
O'Brien, Dave, 37
O'Brien, Margaret, *123*

O'Halloran, Ken, 113
O'Keefe, Bev, 37
O'Reilly, Tony, 175
oils, 59, 61, 150, 228
Oldman River valley (AB), 124
Old South (brand), 151
Oliver, Jamie, 60
Olivier, Alain, 87, 88–89, 100, 101
1.2.3. Frites, 31
onion rings, 181, 183
Ontario Teachers' Pension Plan, 160
Opco (operating company board), 114, 121, 159–61, 234, 234
orange juice. *See* juice, frozen
Orbetta, Oscar, 128
Orchard, Keith, 181
Oreel, Kees, 89, 100, 128
Ore-Ida, 150, 166, 175, 177–80, 181, 182–83
Orr, Ralph, 24
Orton, John, 123
Osaka (Japan), 209
Ostend (Belgium) plant, 84, 222
Othello (WA) plant, 130, 136–37, 172, 177, 198, 221
oven-baked fries, 30–31, 58–59, 59, 60, 61, 84, 85, 89, 150, 189, 229
Oven Chips, 62
Owens, Dick, 170

packaging, 15, 96, 127, 130, 133, 148, 193, 202, 213, 228
Page, Paul, 159
Palazzi, Nino, 87
Palazzi, Rolando, 86–87, 86
Palmer, Joe, 16, 33, 62, 152, 152
Panda potatoes, 135
Pankova, Elena, 96
Pansophic Resource Management System (PRMS), 143
Papa Giuseppe (brand), 120
Parafita, Graciela, 206
Paraguay, 203
Pardon, Erwin, 88, 100
Parfitt, David, 37
Park, Arnold, 37, 160
Partner, Heather, 187–88, 189, 192, 196
Patagonia, 201
Patijn-Lodewijks, Sylvia, 89
Pattison, Jim, 140, 237
Payne, Cindy, 179
Peabody, Don, 159
peas, frozen, 3, 13, 40, 41–42

peel waste, 46–47, 105–6, 109–10, 167, 169
Pellatt, Allan, 110
Pelletier, Ghislain, 135, 136, 137, 197–200, 199, 211, 215, 239
Pelletier, Suzanne, 197
Penola (Australia) plant, 223
Pepperidge Farms, 226
PepsiCo, 226
Perez, Jose Luiz, 200
Peru, 229
pest management, 93, 230
Peterson, Ray, 37
Phillips, Bruce, 122, 128, 231
Pickup, Alan, 63
Pierson, Olof, 9–10, 11
Pillsbury, 140
Pinette, Jean, 37
pizza, 30, 53, 59, 62, 72, 104, 108, 113, 115, 116, 120, 121, 142, 148, 150, 157, 225
plant diseases, 2, 50, 58, 92, 93, 211, 230
Plant X, 132
Plover (WI) plant, 175, 175, 221
Poland, 86, 81, 90, 91, 96, 210, 217
PomFrit (company), 87
Pomona (company), 78, 218
Pop-a-Doodle, 18, 19
poppers, 179
Portage la Prairie (MB) plant, 142, 146, 148, 221, 226
Porteus, Owen, 122, 188, 193–95, 196, 196
Post, Madeline, 37
Potato Allied Services, 49, 55
potato blight, 58
Potato Cakes, 116–17
potato chips, 18, 19
potato flakes, 189, 211
Potato Gems, 119
Potato Kings (hockey team), 26, 26
Potato Processing Technology Centre (Florenceville), 235
Potato Smiles, 205
Potato Tops, 119
potatoes
 discovery, 229
 global production stats, 211
 growing practices, 93
 nutritional value, 229, 229
 varieties, 94, 95, 135, 230
 (*See also* seed potatoes; specific types; table potatoes)
Prater, Steve, 37

Presque Isle (ME) plant, 167
Prince Edward Island plant. *See* Borden-Carleton (PE) plant
private label products, 59, 85, 87–88, 97, 166, 172
Procter, Pam, 63
Pronchenko, Svetlana, 96
Pryde, Rick, 151
punch-card system, 145, 145
Pune (India), 215, 216
Putin, Vladimir, 140

Quebec City (QC), 142
Quebec Major Junior Hockey League, 26
Queen's Award for Enterprise Innovation, 62–63, 62
Queen's University, School of Business, 152
quick-service chains, 5–6, 22, 51, 79, 82, 87, 105, 112, 118, 119, 131, 183, 185, 192, 208, 209, 210, 213

Rastogi, Anil, 67, 143, 143, 145, 146, 149, 239
Raw Material Utilization (RMU) program, 131–32
Reid, Reg, 37
Reijula, Peter, 174, 181, 182–83, 184, 230
Renault, Stéphane, 101
Republican League (hockey), 26
Reputation Institute, 237
restaurants, fast food. *See* quick-service chains
Rice Lake (WI) plant, 175, 179, 221
Richardson, Colin, 148
Richmond, Gerard, 122
Rigo, Christophe, 100
Rioux, Arthur, 37
Ritchie, Cedric, 31–32, 53, 146
R.M. Gow (company), 114, 115
Robinson, Ian, 169, 213, 219
Robinson, Mick, 63
Rodda, Milton, 106–7, 106, 111–12, 123
Roelants, Patricio Gonzalez, 207
Rogers, David, 128, 132
Roos, Anton, 37
Roptin, Yves, 100
Ross (company), 59
Ross, Walter, 33, 152
Rösti Ecken (hash browns), 85–86
Roy, Margaret (daughter, Andrew McCain Sr.), 162

Roy Thomson Hall (Toronto), 25
Roynat Capital, 237
Ruff, Brian, 235
Ruff, Winston, 37
Rush, Dominic, 214
Russet Burbank potato, 12, 13, 51, 52, 53, 92, 94, 95, 112, 135, 136, 176, 199, 211
Russia, 91, 92, 95–96, 95, 96, 211

Safries, 115
St. Amand, Carol, 142
Saint John River (NB), 3, 3, 10, 12, 32, 50, 136
Saint John Sea Dogs (hockey), 26
St. Lucia, 219
St. Michael's Hospital (Toronto), 168
Sakina, Svetlana, 96
Salvesen Group, 55
Sameday Right-O-Way, 154
Sanchez Acosta, Enrique, 201, 207
Sanchez, David, 178, 180, 153, 218, 220, 239
Santana potato, 95
satellite imagery, 233
saturated fats, 228
Scarborough (UK) plant, 39–40, 40, 45–52, 58, 62, 72, 156, 222
Schacht, Reinhard, 74
Schaeffer, Fred, 138, 238
Schelling, Friedbert, 74
Schiller, John, 153
Schmidt, Josef, 74
Schnetkamp, Ernst, 74
Schnetkamp, Hildegard, 74
Schnetkamp family, 75
school lunches, 60, 189, 205
Schultz, Theresa, 179
Schwartz, Nancy, 229
Scioli, Gustavo, 199, 201, 204, 207
Scioli, Sergio, 199
Scotiabank, 8, 31–32, 53, 146
Scotland, 43, 53
Sebago potato, 112
seed potatoes, 2, 7, 12, 34, 53, 94, 95, 190, 190, 197, 200, 212–13, 215–16
Seeley, Gail, 33
Seeley, Ken, 37
Seoul (South Korea), 209
Serra, Pablo, 135
Shanghai (China), 210, 211, 211, 213
Shepody potato, 13, 94, 95, 135, 174, 199
Shirmazanyan, Karina, 96

INDEX   249

Simplot, Jack, 6–7 (*See also* J.R. Simplot Dehydrating Company)
Singapore, 27
Singer, Dan, 215
Sissens, John, 37
Sitnik, Georgiy (Gera), *95, 96*
Skinner, Jim, 176
Skorick, Bill, 178
SKUs (stock keeping units), 115
Slipp, Leonard, 37
slogans, 104, 191, *191*
Smith, Peter, 37
Smithton (Australia) plant, 112, *113*, 194, 223
snack products, 19, 59, 182 (*See also* appetizers)
Sneep, Folkert, 84, *88*, 156
So Good for You campaign, 62
Soerel, Furny, 100
South Africa, 19, 54, 96, 157, *157*, 187 (*See also* McCain South Africa)
South America, 151, 173, 197, 218, 219, 240 (*See also* McCain South America)
South Korea, 209, 210
Soweto (South Africa), 187
Spain, 62
Spavold, Stan, 37
Springs (South Africa) plant, 194, 222
Spunta potato, 199
Stam, Maarten, 128
Star, The (McCain newspaper), 14, 15, 24, 27, 28, 44
Stewart, Graeme "Bennie," 123
Stronach, Frank, 237
Strong, Marilyn, *17*, 140, 149, 159
Strzelin (Poland) plant, 91, 222
Stybr, Percival, 74
Subway (chain), 184
Sudan, Ana, *207*
Sunny Orange (brand), 169
Superbrands Organization, 62
Superfries, 30–31, *31*, 58, 229
Suriname, 219
Sustainable Agricultural Initiative Platform, 230
sustainable agriculture, 229–33
Sutherland, Jed, *9*, 55, 161
Sutherland, Marie (McCain) (sister, Harrison, Wallace), *9, 16*, 55
Suzuki, George, *208*
Sweet Potato, 180, *180*
Swisher, Jerry, *173*
Sysco, 180

table potatoes, 2, 12, 200, 203, 211
Taggares, Peter, 77, *172*
Taiwan, 183, *209*, 210, 213
Tasmania, 112, *112*, 113, 118, *121*, 194
Tater Meal, *167*, 169
Technico, 190
Tellier, Paul, 25, 99, *161*, 234, *234*
Terry, Bruce, 28–29, 32, 99, 141–43, 146, 236
Tetley, Barry, 37
Tetra Pak juice, 170–71
Théry, Philippe, 100
Thiel, Edgar, *74*, 90
Thiers, Alain, 79, 80
Thomas Equipment, 27, *45*, 48, 60
Thomas, Les, 37
Thomas, Vernon, 2
Thompson, Bob, 37
Thompson, Ernie, 37
Thompson, Keith, 106–7, *110*
Thomson family, 25
Thomson, Ken, 237
Thorne's Hardware, 1, 3
Thornley, Dell, *95*, 176
Timakova, Nadia, 96
Timaru (NZ) plant, 114, *120*, 223
Tishkina, Irina, 96
tissue culture, *94*, 215
Tokyo, *208, 209*
Tol, Paul, *217, 219*
Tompkins, Allen, 37
Tompkins, Lloyd, 37
Toronto-Dominion Bank, 160
Toronto Maple Leafs, 26
Toronto (ON) plant, *221*
Toronto Star, 34, *137*
Toronto Symphony Orchestra, 25
Total Quality Management (TQM) system, 129
Tour Eiffel plants (QC), *142*
Toxopeus, Pieter, *95*, 96
trans-fatty acids, 228–29, *228*
Trass, Ad, 37
Trudeau, Pierre, 149
Turner, Fred, 66
Turner, Paul, 122
Twomey, Jeff, *128*

Ukraine, 96, 211
Unilever, 113, 202, 203, 230
Universal, *172*
Uruguay, 201, 203
U.S. Food and Drug Administration (FDA), 169, 170

Valley Farms (Canada), 50
van Dalen, Dick, *72*
van den Boom, Iet, 72, *72*
van den Hoek, Han, 100, *156*, 176, *190*, 198–99
van der Neut-Kolfschoten, Jan, *85*
van der Wel, Paul, *75*, 80, 82–86, *82, 85, 88*, 89–91, 101
van Gils, Frank, 122
van Leersum, Tony, *87*, 138, 140, 142, 198–99, 200, 202–3, *204, 205*, 230–31, *230, 235*
van Lipzig, Pieter, *128*
van Rijn, Cees, 89
van Rouwendaal, Hans, 89
van Schaayk, Frank, 89, *161, 173*, 177–78, *177*, 180, *181*, 182, 184–85, 232, 238
van Tuyl, Henk, 76–77, *76*
Varnis, Damien, 37
Vatican, 86
vegetables
 frozen, 13, *13*, 21, 41, 60, 104, 113, 114, 117, 120, *121*, 187, 188, 194
 roasted, 183–84, *185*
Veraart, Yke, *74*
Verloop, Herman, *76*
Vermont, Nick, 54, *56*, *56*, 59, 63, 64, 66, 96, 238
Vesey, Jeff, 37
Vlasikhina, Tatiana, 96
Volkova, Viktoria, 96

Wagner, Stanley, 25
Waldner, Clarence, *137*
Waldner, Eil, *137*
Wales, 43
Walker, John, 37
Walker, Val, *63*
Walsh, John, 99, *168*
Walsh, Sherry, *168*
Wang Rengui, 211, *211*
Washburn (ME) plant, 166–67
waste treatment, 46–47, 81, 105–6, 110, 231
wastewater, 81, 105, *133*
water gun knife, 130–31, *131, 133*
water pollution, 105, 109–10
Weenink, Bert, *196*
Weinreich, Dieter, *74*
Wendouree, Lake (Australia), 118, *119*
Werkendam (Netherlands) plant, 72–73, *73*

West Free State Seed Growers Association (South Africa), *157*
West Germany, 90
White, Bud, 37
White, Florence, 22
White, Gilbert, 37
Whittaker, Gilbert, 37
Whittlesey (UK) plant, 53–54, *54, 55*, 62, 76, 222, 231
Wieland, Randy, *178, 179, 181*
Wilkinson, Quinton, *111*, 115, 116
Wilmot, Ian, 37
Wilmot, Ken, 47, *63, 65*, 128
Wilson, Bob, 37
Wilson, Roger, 161
Wilson, Trevor, 37
windmills, 231
windrowers, *93, 164*
Winterberg (Germany), *74*
Wishart, Bob, 31
Wishart, Don, *20, 26, 31*, 159
Wismer, Janice, xii–xiii, *xii*, 100, 229, 232, 239
Wombourne (UK) plant, 222
women in workforce, 5, 49, 51, 79, 105, 227
Wong Wing Foods, 151, *151*
Woolworths (chain), 120
World Hockey Association, 26

Yamaguchi, Yon, *208, 208*
Yee, Lisa, *217*
Young, Donald, 13, *135*, 198
Young, John, 61, 63
Young, Victor, *161*, 234–35, *234*
Yulina, Elena, 96
Yung, Steve, 115, 116, 118, 119–20, 123, 239

Zanolli, Néstor, *206*
Zavgorodniy, Dmitry, 96
Zeropac, 22
Zilinksi, Jean Pierre, 101
Zuiderzee. *See* IJselmeer lake
Zwick, Roland, *74*